HAUNTED COLLEGES AND UNIVERSITIES

Creepy Campuses, Scary Scholars,
and Deadly Dorms

Retold by Tom Ogden

gpp

Guilford, Connecticut

For Dylan, Jordyn, Peyton, and Brayden

To buy books in quantity for corporate use
or incentives, call **(800) 962-0973**
or e-mail **premiums@GlobePequot.com.**

Editor: Meredith Dias
Project editor: Lauren Brancato
Layout artist: Lisa Reneson
Text design: Sheryl P. Kober

Library of Congress Cataloging-in-Publication Data is available on file.

ISBN 978-0-7627-9155-2

Printed in the United States of America

10 9 8 7 6 5 4 3 2 1

CONTENTS

Contents

Part Two: Southern Spirits

Part Three: Mysteries of the Midwest

ACKNOWLEDGMENTS

Because I am a graduate of Penn State University, which has plenty of ghost stories, this project has been a labor of love from the very beginning.

I'd like to thank Joan Lawton, first and foremost, for suggesting that this would be a perfect book for me.

Thanks go out to Chuck and Bambi Burnes, Larry Cimino, Jean and Brian E. Hickey, Jim Petcoff, and Kim Roach for proposing several schools and sharing their experiences when I was compiling my list of haunted institutions.

Although I contacted many colleges and universities directly for information and clarifications, I'd especially like to thank the following for their assistance: Sharon S. Brown, assistant to the chair of the Department of Communications, Boise State University; Carol Dempsey, School of Drama, University of Washington; Jim Doran, archives associate, Boise State University; Steve Fisher, University of Denver; Sam McCord, ETSU Library, Eastern Tennessee State University; Andrew Prellwitz, archivist, Ripon College; John T. Rogers, communications and media relations manager, Johnson & Wales University; John Seden, facilities manager, San Francisco Arts Institute; and Christine Stamper, Communications Department, California State University, Stanislaus.

Thanks, too, to Mark Willoughby, Michael Kurland, Linda Robertson, and David Shine for their advice and feedback on the manuscript during the two-year writing process.

Finally, thanks to my editor Erin Turner, project editor Lauren Brancato, copyeditor Kate Hertzog, and Jane

Sheppard for her cover design, along with all the rest of the Globe Pequot Press team. Most of all I must thank developmental editor Meredith Dias, whose necessary work on my manuscript went beyond the call of duty. Without her insights and incredible assistance, this book never would have made it to print.

INTRODUCTION

Going away to college is stressful enough. Most undergrads are still teenagers, with all the accompanying angst and confusion that entails. For many of the students, it's their first time living away from home and having to cope on their own. Suddenly, they have to get *themselves* out of bed in the morning; they have to learn to do laundry, budget their time, clean their own rooms.

And then on top of that, they have to deal with *ghosts*?

That's right: Ghosts are said to haunt hundreds of the four-thousand-plus colleges and universities in the United States. Obviously teens and young adults are thrilled and excited by such titillating fare. But what is it about college ghost stories specifically that make students want to pass them down from one class to another? Is it just tradition?

For many it's a temptation impossible to resist. They know that many campus newcomers are feeling vulnerable, or secretly petrified about being away from home. It's too much fun not to scare them—and in the process alleviate their own anxieties. This may seem like hazing (however mild), but for the initiates, the indoctrination into their school's folklore provides a real sense of belonging. It also makes them the torchbearers of the tales to the next generation of students.

Parapsychologists have tried to categorize the many types of spirits said to haunt institutions of higher learning. (For some reason there are an inordinate number of ghost stories involving suicides—so many that if they had all actually occurred, it wouldn't have gone unnoticed. In fact, it would be seen as a national epidemic.) Among the archetypes are:

- Brokenhearted young lovers who pine away or kill themselves
- Murder and accident victims who don't know they've Passed Over
- Professors who apparently think tenure continues into the Next World
- Sports stars reliving their glory years
- Prized employees who just aren't ready to retire
- Alumni giving a whole new meaning to homecoming
- Native Americans who lived on land where the school now sits
- Soldiers who drilled, fought, or died on the grounds
- Souls buried in campus cemeteries or in unmarked graves
- Spectres from campus buildings that once were private homes

In addition, there are always the entities that can't be identified or whose presence can't be explained. As for why the spirits chose not to "graduate" to the Other Side, it seems their reasons are as varied as the ghosts themselves.

After years of being hidden in the shadows, these juicy tales of terror are now seeing the light of day. Students are starting to talk about their personal encounters with ghosts on social media. More and more colleges and universities are including the legends on their websites or exploring them in courses on comparative religion, psychology, sociology, and anthropology. Several campuses have student ghost hunter clubs. There was even a short-lived television series on Syfy called *School Spirits* that investigated hauntings on college and university campuses. And, of course, now there's *Haunted Colleges and Universities*.

Readers of the Globe Pequot Press Haunted books will immediately notice that the format of this one is completely different from others I've written for the series. During my research, I wasn't finding just two or three dozen stories. I was finding *hundreds*. So instead of highlighting just a few hauntings, in this work I've tried to include as many legends as space would permit. In the end, more than two hundred schools—many of them with multiple haunted sites on campus—made it into this book.

I've limited myself to post-secondary schools in the United States, and all of the institutions are still educating students. Several fascinating ghost stories were excluded simply because the college is closed, the spirit activity has stopped, or the once-haunted building has been torn down.

To make *Haunted Colleges and Universities* more manageable, I've separated the book into four sections. Believe me, it was by no means easy to decide where to draw the lines, especially with regard to border states. After much consideration, I used the regions of the country as defined by the US Census Bureau.

The first section, "Nightshades of the North," concentrates on New England down to Pennsylvania. Part Two, "Southern Spirits," features phantoms south of the Mason-Dixon Line from the Atlantic to the Rockies. Ghosts that haunt the Central States show up in "Mysteries of the Midwest," and "Wraiths of the West" showcases spectres from the Rocky Mountains to the Pacific shore, along with those in Alaska and Hawaii.

Each listing begins with the college or university's name along with its address, main phone number, and website. This is followed by a short summary of the school's history. Every attempt has been made to verify the accuracy of basic information regarding the school and the hauntings. Where there has been conflicting data, I've sided with student and local newspapers, the school's website, and campus archivists, historians, or other representatives. To help you pinpoint the individual haunted sites, I've boldfaced their names the first time they appear in the text.

While these tales are comprehensive and exhaustively researched, they are by no means definitive. Legends change as they're retold over time. Things that people are absolutely sure of one minute turn out not to be true the next. Spirits go dormant. New hauntings pop up. Campuses move; buildings are torn down or renamed. Please send me your corrections for future editions.

Please note that the inclusion of a college or university or any individual landmark should in no way be construed as permission for you to enter or trespass on university property. Many campuses restrict their visitors to students, faculty, staff, and others who have legitimate business there. Check the school's website for visitation policies before making plans to show up. Consider taking a campus tour if one is available. Also, several college towns offer ghost tours that mention the hauntings on campus.

In closing, this book is perhaps the largest compilation of haunted colleges and universities in a single volume, but there always will be another new anomaly to be uncovered, another variation of an urban legend, another personal experience to be revealed. If you have a story you'd like to share, please send it to me in care of the publisher.

Maybe there'll be enough ghost stories for a Volume II!

Part One

NIGHTSHADES OF THE NORTH

The birthplace of the nation, the American Northeast, has more halls of higher education per square mile than any other section of the country. Is it any wonder that it also has more hauntings than many other parts of the country?

Although the Northeast has some of the country's oldest spooks, you couldn't tell by looking at them. Many of them look as young as they did when they were alive and first entered these school yards.

If you've got a hall pass to the Spirit World, let's begin Orientation.

CONNECTICUT

YALE UNIVERSITY

38 Hillhouse Avenue, New Haven, CT 06511; (203) 432-9300
www.yale.edu

Yale University was founded as "Collegiate School" in 1701 in the colony of Connecticut, making it the third-oldest institution of higher learning in the United States. The private Ivy League school was renamed Yale College in 1718 for Elihu Yale, a governor of the British East India Company and a major donor in the school's early years. It became a university in the 1930s.

Yale's main haunting takes place inside a 2,695-seat concert hall that was built in 1901 to celebrate the school's bicentennial. **Woolsey Hall,** as it's known, was part of a three-building complex. Its claim to fame is the magnificent Newbury Memorial Organ, one of the world's largest pipe organs. Students, faculty, and custodians have reported hearing organ music in the hall when no one was at the keyboard.

Current suspicion regarding the instrument's phantom musician falls on Harry B. Jepson, Yale's main organist before the world wars. He died in 1952, and it's believed that he's now returned to play to his spirit heart's content.

MAINE

UNIVERSITY OF MAINE AT FARMINGTON

224 Main Street, Farmington, ME 04938; (207) 778-7000
www.farmington.edu or www.umf.maine.edu

The University of Maine at Farmington was the first public institution of higher learning in Maine. The liberal arts university opened in 1864 as Western State Normal School and graduated its first class two years later. It became part of the University of Maine system in 1968.

Two buildings on campus are haunted. **Mallet Hall,** a three-story, 122-student coed dorm, has a number of spirits. The second and third floors are considered to be the most active, but ghost phenomena have occurred throughout the building. Students sense a negative, if not quite evil, presence in the basement, and the spectre of a female student who hanged herself in her room returns to visit it now and then. The second floor is home to an unseen little girl who's been named Mary. She opens and shuts doors, rifles through people's bureaus, and strews clothing and other items around the rooms.

Nordica Auditorium in Merrill Hall is home to its namesake ghost, Lillian Nordica, who performed there in 1911. Madame Nordica, as she was called, made her operatic debut in Brescia, Italy, in 1879 and became known for a large, varied repertoire. She was shipwrecked while on a world tour and died on the island of Java on May 10, 1914.

Today, Nordica's disembodied bel canto voice is heard in the main performance hall when the lights are out and the space is all but empty. It's a regular occurrence and most often happens around midnight. Sometimes the soprano's presence makes students want to sing out themselves. Other ghost activity in Nordica Auditorium include the standard flickering lights and creaking floors.

MASSACHUSETTS

Boston University

957 Commonwealth Avenue, Boston, MA 02215; (617) 353-2000
www.bu.edu

Boston University, or BU for short, has its roots in a theological school, the Newbury Biblical Institute. A group of Boston Methodist ministers founded the school in Newbury, Vermont, in 1839. Its campus along the Charles River was established around 1937.

Among BU's dorms is the very haunted **Kilachand Hall,** whose resident ghost is a celebrity: Nobel Prize–winning playwright Eugene O'Neill. Over his lifetime he wrote thirty-eight plays, four of which won the Pulitzer Prize for Drama. O'Neill died of bronchial pneumonia on November 27, 1953, at the age of sixty-five in Suite 401 of what was then the Shelton Hotel. O'Neill's last words, uttered three days before he died, have become legendary: "I knew it, I knew it. Born in a hotel room and, goddammit, died in a hotel room."

Kilachand Hall, renamed in 2012 for trustee and donor Rajen Kilachand, currently houses approximately 420 students, mostly upperclassmen, many of whom request it because of the O'Neill connection. Even before Boston University acquired the hotel, it had a reputation for being haunted. O'Neill's widow claimed she talked to her husband's spirit in the room after his death. Students say the lights on the fourth floor are dimmer than elsewhere in the building, although it may seem they're less bright because of higher ceilings. Residents answer the sound of knocking or scraping at their doors (like a key being fitted into a lock) only to find no one there. Sometimes there is rapping on the walls.

Toilets flush on their own. Lights flicker in the rooms, window shades roll up without being touched, and occasionally an unexplainable, roaring gust of wind will blow under the door from the hallway. The elevator sometimes stops on the fourth floor without being called or will refuse to stop at all. Finally, a ghost (though not identified as O'Neill) was seen running into one of the student suites twice in 1994.

The rooms have been slightly renumbered since the Shelton Hotel days. Various sources report the suite in which O'Neill passed away as now being 405, 417, or 419. Oddly, those rooms seem to be among the least haunted on the floor.

Myles Standish Hall has a similar history to Kilachand Hall. Boston University bought the former Myles Standish Hotel in 1949 for use as a dormitory. Baseball great Babe Ruth was a frequent guest at the hotel, and his favorite room was 818. Supposedly his spectre occasionally shows up there. The ninth floor may be haunted by Arthur Miller's uncle, who was said to be the inspiration for the Willy Loman character in *Death of a Salesman*. The man committed suicide in his ninth-story apartment. Students now report cold spots, furniture that rearranges itself while they're away, and bureau drawers opening themselves.

Construction began on the **Boston University Theatre** in 1923. It opened its doors in November 1925 as the Repertory Theatre of Boston, the first tax-exempt civic playhouse in the United States. It was intended as the permanent home of the Henry Jewett Players. Jewett, an Australian-born actor, formed his own troupe in Boston around 1910, and the company remained active until shortly before Jewett's death in 1930. The auditorium later became a cinema.

Boston University bought the playhouse in October 1953 for the School of Theatre Arts program within its College of

Fine Arts. Students blame Jewett's ghost whenever some of their classwork is tampered with or goes missing. The actor's apparition actually shows up from time to time, always dressed in Elizabethan costuming.

Finally, from 1947 until 1973, Boston University owned the former Charlesgate Hotel for use as a female dorm. During that period there were rumors that it was haunted, but most of the stories surfaced during the years it was owned by Emerson College. The building's history and the manifestations that took place there are detailed in the Emerson listing.

EMERSON COLLEGE

120 Boylston Street, Boston, MA 02116; (617) 824-8500
www.emerson.edu

Located in the Back Bay area of Boston, the building at 4 Charlesgate East is now filled with luxury condominiums. During different periods in the twentieth century, however, it was a hotel and then a residence hall for students, first for Boston University and later for Emerson College. And during both go-rounds it was haunted!

The Charlesgate Hotel opened to the public in 1901. There were rumors from the very beginning that some guests had a dark side and liked to dabble in the occult. It was whispered that large, unexplainable black shapes floated in the hallways and sometimes attacked visitors in their beds. There also seemed to be an unusually high number of deaths in the hotel, especially suicides.

Boston University bought the property in 1947, changed its name to **Charlesgate Hall,** and turned it into a female dormitory. It didn't take long for its sinister reputation to surface. A closet on the sixth floor radiated an evil aura, supposedly related to a suicide that had occurred in the hotel years before. There were elevator accidents, though none fatal. It's said that a secret room was discovered behind a closet, and everyone who investigated it got sick.

After BU sold the building in 1973, it operated as a rooming house for a number of years. Emerson College bought the building in 1981 and once again made it a residence hall. That's when the ghost stories really began in earnest. Invisible spirits pulled blankets off students as they slept. One freshman woke to see a male ghost hovering in the air. Doors would slam. Lights would turn off. Paint would be scratched from walls. Unknown noises could be heard. More hidden rooms were found. The apparition of a man in black appeared in the elevator and in the halls, especially on the seventh floor.

It was claimed in a 1981 issue of the student newspaper that a malevolent creature lived in the basement. In 1987 student Cindy Ludlow was sleeping in a bottom bunk in Room 327 when she felt the bed move as if someone were crawling into the top bunk. In the morning the upper bunk's sheets were wrinkled, but the bed was empty; the roommate had never come home the night before.

Ouija board sessions became very popular in the dorm throughout the 1980s, and several students claimed they were communicating with the dead—and not all of them turned out to be friendly phantoms. As a student was changing a flickering bulb in the bathroom, he looked down to notice that somehow a pool of water had gathered around his feet. One wrong move and he could be electrocuted! Meanwhile his friends were playing with a Ouija board in the next room, and it kept spelling out "HA." When the students asked the spirit what was so funny, it spelled out "AC DC" over and over.

Emerson sold Charlesgate Hall in 1995. Three years later new owners converted the building into high-end condominiums. If there are any ghosts still roaming the old Charlesgate Hotel, none of the current residents is talking.

HARVARD UNIVERSITY

Cambridge, MA 02138; (617) 495-1000; www.harvard.edu

Harvard, founded in 1636 by the Massachusetts Bay Colony, is the country's oldest Ivy League institution and one of the most prestigious universities in the world.

University Hall, constructed in white granite, was built between 1813 and 1815. Until 1849, its first floor was the College Commons, or dining room. The spectral sound of meals being served and rowdily consumed can still be heard near the doorway at the southwest corner of the building.

Thayer House, built in 1870 and located on Harvard Yard, is a coed dorm for first-year students. Its ghost wears Victorian-era clothing and is thought to date from the building's pre-Harvard years as a textile mill. Some students have seen a group of similarly clad phantoms, believed to be former textile workers, crowding the dorm's entranceways at night. Other spirits hang out along the wall where there might have been doors at one time. Most of the outdoor sightings take place in the winter, but their frequency dropped off precipitously when exterior safety lighting was installed.

The **Harvard Lampoon Building,** also known as the Lampoon Castle, was completed in 1909. At the time, it was the most expensive college newspaper building ever constructed. Several staff members have seen an anonymous male apparition passing down its halls.

Massachusetts College of Liberal Arts

375 Church Street, North Adams, MA 01247; (413) 662-5000
www.mcla.edu

Founded in 1894 as the North Adams Normal School, the Massachusetts College of Liberal Arts awarded its first baccalaureate degrees in 1932. It began a graduate program four years later. The school has approximately two thousand students.

Berkshire Towers is a twin-towered residence hall set up with suite-style rooms with separate areas for male and female students. Room B8 is haunted by an unknown female ghost. She makes herself known by playing with the doorknob and jangling keys. Residents in the room also hear the spirit's disembodied footsteps.

Smith College

Northampton, MA 01063; (413) 584-2700; www.smith.edu

Smith College is the largest of the Seven Sisters, an informal association of seven prestigious, traditionally female liberal arts colleges founded in the Northeastern United States in the mid-nineteenth century. (Two of the schools—Radcliffe, which merged with Harvard College, and Vassar—are now coeducational.) Smith was chartered in 1871 and opened in 1875.

Sessions House, a residence hall, is the second-oldest building on campus, built in 1710 by Lieutenant Jonathan Hunt and acquired by the college in 1921. The staircase was specially designed with a hidden passageway that would allow the family to hide if they were attacked by marauding Indians. During the Civil War the house's secret pathway was used by runaway slaves on the Underground Railroad. Some of the paranormal activity in the house is said to be caused by revenants of escaped slaves who died when a tunnel leading into the cellar collapsed.

The most popular ghost story about Sessions House, however, concerns clandestine trysts between Hunt's granddaughter Lucy and British soldier General John "Gentleman Johnnie" Burgoyne. Years after their deaths a ghost appeared in the house. At first people thought it was the soldier's spectre coming back to look for Lucy. Over time, folks began to say that, no, it was Lucy's apparition. There are also those who think Lucy and Johnnie's spirits are both present, happily reunited in the Afterlife.

In 1996 the college did a thorough inspection of Sessions House for any concealed rooms or channels. While no full walkways were found, a few large gaps were discovered—enough to suggest that bigger spaces might have existed at one time.

Elsewhere, at the residence hall known as **150 Elm Street** there are inexplicable knocks on the walls and ceilings after the lights go out, and at least one door refuses to stay closed. On one occasion, a bookcase somehow moved itself across an empty room on the second floor and wedged up against the door, preventing anyone from opening it.

Residents on the top floor of **Baldwin House** hear footsteps and furniture moving in the attic, even when the room is locked. The garret's light turns itself on, the door slams shut as people enter the room, and students have seen wet footprints heading to the attic from where a bathroom used to be located. Lights on the third floor work themselves, and there's been talk of an unrecognizable apparition walking through dorm room walls. Some have suggested that the spirit is a former housemother.

Smith College acquired **Chase House** in 1968. Before that it was the Mary A. Burnham girls' school, which dated from the 1870s. Before that it was a boardinghouse for working women. Folklore has it that one of the unwed women who lived there became pregnant. After giving birth, she had a friend kill the baby and then committed suicide. Her unseen apparition paces the halls of Chase House, cradling the child in her arms. Residents hear the woman's footsteps and sometimes hear the infant's cries as well.

Northrop is haunted by the phantom of a former student that everyone calls Francine. Supposedly she went to Italy during her junior year and fell in love with a boy named Francino. She returned, and the two kept in touch for a time, but soon Francino's letters stopped coming. Then one day Francine was gone, without leaving a message. When she never came back, she was presumed dead. After a while, students started to notice that Francine's old rocking chair would begin to rock on its own. Even new rocking chairs brought by other students would start to move.

The identity of the phantom that haunts **Park House** is well known. It's Jeanne M. Robeson, a senior who died in her room on November 13, 1925. She had turned on her gas stove to heat up her iron but never lit the flame. It's unclear whether she did it intentionally, forgot, fell asleep, or was knocked unconscious, but she died of asphyxiation.

The college has owned **Talbot House** since 1921. Built in 1909, it used to be part of the Capen School, which was run by Miss Bessie Capen and catered to children. One of the students, Thomas, was constantly bullied by the other boys for being overweight. When they finally invited him to play a game, he was thrilled and immediately agreed. The boys led him into the attic and locked the door behind him—and they never came back. Thomas was found several days later, dead of dehydration—which might explain why his spirit now spends so much time playing with water in the fourth-floor bathroom. He turns on the faucets full blast, flushes toilets, and is seen washing his hands. He's even carried on conversations with others in the restroom. He apparently "lives" in the attic; residents on the fourth floor hear him moving around overhead in the garret. They also hear him knocking from the inside of the locked attic door.

The other ghost at Talbot House is an enigmatic Woman in White with long brown hair. Her spectre is seen crossing the front porch, waiting under an adjacent streetlight, or standing in the parking lot between Talbot and Lamont House. She never hangs around too long. If she becomes aware that she's being watched, she instantly disappears.

And then there's **Wilson House.** Built on the West Quad in 1926 and named for Martha Wilson, an illustrious alumna, the four-story residence hall has a distinctive bell tower. The ghostly presence that haunts the building's first floor is unknown, but residents hear its disembodied footsteps. Windows open on their own, and sometimes all the doors will suddenly slam shut at the same time.

STONEHILL COLLEGE

320 Washington Street, Easton, MA 02357; (508) 565-1000
www.stonehill.edu

Founded by the Congregation of Holy Cross in 1948, Stonehill College is a private Roman Catholic liberal arts school. **Donahue Hall** predates the college, having been the Seminary of Our Lady of Holy Cross from 1935 to 1948. Today it holds the college's administrative offices, and the Chapel of Our Lady of Sorrow is located on the first floor.

The building was constructed by successful businessman Frederick Lothrop Ames Jr. on 540 acres he purchased in Easton. The centerpiece of his grand estate, completed in 1905, was a fifty-room mansion that he called Stone House Hill House. This residence would eventually become Donahue Hall. On November 6, 1932, Ames was at the controls of his own airplane when he crashed, killing everyone on board. Some say he was attempting daredevil stunts and failed to pull out of a turn. Others blame the accident on a servant who failed to light the landing strip on the Ames estate.

It's uncertain exactly when Ames's ghost began to haunt Donahue Hall. His apparition has been seen only a few times, but people are aware of his presence. More often, the spirit materializes as a blue haze that rises out of a pond on the college grounds. The mist, which is generally diamond shaped and about ten feet long, floats all over campus.

There have also been sporadic claims of a female apparition seen at Stonehill College, including inside Donahue Hall. Some versions of the story have identified her as someone from the Ames family. One story says she drowned in the pond, precipitating the ghostly fog. Another erroneously states that she died in the 1932 plane crash. None of the legends has been corroborated.

WELLESLEY COLLEGE

106 Central Street, Wellesley, MA 02481; (781) 283-1000
www.wellesley.edu

Established in 1870 by Pauline and Henry Fowle Durant, Wellesley College is one of the famous Seven Sisters. The

500-acre liberal arts school is located just west of Boston and has about 2,400 students.

Founders Hall, the oldest academic building on campus, houses several departments, most of them in the humanities. The building is haunted by a Revolutionary War messenger. It's thought that the boy was killed somewhere on the campus grounds during the War for Independence. When he's seen, the courier is still carrying a communiqué in his hand. He roams the hallways of the building, apparently looking for the intended recipient of the message. The Founders Hall apparition is a perfect example of a soul that returned from the Beyond or chose not to Cross Over because it has unfinished business or a message to impart.

Tower Court was constructed on the site of College Hall, the school's original structure that was destroyed by fire in 1914. Students in the residence hall can hear one of the elevators going up and down all night regardless of whether or not anyone has called the car. Supposedly the phenomenon is caused by a maid who fell to her death in the elevator shaft sometime in the early twentieth century.

Beebe Hall, located on the Hazard Quad, has two ghosts. One is a Woman in Black, about whom the students know nothing. The other, who is more sensed than seen, is a former house president who died under mysterious circumstances. Either she committed suicide or, as rumor has it, she was killed by the elusive Woman in Black.

An urban legend suggests that during the construction of **Claffin Hall** a beam fell loose, struck, and killed the Durants' daughter, Alice. The living room of the residence hall is decorated with woodcarvings based on "Alice in Wonderland," the little girl's favorite story. There have been hints that the child's ghost has returned to the room.

Completed in 1923, Alumnae Hall is the college's primary venue for special events and the performing arts. The 1,300-seat **Barstow Auditorium** is on the main level, and the "black box" **Ruth Nagel Jones Theater** is located downstairs. The theaters' primary ghost may be unique in that it was never a real person at all. "Rob" was supposed to be a character in a play that was performed in the Jones Theater in 1992, but the role was cut from the script. Nevertheless, the name still got into the program. Somehow Rob came to life. The spectre began haunting the Jones Theater, occasionally taking the form of a boy or a shadowy man wearing a top hat. His main prank was to mess with the sound and lights. People also had to put up with spooky noises, cold spots, and objects moving on their own. The irksome spirit subsequently began to pull the same shenanigans in the Barstow Auditorium upstairs. Two other phantoms have haunted the Barstow since 1996. One is a woman; the other is a man in dark attire, possibly a suit, and wearing a hat.

All the ghostly activity in the theaters has lessened in recent years. Some think it's stopped completely, but ghost enthusiasts know to never say never.

NEW HAMPSHIRE

COLBY-SAWYER COLLEGE

541 Main Street, New London, NH 03257; (603) 526-3000
www.colby-sawyer.edu

Every square inch of Colby-Sawyer College seems to be haunted. The school was founded as the coeducational New London Academy in 1837. In 1928 the school became a junior college for women only. Baccalaureate programs were added to the curriculum in 1943. It was finally rechristened Colby-Sawyer College in 1975 and became coed again in 1990.

The **Quad** has its share of ghosts. The disembodied sounds of people marching in procession are heard there, especially early on foggy mornings. The haunting is thought to be a carryover from when students practiced drills on the field while preparing to leave for combat during World War I.

Colgate Hall, which opened in 1912, is now classroom and administrative office space. An unknown male phantom with gray hair and a solemn expression on his face wanders Colgate's halls, always wearing a dapper suit or coat and a wide-brimmed hat. He's been seen peering over railings and out of the building's central tower. Some think the ghost may be Governor Anthony Colby.

Many of the college dorms have spectres. **Austin Hall** offers three- and four-person-occupancy rooms. There are no specific details about its ghost, only general reports that the third floor is haunted.

Best Hall, built in 1954, houses more than a hundred students. Its spectre is female, young but older than a student, and dressed in a gray gossamer gown from the late nineteenth or early twentieth century. Her blouse and skirt always seem to be fluttering as if blown by a breeze. Sightings are always brief. The spectre wafts through the corridors and dissipates into thin air as people watch. Some have nicknamed her Mara or Maura.

Burpee Hall is mostly coed, although one floor is for women only. The spectre is a female field hockey player, and usually residents only hear her. When she does appear, it's no more than a shadow. Most often she manifests on an upper floor.

Colby Hall is a three-story residence hall. Students hear phantom footsteps and rattling doorknobs. Some feel surprising gusts of wind even when windows and doors are closed. A spectral cat has also been seen, although if chased it will dart around the nearest corner and vanish, or it will walk through a wall or closed door to get away. Even when the feline doesn't materialize, its mewing has been heard echoing down the halls.

McKean Hall has three floors, with the second story reserved for men. Its resident ghost is Gilbert Ross, who was supposedly executed for witchcraft in the 1700s on the very spot where McKean now stands. The apparition has a pale complexion, a cruel expression, and is forever dressed in black. People usually notice his reflection in a window or catch him out of the corner of their eyes. When seen face-to-face, he'll instantly disappear.

The basement and first and third floors of **Page Hall** are for female students. The second floor is set aside for men. A strange aura felt throughout the building is thought to be a young woman who was a student in the 1960s. She was known to be wacky and would cover herself in Jean Naté perfume and roam the second floor with a loose noose around her neck. A different, more uncomfortable presence is sensed in the basement.

Shepherd Hall's first and third floors are for women; the others are coed by room. The building has a banshee in the basement, and, like Page Hall's ghost, it's never seen.

The playful spirit of a young boy appears in the loft area of the **Susan Colgate Cleveland Library,** which was once a barn but is now totally renovated and repurposed. The lad may be the same shade who rearranges history books, putting them out of order, when no one's around.

The 650-seat auditorium in the **Sawyer Fine Arts Center** has two spectral entities. Like other theater ghosts, one of them fiddles with the lights and plays with objects. The second spirit makes a distinct rapping sound, so it's thought to be a professor who had the nervous habit of tapping his fingers as he talked. The noise is especially apparent near the teacher's former office.

DARTMOUTH COLLEGE

Hanover, NH 03755; (603) 646-1110; www.dartmouth.edu

Dartmouth College, an Ivy League school, was founded in 1769 by Eleazar Wheelock, a Congregational minister. Though easily accessible by Interstate 91, the school's 269-acre campus is far removed from any major metropolitan area. All the better for the ghosts to come out and play.

The departed spirits thought to live on at **Alpha Theta** all met their maker at the fraternity house on the same night. The ghost story dates from a tragedy in 1934 when the building was occupied by a Theta Chi fraternity. On Saturday night, February 24, nine young men sleeping in the house died in their sleep of carbon monoxide poisoning caused by an improperly banked coal furnace. (According to some tellings of the story, all of the victims were fraternity brothers. In other recountings, two of them were overnight guests.) The other eight members of the fraternity survived only because they were away for the weekend.

Everyone at Dartmouth—indeed, the entire town—was shaken. Over the next few years, with such a stigma over its head and rumors that the house was haunted by the victims, the fraternity had difficulty finding pledges. It was decided that the only way to prevent Theta Chi's demise would be to tear down the notorious building and erect a new frat house. The structure at 33 North Main Street was razed in 1940, and a new home went up on the same site.

But was that enough? Some portions of original foundation remained, and apparently so do some of the building's ghosts. The leftover stones are now part of the laundry room located in the basement by the back stairs, and some members of Alpha Theta say they feel uneasy whenever they're down there. Supposedly laundry will move around by itself, and food shows up that has no reason for being there. A few guys have walked into rooms that no longer exist, and others have reported running into male spectres wearing 1930s attire—some of them recognizable from old college yearbook photos as having been among the fatalities.

Panarchy, the college's first undergraduate society, had its beginning in the Greek system. Early in the 1900s the fraternity bought the house at 9 School Street, where it still resides, an 1835 Greek Revival building that was once a physician's private residence. There were whispers that the good doctor imprisoned his daughter, a schizophrenic, in the attic. Left to her own devices, she committed suicide there. Her troubled presence is said to still haunt the room.

With its central location and tall spire, the Baker Memorial Library (renamed the **Baker-Berry Library** in 2002) is one of the most noticeable buildings on campus. The first account of a library ghost dates from the 1940s and appeared in the *Library Bulletin*. The newsletter reported that a staffer was surprised by a spectre dressed in gabardine in the stacks on the third floor. As recently as 2002, a student claimed an entire shelf of books on the seventh floor dissolved into nothingness. People also have heard strange noises coming from the room directly below the tower.

KEENE STATE COLLEGE

229 Main Street, Keene, NH 03435; (603) 352-1909 or (800) 572-1909; www.keene.edu

Established as a teachers college in 1909, Keene State College is now a full liberal arts institution offering at least forty degree programs.

Its most famous spirit, Harriet Lane Huntress, was an important administrator in the New Hampshire Department of Education. The spectre haunts her eponymous **Huntress Hall,** which is located on the Quad.

Apparently Huntress wasn't too happy when the dormitory began to board men. That's when people started hearing the racket coming from the attic. Some thought it sounded like a person loudly rolling around in a wheelchair, and a legend was born. Supposedly it was Harriet Huntress, making a fuss to protest the mingling of the men and women. However, after the war when the dorm went back to being a female residence hall, the noises didn't stop. In fact, they've gotten worse over the years. Students now also report hearing the echo of chains being dragged across the garret floor. On rare occasions, the clanks and clatter are heard from other areas of the building as well.

The hall was renovated top to bottom in 2009. It houses 154 students and is once again coed—which may be why the paranormal activity continues. The ghost *has* been investigated. In the 1970s, a wheelchair was discovered in the attic, stored away and not recently used, but it never belonged to Huntress. New Hampshire Paranormal (NHP), a ghost hunter group, was given access to the hall during one of the school breaks but found nothing. The Travel Channel also visited the building for its 2004 production *Haunted Campuses*.

There is one more spot at Keene that's said to be haunted. The **Brickyard Pond** is a large greenish pool more or less bordered by Wyman Way, Main and Appleton Streets, and the Ashuelot River that meanders through town. It's said that students can sometimes gaze into the water and see a gleaming spectral horse ridden by a young couple.

Mount Washington College

3 Sundial Avenue, Manchester, NH 03103; (603) 668-6660
www.mountwashington.edu

Mount Washington College takes up about a third of a major business complex known as the **Mount Washington College Center of Commerce and Education.** Legend has it that at least two ghosts wander the halls, but both of them are pre-secondary age. One is a little boy who bounces a ball on the third and fourth floors. Both the boy and the ball will vanish on a moment's notice. A young girl is seen in the corridors as well. She allegedly died in the building—somehow of hypothermia. (One version of the tale has her dying outside the building while writing a plea for help on the window.) There are also stories of disembodied blue eyes staring in through the windows and the sound of a wet finger trailing down the glass.

Plymouth State University

17 High Street, Plymouth, NH 03264; (603) 535-5000
www.plymouth.edu

Plymouth State University can trace its origin to 1808 and Holmes Plymouth Academy, which was one of the country's first teachers preparatory schools. As it grew, the institution also diversified its programs, becoming first a teachers college, then a state college, and finally (in 2003) a state university.

Because of the cold winters, a **tunnel system** was built to connect five dormitories: Blair, Mary Lyon, Hall, Memorial, and Rounds. At some time in the unknown past, a young man from **Blair Hall** and a girl from **Mary Lyon Hall** allegedly became lovers. One night they were meeting for a tryst in the tunnels when the section they were standing in collapsed. Both were killed.

Now the male student causes mischief in his old dorm. The young lady from Mary Lyon Hall, however, mostly haunts the tunnels, supposedly seeking her old beau. She or some other spirit also haunts the basement of Mary Lyon Hall. Students have reported being uncomfortable whenever they're down there, and they try to leave as soon as possible.

Meanwhile, **Hall Dormitory** also has a phantom. The building's ghost is thought to be a male student who hanged himself in the attic. Years later, a punching bag was hung from the beam that the boy used to end his life, and students were stunned when it began to sway by itself. The lad's spectre is seen in the halls, always wearing jeans and a flannel shirt. Other strange activity includes the sound of a ball being bounced on the floor, and even when students know they're alone they sometimes feel that someone or something is in the room with them.

Saint Anselm College

100 Saint Anselm Drive, Manchester, NH 03102; (603) 641-7000
www.anselm.edu

Saint Anselm College and an attached Benedictine abbey were founded in 1889. The state granted the school the right to award degrees in 1895. The first academic building, **Alumni Hall,** was nearing completion when it burned to the ground in 1892. Rebuilt, it was dedicated a year later to officially open the college. Its bell tower was constructed in 1912, and a new wing, the Chapel Arts Center, was added in 1923.

Today the building is primarily used for administrative and faculty offices, although there are also a few classrooms and a women's residence area known as "The Streets."

According to legend, a monk once killed himself by jumping out a fourth-story window in Alumni Hall. His spectre now haunts the entire building—especially the fourth floor, from which he took his fatal leap.

UNIVERSITY OF NEW HAMPSHIRE

105 Main Street, Durham, NH 03824; (603) 862-1234; www.unh.edu

When the University of New Hampshire started out in 1866 it was an agricultural school affiliated with Dartmouth College. Today it's the largest university in the state.

At first there was no on-campus housing, so few women were attracted to the college. To help remedy that, construction began on **Smith Hall,** the first female dorm, and it was completed in 1908. No one knows when stories about a ghost in Smith Hall began, but they seem to have been around forever. The spirit is said to be a good-looking young woman, but no one has been able to identify her. She comes and goes, walks the corridors, and is responsible for the sound of footsteps in the attic.

NEW JERSEY

DREW UNIVERSITY

36 Madison Avenue, Madison, NJ 07940; (973) 408-3000
www.drew.edu

Drew University was founded as Drew Theological Seminary in 1867. Affiliated with the United Methodist Church, the institution attained university status in 1928 and added a graduate degree program in 1955.

Built in 1893, **Hoyt-Browne Hall** is one of the school's oldest dormitories, housing mostly upper-level students, especially seniors. The first floor is set aside for male students; the second and third floors are coed. The fourth story houses females only, and that's where the ghost lives. Drew University even mentions her on its website. Her name is Carol, and she was a student who killed herself by leaping from the fourth floor to the ground below. Fortunately, all of her activity is playful in nature. Mostly she rearranges the furniture when no one's at home.

PRINCETON UNIVERSITY

Princeton, NJ 08544; (609) 258-3000; www.princeton.edu

One of the eight Ivy League institutions and one of the nine US colleges founded before the Revolution, Princeton University was established as the College of New Jersey in 1746. It moved to Newark the next year and settled in Princeton in 1756. The name was changed to Princeton University in 1896.

Murray-Dodge Hall is actually made up of two buildings joined by a cloister. Murray Hall, built in 1879, now houses the university's **Hamilton Murray Theater.** Dodge Hall, constructed in 1900, is home to the chaplains, their dean, and student religious and service clubs.

Most of the school's spectral activity takes place in and around the theater space. The oil portrait of Hamilton Murray hanging in the hall is said to glow at night, and students often sense his presence near the painting. Props move by themselves on the stage. Tools will vanish while sets are being built, only to show up later somewhere else. During dress rehearsals for new productions, the ghost of a young man wearing a long coat and top hat sometimes materializes in the auditorium stage left. He'll disappear just as quickly, even while people are staring at him.

NEW YORK

CORNELL UNIVERSITY

410 Thurston Avenue, Ithaca, NY 14850; (607) 255-5241
www.cornell.edu

Founded by Ezra Cornell and Andrew Dickson in 1865, Cornell University is a private Ivy League school with approximately twenty-one thousand undergraduate and graduate students.

One of Cornell's most popular (and colorful) professors at the end of the nineteenth century was Hiram Corson, who taught English literature from 1870 to 1903. Corson was a firm believer in the Afterlife and the ability to communicate with those on the Other Side. Robert Browning, Henry Wadsworth Longfellow, Alfred Tennyson, and Walt Whitman were just a few of Corson's "spiritual visitors," as he liked to call them. No one but Corson knows if he actually talked to the dead, but there *are* plenty of phantoms on campus.

The **William Straight Hall Student Union,** commonly referred to as "the Straight," is a six-story Gothic structure modeled off Hart House at the University of Toronto. Ghosts at the Straight are pretty easy to pick out: They're the handsome young men walking around in tuxedos.

The **Sage Chapel** is one of Ithaca's most popular wedding venues, but there's not a lot of "backstage space" in which to get ready. As a result, bridal parties frequently dress and prepare in the crypt, where the university founders and numerous donors and supporters are entombed. Legend has it that sometimes the spirits will rise from their eternal rest long enough to sanctify the nuptials.

Built in 1961, the **John M. Olin Library** contains materials on the humanities and social sciences. According to campus gossip, the angry spirit of a female student causes trouble for newcomers to the stacks. Supposedly she was killed in the library, but according to the college and local police there's no record of such a death.

The **Agriculture Quadrangle,** or Ag Quad, is surrounded by buildings associated with the New York College of Agriculture and Life Sciences. A group of spectral gentlemen wearing top hats and dressed in nineteenth-century attire materializes there whenever a major building on campus is about to be razed. The ethereal protestors showed up before the demolition of both Roberts and Stone Halls, for example. The original dean of the college, Isaac P. Roberts, who wore a signature stovepipe hat, is thought to be among the revenants.

The **Alice Statler Auditorium,** part of the Cornell School of Hotel Administration, is used for lectures, presentations, and special events. Custodians have seen Alice Stratler's apparition walk through walls in the auditorium, and she's even grabbed at them when their heads were turned. There have also been reports that Alice strolls down the halls in the Statler Hotel on campus.

Ecology House started out as a hotel in the 1950s. Cornell acquired the building in 1964 and used it as a residence hall for upper-level women and doctoral students. A fire broke out on the morning of April 5, 1967, and six undergraduate women, three graduate students, and a professor were killed. Their spirits now haunt the premises. There are strange lights, and apparitions of the victims turn up in their old rooms. People hear disembodied voices and footsteps as well as the barking of a dog that some say died in the flames.

Unlike most of the other dormitories at Cornell, **Risley Hall** is a themed dormitory that houses students with a common interest. The Tudor Gothic building, modeled on England's Hampton Court Palace, has a "house ghost" wandering the halls: none other than Prudence Risley herself. "Auntie Pru," as the kids refer to her, creates cold breezes, plays with the lights, and makes strange noises.

Fordham University

441 East Fordham Road, Bronx, NY 10458; (718) 817-1000 www.fordham.edu

Fordham University, founded in 1841, has about 6,000 undergraduate and graduate students; about 2,900 of them live on campus.

Collins Auditorium was built in 1904 and named for John Collins, S.J., a former university president. Students hear inexplicable whispering in the hall and sometimes see a male spectre walking in the balcony. There are also cold spots throughout the building. Sometimes cast and crew will come to dress rehearsal to find that set pieces have somehow moved on their own—an activity usually blamed on Father Collins.

Finlay Hall is a four-story residence hall. At one time the building was part of the medical school, and several dorm rooms still have remnants of the loft areas where students observed dissections of cadavers. Residents have woken up during the night to see the visitants of long-gone students dressed in lab coats staring down at them. Other residents have felt themselves being choked or a cadaver tag being tied to one of their toes. Security guards in the basement have seen doors slam and chairs move by themselves.

Martyr's Court is a huge multistory dorm built in 1951. Among the many hauntings in the three-sectioned complex is the apparition of a young blonde girl who is seen in the showers, standing discreetly behind a curtain, immobile and staring straight ahead. A phantom man walks past open doorways, heading toward the wall at the end of the corridor. If students get up to check on the stranger, there's never anyone in the hall. Then there's the sound of children's laughter that seems to come from inside the walls.

O'Hare Hall, built in 2000, is named for former university president Joseph O'Hare. A worker who was killed during the building's construction has returned to wander the halls. He must think he's still on the job, because residents hear him hammering and banging away at the walls.

NEW YORK UNIVERSITY

70 Washington Square South, New York, NY 10012; (212) 998-1212 www.nyu.edu

Founded in 1831, New York University (known as NYU) is one of the largest private universities in the United States, with about fifty thousand students in its undergraduate, graduate, and non-credit programs. Its main campus is at Washington Square in Greenwich Village.

Brittany Residence Hall started out as the Brittany Hotel before the university acquired it. Constructed in 1929, the building had a speakeasy in its penthouse during the Prohibition era. According to current residents, modern times haven't stopped some of the early-twentieth-century revelers. Students throughout the building hear music from the Jazz Age coming down the halls as well as the sound of dancing feet. Sometimes they see inexplicable lights as well.

D'Agostino Residence House is one of the residence halls set aside for NYU law students. An apparition in eighteenth-century garb, sometimes on foot and sometimes in a carriage, has been seen waiting outside the dormitory. The spirit often strolls Third Street along the front of the residence hall between MacDougal and Sullivan Streets. Sometimes he'll simply stand at the corner of Third and Sullivan. The storied Café Bizarre used to be located at the intersection, and before the club was torn down to make way for the dormitory, the wraith would sometimes go inside and take a seat. Some people think the spectral stranger may be Aaron Burr, who owned carriage houses located on what is now Third Street.

The **Brown Building of Science** is a classroom, laboratory, and research facility for New York University students, but on March 25, 1911, it was the ten-story Asch Building—the site of one of the worst industrial tragedies in American history. The Triangle Shirtwaist Factory, located on the eighth through tenth floors, caught fire. In the end, 123 women and 23 men, ranging in age from fourteen to forty-three, were dead from either fire, smoke inhalation, being trampled or crushed, or jumping to their deaths. Today, people out on the street occasionally hear the screams of the trapped, injured, and dying or smell smoke and burning flesh—especially on the anniversary of the disaster. Some students and staff on the upper floors are intermittently overcome with an irrational need to flee the building. Others are suddenly overwhelmed by an intense sadness or feeling of hopelessness. At least one female wraith has been spotted on the eighth and ninth floors. People outside the building also encounter the phantoms of parading union members who picketed the Triangle Shirtwaist Company for better working conditions back in 1909.

NIAGARA UNIVERSITY

5796 Lewiston Road, Niagara University, NY 14109; (716) 286-8700
www.niagara.edu

Niagara University was founded as Our Lady of Angels Seminary in 1856. About half of the 3,300 undergraduate students live on campus, located on the US side of Niagara Falls overlooking the gorge.

Clet Hall, constructed in 1862, was the first building on campus. On December 5, 1864, a fire swept through Clet Hall, and a student from Brooklyn named Thomas Hopkins rushed into the building to make sure everyone had escaped. Unfortunately, he was the one who didn't make it out alive. According to legend, Hopkins has returned to watch over students. That being said, he's apparently also quite a prankster and will play tricks on residents if he thinks they're getting out of line.

RENSSELAER POLYTECHNIC INSTITUTE

110 Eighth Street, Troy, NY 12180; (518) 276-6000; www.rpi.edu

Rensselaer Polytechnic Institute was founded in 1824 by Stephen Van Rensselaer as a technological school and research laboratory.

West Hall is home to the Arts Department as well as administrative and financial offices, but during the Civil War the building was turned into a hospital. Soldiers who had mental or emotional problems due to their war experiences—what today would be called post-traumatic stress disorder—were housed in the basement.

West Hall is haunted by a female spectre nicknamed Betsy. Supposedly she was a nurse who tended to the mentally unstable patients, but the strain eventually caused her to go mad. Her ghost has returned to look after the long-gone wounded and shell-shocked, but she never materializes. Instead, students and staff hear Betsy's disembodied, barely audible murmurs as she passes them in the halls.

SAINT LAWRENCE UNIVERSITY

23 Romoda Drive, Canton, NY 13617; (315) 229-5011 www.stlawu.edu

Saint Lawrence University, founded in 1856, is New York's oldest coeducational university. St. Lawrence, as the spelling of the school's name is usually abbreviated, has approximately 2,400 undergraduate students and 90 or more students in its graduate program.

In addition to its dormitories and other housing, the university has several Theme Cottages in which residents share a common interest. **The Hub** is techno-centric,

offering (according to the university's website) "gaming ori-
ented events" that "celebrate 'nerd' culture." The two-story
building was acquired by university president John Stebbins
Lee in 1860, and he and his wife raised five children there.
Modern-day residents and visitors have spotted a female
apparition just as it dashes around a corner or into the next
room. The spectre is always wearing a long, white dress with
a red petticoat. A playful sprite, she turns off stereos if the
volume's too high and slams doors.

Legend has it that the ghostly gamine is Francine, one of
the Lee daughters who supposedly died in the house while
still a fairly young girl. Others have said that it's her sister
Gertrude. Neither explanation holds water, though: Francine
grew up, graduated from St. Lawrence, married, and moved
to Cambridge, Massachusetts. Years later, she became one of
St. Lawrence's trustees. In fact, Whitman Hall is named for
her. Francine's sister Gertrude *did* die in the house, but not
until she was a much older woman. So who is the ghost?
Perhaps we'll never know.

One part of the equation may have been solved, though.
Folklorists believe the story about a red petticoat stems from
a former dean of women who didn't allow female students
to wear loud colors. She thought they were too excitable for
the male students.

Skidmore College

815 North Broadway, Saratoga Springs, NY 12866; (518) 580-5000
www.skidmore.edu

Skidmore College, a private liberal arts school, grew out of
the Young Women's Industrial Club that was established in
1903. The group formed the Skidmore School of the Arts in

1911 and was chartered as a four-year college offering baccalaureates in 1922. The institution became coed in 1971.

Wilmarth Hall, one of the residence halls, was completed in 1968. It suffered a tragic fire two years later in which one student was killed. Residents still see her soul wandering the halls. Even if students don't spy her, they sometimes still hear the distinctive tapping sounds she makes as she walks the corridors.

Union College

807 Union Street, Schenectady, NY 12308; (518) 388-6000
www.union.edu

Union College is a private liberal arts school founded in 1795. It has been coeducational since 1970.

Jackson's Garden is eight acres of lush formal gardens and wooded glen created by Professor Isaac Jackson in the 1830s on the north side of campus. One of its prettiest features is a small creek, **Hans Groot's Kill,** that runs from east to west, cutting the garden almost exactly in half. There's been a ghost story about the waterway for more than two hundred years! On the night of the first full moon after the summer solstice, the apparition of "Alice" can be spied soulfully strolling along the path of Hans Groot's Kill in the center of the garden. It's also sometimes possible to see her walking along the Mohawk River about two thousand feet from the northwest edge of campus. The young woman can be recognized by her seventeenth-century clothing, the black and blue marks on her neck, and the sound of her mournful cries and groans.

According to legend, Alice was accused of witchcraft and burned at the stake next to the meandering creek.

A variation of the tale further identifies the girl as the daughter of prosperous Dutch settler Jan van der Veer. Jan hoped to find a fine husband for Alice, but she wasn't interested in any of her father's choices. She had found her own beau. When the father caught Alice and her boyfriend on the banks of the Mohawk, he shot the interloper and started to drag his daughter home. A mob grew up against him. Someone in the crowd cried out that Jan was a witch, and within minutes he had been tied up and burned at the stake. When Alice started screaming, the crowd decided that she was probably a witch, too! The horde hauled her to the gardens and either hanged her or burned her at the stake.

It's uncertain why Alice—if that was her name—has chosen to come back from the Beyond to return to the site of her horrific death. Perhaps her spirit wants to remember the tranquil times before her world turned upside down.

A totally unrelated spectre, a seemingly deaf professor, has been encountered at one of the entrances to Jackson's Garden, acting for all the world like its caretaker. Could it be Isaac Jackson himself?

United States Military Academy at West Point

West Point, NY 10996; (845) 938-4011; www.usma.edu

Technically known as the United States Military Academy at West Point, the school goes by many names, including the Academy, the Point, Army (when talking about its sports teams), and, of course, simply West Point. Founded in 1802, it is a four-year coeducational federal service academy, meaning that graduates are enlisted into the armed services, most often as second lieutenants in the army. Its campus, which is a national landmark, is located about fifty miles north of New York City on the Hudson River.

Although ghost hunters probably won't be allowed to go in and check the facilities anytime soon, at least one location on the grounds is rumored to be haunted. The official **residence of the Superintendent** is home to a spectre known as Molly, a maid from sometime in the distant past. Instead of straightening up the house, however, the ethereal servant likes to undo freshly made beds.

WELLS COLLEGE

170 Main Street, Aurora, NY 13026; (315) 364-3266; www.wells.edu

Wells College, a private liberal arts school, is located in the Finger Lakes district of upstate New York. It was established as a women's college in 1868 by Henry Wells, who also founded the Wells Fargo and American Express companies. The school became coeducational in 2005.

Main Building, constructed in 1890, is a four-story, coed residence hall accommodating about 180 students. The four ghost stories associated with it all have to do with an illness that swept through campus or a fire in the building. No dates ever seem to be associated with the tales, other than the fact that they happened "long ago."

Residents of **Main 220** have reported paranormal activity ever since a student killed herself in the room. The suicidal girl had become involved in the occult, leaving her depressed and mentally unbalanced. Subsequent boarders in the room have looked into the mantel mirror and seen a reflection of the dead girl sitting alone in a corner of the room. On a few isolated occasions, the girl's apparition briefly materialized. Cold spots also appear in the chamber.

According to legend, a cholera epidemic hit Wells College at some point. Those who became sick were treated in a makeshift hospital on the fourth (and possibly the third) floor, and one female student was isolated in what was then **Main 305.** Its window faced south toward Morgan Hall, so the girl's fiancé would go to the top floor of Morgan and wave to her. One horrific night as he watched, a rapid fire passed through Main and the woman was killed. According to recent residents of Room 305, the fire victim is still there. She's never destructive, but the spirit will rap on walls, move small personal belongings, create odd sounds, and generally make those who live in the room feel uneasy.

A similar ghost story suggests it may have arisen from the same cholera outbreak. In the second tale, the epidemic was so severe that the school had to bring in additional nurses. When the fire broke out in Main Building, the health providers tried to get as many patients as possible to safety. Tragically, many students and nurses died. Nowadays, students living in Main Building who are sick enough to stay bedridden say that they've sometimes been visited by one or more of these Angels of Mercy, as the phantoms have been called. The spectral saviors will take the students' pulses, check their temperatures, or even stroke the students' hair and fevered brows as they fall asleep.

Morgan Hall also succumbed to flames in 1925. To speed students out of the burning building, Max, a security guard, pushed students down the staircases. His method was rough but effective: Everyone survived . . . except Max. Today, kids walking down the stairs in Morgan sometimes feel a disembodied hand give them a sharp shove from behind. Most residents of the hall have heard about Max, though, so they know he's just trying to help them out.

A female science student in **Zabriskie Hall** had a tendency to burn the midnight oil. At first she was flattered that one of the professors was taking a scholarly interest in her results, but then she discovered he was publishing her findings as his own. When she confronted him about it, he stabbed her to death and left the weapon in her back as he fled. Today the girl's apparition comes up to students and asks them to remove the knife. Then she attacks anyone who is kind (or foolish) enough to try to help her.

Most seniors are required to write a thesis about their experiences at Wells. One girl residing in the **South Wing of Dodge House** became so obsessed with the paper that her fellow students could hear her typing away hour after hour, morning, noon, and night. They started calling her the "Mad Typist." Finally, some friends convinced her to take a break. Coming back that night from the Fargo Bar & Grill, a motorist careened onto the sidewalk and killed her. To this day, students living near her old room feel the victim's presence standing behind them whenever they get stuck on a writing project.

There's an urban legend that one year, back when **Pettibone House** was a residence hall, three senior girls became particularly close friends. Two of the girls were unpacking after returning from Spring Break when the third arrived, looking rather sad. The girl confided that she was afraid they would grow apart after graduation. Her two BFFs assured her that would never happen, and, comforted, the girl left the room. When several hours passed and she didn't come back, the others became curious and started looking for her. They found out that their friend had never made it to the dorm. She had been killed in a car accident on her way back to college. The girls had been talking to her ghost.

Pettibone House was built in 1857 as a private residence by George Pettibone. Henry Wells purchased it for use by the university in 1869, but according to rumor, at some point prior to that, Wells was having an affair with a woman living with the Pettibones. When Mrs. Wells found out about it, she stormed down to the bridge in front of the Wells's home, known as Glen Park, where she knew the hussy would be meeting her husband. She stabbed the woman to death. Students crossing the **Glen Park Bridge** today know to beware if the lights go out. The ghost of Mrs. Wells may be right behind them, ready to strike from beyond the grave.

There are also hauntings at Glen Park, now a residence hall. People sometimes see a dark figure standing in the tower atop the building. Most assume that the apparition is Mrs. Wells, looking for her husband's return. Some think, instead, that it's the spirit of a Civil War–era nurse waiting for her husband to come back from war. On one occasion in the mid-1990s, residents at Glen Park went down to the basement where they stored their bicycles, only to discover that they had melted together into a giant metallic heap. Several theories were suggested as to what could have caused the freakish manifestation—including the possibility of underground hot springs or perhaps someone buried beneath the cellar floor—but, in the end, none of them could explain the phenomenon.

PENNSYLVANIA

Bucknell University

701 Moore Avenue, Lewisburg, PA 17837; (570) 577-2000
www.bucknell.edu

Founded in 1846, Bucknell University is a private liberal arts institution with approximately 3,500 students. Originally known as the University of Lewisburg, the name of the school was changed to honor a charter member of the board of trustees, William Bucknell.

Hunt Hall, built in 1928 and fully refurbished in 2003, houses 150 students and provides common rooms for the university's sororities. A female spirit has called the dormitory home since the mid-1980s. She mostly sticks to the third and fourth floors of "Haunt Hall," as it's been nicknamed. The ghostly visitor usually remains invisible, but people smell a delicate perfume when she walks by. She opens and shuts cabinets, shifts around furniture, pulls posters and other objects off the walls, moves plants, and turns on lights and music players. More extreme activity has included tossing CDs around the rooms. On one occasion she even made an unplugged telephone ring. In the summer when residents are away, she turns her attention to the custodians and plays with their tools and moves their equipment. The apparition doesn't materialize often, only every two or three years. When she does she's wearing a red or green raincoat, although she's been known to try on students' dresses and parade down the hall in them.

Everyone agrees that the phantom is a former student, and many folks call her Angela. The most popular tale about her past is that she died in an automobile accident on her way back to school after attending funerals for her mother and brother. Others believe she died in a carriage accident back in the nineteenth century or that she fell into a nearby creek and drowned.

EAST STROUDSBURG UNIVERSITY OF PENNSYLVANIA

200 Prospect Street, East Stroudsburg, PA 18301; (570) 422-3211
www.esu.edu

East Stroudsburg University of Pennsylvania began as East Stroudsburg Normal School, a teachers training school, in 1893. Today there are more than seven thousand undergraduate and graduate students on its 213-acre campus, located about two miles from the New Jersey border.

When it opened in 1929, the **Abeloff Center for the Performing Arts** was known simply as "the auditorium." No one has ever seen the building's wraiths, but people have heard their voices in the halls. Objects will disappear and then show up elsewhere—if they come back at all. There are also cold spots and odd odors.

The new **Fine and Performing Arts Center,** constructed in 1979, contains two legit theaters, a concert hall, "black box" experimental theater spaces, rehearsal rooms, a gallery, classrooms, and offices for the Art, Music, Theater, and Communications Studies Departments. With all that going on in one building, who would have thought there would be room for spooks as well? But there is! The first phantom is Sarah, a young woman who hanged herself from the lighting grid over one of the stages soon after the theater opened. People have seen her apparition, and it's probably her ethereal voice that they've heard in the building. Sarah likes to snatch at people, but most of her activity involves playing with the lights and causing other technical problems during performances. Another ghost, "Ice Cold," has an entirely different personality. The temperature drops whenever she's in the room— hence her name—and her actions are more poltergeist-like than Sarah's—in other words, she's mildly destructive. She'll move or deface objects, switch around plaques and name-plates, and just be a general nuisance.

Kemp Library was built at the same time as the Fine and Performing Arts Center. Two spirits are commonly seen there, but no one knows why they're in the building. One is an African-American boy, about nine years old, and he only appears among the books in the history section. The other apparition is a black cat that weaves its way among the archived government documents.

Shawnee Hall, constructed in 1952, is the oldest dormitory on campus. The coed residence hall has a phantom in its basement, thought to be a former custodian who died somewhere in the building. Mostly only his voice is heard.

Phi Sigma Kappa fraternity house has a presence in the form of an adult female ghost. The guys have given the soothing spirit the sobriquet Mrs. Booth, and she may have been the owner of the building at one time. She materializes by a fireplace, so the frat boys think her ashes are interred somewhere inside it. Her spectre also wanders the second and third floors.

The nearby **Sigma Pi fraternity house** is haunted by a banshee named Margie. She's been really unpleasant—let's leave it at that—to anyone staying in one particular room on the third floor ever since it was renovated in the 1960s. During the room's makeover, someone found Margie's cremation urn behind one of the walls and accidentally spilled its contents. Not good.

FRANKLIN & MARSHALL COLLEGE

415 Harrisburg Avenue, Lancaster, PA 17603; (717) 291-3911
www.fandm.edu

Franklin & Marshall College, founded in 1787, is a four-year private coeducational liberal arts institution. The school evolved from the 1853 merger of Franklin College, founded by Ben Franklin and others in 1787, and Marshall College, established by Supreme Court Justice John Jay Marshall forty years later.

A staggering number of its buildings are haunted. In the **Barshinger Center for the Performing Arts,** people have reported that if they stand on the stage and look out into the empty, dark auditorium at night, they will sometimes see two small lights moving back and forth at the back of the house.

Franklin & Marshall provides residence halls for students with similar interests to live together in what are called "college houses." Legend has it that in **Bonchek College House,** a female student overcome by stress killed herself in her room in the 1970s. Ever since, residents in the hall have been able to hear her frustrated screams during final exam weeks in the fall semesters. People assigned to her old room have woken up to find a pool of blood on the floor. The girl's angst-ridden apparition even turns up in the hallways periodically, usually carrying a physics book.

Built in 1856, **Diagnothian Hall** currently houses the registrar's office on its first floor and a large lecture hall–style classroom on the second. During the Civil War the building served as a hospital. The moans and rattles that pervade the place were reportedly first heard one night when a music professor was playing a recording of a war-related song, Sousa's "Red Cross Nurse." (That would put the initial haunting sometime between 1977 and 2001, back when the hall was home to the music department.) In addition to the disturbing sounds of patients in pain, people hear doors slam and experience other mild paranormal activity.

The former **Distler House**, built in 1891 to serve as the college's first gymnasium, is now a bookstore and the Jazzman's Cafe. Visitors hear spectral sounds at night that date from the building's days as a fitness center. People have heard scrambling noises from the perimeter of the upper level, where the indoor track used to be. There are also spectral grunts and groans that sound like workouts, wrestling, and horseplay.

Shadek-Fackenthal Library was constructed in 1937. Its ghost is thought to be Dr. Harvey Bassler, who died in a car accident on March 14, 1950. He was known for displaying his Pennsylvania Dutch artifacts in the northeast corner of the Fackenthal Library, as it was then called. Soon after Bassler's death, his stooped, aged apparition started appearing in the area in which he had shown off his collection. Weird things started happening elsewhere in the building, too. Books turned up in the wrong places or would fall from shelves; elevators stopped on the wrong levels; and people heard strange sounds. The activity lessened after the Shadek wing was added in the 1980s, but Bassler's spirit still turns up from time to time. Another oddity: Three days before Bassler's accident, he had a premonition that he was about to die. He wrote a letter to the caretaker of his farm telling him where he could find money that was due him.

Wohlson House began life in 1929 as the Lambda Chi Alpha fraternity house. After fifty-three years it was turned into the admissions office in 1982. Folks think its ghost is a Lambda Chi who either drowned somewhere in the building or died from falling down the cellar stairs. The spirit's identity is unknown, but he's been nicknamed Bob. He slams doors in the middle of the night and sometimes turns out all of the lights in the building at the same time. (Supposedly, if you chide him by name, he will turn the lights back on.) At least one woman has told of being alone in the basement and hearing a loud thud on the steps behind her. Two others in the cellar saw an unfamiliar male figure, presumably Bob, walk across the room and pass through the wall.

GETTYSBURG COLLEGE

300 North Washington Street, Gettysburg, PA 17325 (717) 337-6300; www.gettysburg.edu

Gettysburg College was founded in 1832. There are about 2,700 students on the 200-acre campus, which is less than half a mile from the famous Civil War battlefield.

Brua Hall, built as a chapel in 1890, is home to the Theatre Arts Department. It's rumored that the spirits of several slain soldiers have wandered into the building over the years, but the one that shows up most often is an officer, not elderly but no longer young, who's been nicknamed "The General." He's been seen peering out of a window on the east side of the building, and his ghost materializes in the middle of the stage sitting in a chair. (The chair is a ghost as well!) His shadow is sometimes cast against the back wall as he walks across the catwalk above the stage.

Stevens Hall opened in 1868 as a preparatory school for the college. Now the fourth-oldest building on campus, it was named for Thaddeus Stevens, a cofounder of the college and the author of the Fourteenth Amendment of the Constitution. The hall's ghosts are all children, seen for the most part on the third floor. Their apparitions have been caught going through closets, and one of the spirits, a little girl, likes to stare at herself in mirrors.

The most famous ghost of Stevens Hall—and perhaps the best known at the whole college—is the so-called Blue Boy. Legend has it that during a period that Stevens Hall was a female dormitory, a young boy simply showed up at the door. One version of the story says he was abused at home and was a runaway; another says he was an orphan. Either way, the young ladies who lived there took a liking to the waif and offered to hide him. One night during a freezing snowstorm he had to go out on a window ledge to hide from the headmistress during room checks. When the girls were finally able to open the window to let him in, the boy wasn't there. They ran outside to see if he had fallen, but he was gone. And he was never seen again—at least not in his mortal state. His spectre, tinted blue as if suffering from hypothermia, appears inside and around the perimeter of the building. On occasion he appears on the window ledges of the third floor, staring in at residents through the glass.

Pennsylvania Hall, also known as Penn Hall and Old Dorm, opened in 1837. It's said that the ghost of one or more Union sentries can be spied standing atop the cupola in the evening, especially at midnight. Students have also claimed that the apparitions sometimes float above the circular, flat-top tower. One professor claimed that he recognized the apparition of General Robert E. Lee on the cupola, but it's improbable that Lee was ever in the building.

After working late in Pennsylvania Hall one night in the mid-1980s, two college administrators took the elevator down from the fourth floor, but instead of stopping at the ground level, the lift continued to the basement. When the doors opened, the men were looking out on a makeshift hospital filled with surgeons, orderlies, nurses, the wounded, the dying, and the dead—just as the room had appeared during those dreadful days in July 1863. Someone rushed up to the pair and tried to press them into service. He needed help holding down a patient's leg during an amputation. Fortunately the doors to the elevator closed, and the administrators were whisked up to the first floor. Suspecting they had been the victims of a gruesome prank, they called a security guard. When the trio investigated, however, there wasn't a trace of what the two men had experienced only minutes before.

The episode may not have been a haunting but an instance of a related but much rarer phenomenon known as retrocognition. Also known as postcognition, it is a sudden displacement in time in which the past and the present briefly coexist. In his general theory of relativity, physicist Albert Einstein hypothesized that space and time can twist, warp, and bend. The Gettysburg College administrators weren't transported back or even seeing into the past, but perhaps a strand of time had become looped in such a way that, for a few short seconds, the past and present had intersected.

Kutztown University of Pennsylvania

15200 Kutztown Road, Kutztown, PA 19530; (610) 683-4000
www.kutztown.edu

Kutztown University of Pennsylvania started out as a teachers training school in 1866. It became a state college in 1960 and took its present name in 1983. There are more than nine thousand undergraduate students and a thousand-plus students in the university's graduate programs.

The central administration building, **Old Main,** was constructed in 1866. According to legend, in June 1895 a student named Mary Snyder died on the fifth floor just a few days before graduation. Most people say her death was due to heart failure, although others claim she committed suicide because she was either pregnant, terminally ill, or had just been dumped by her boyfriend. Even those who say she killed herself can't agree how she did it; it could have been by hanging herself or by jumping down an empty elevator shaft. Regardless, people blame Mary's spirit for all the minor inexplicable annoyances that occur in the building.

LEBANON VALLEY COLLEGE

101 North College Avenue, Annville, PA 17003; (717) 867-6030
www.lvc.edu

Founded in 1866, Lebanon Valley College is a private liberal arts institution located about twenty miles east of Harrisburg, Pennsylvania. For several years, one of its professors, Dr. Lou Manza, has taught "Paranormal Phenomena—A Critical Examination" as an advanced psychology class. There is also an annual ghost tour on campus during Oktoberfest.

Mary Green Hall opened in 1957. More than two hundred people have said they've seen the dormitory's ghost, known only as "Mary Green Girl." The spectre is a young lass whose lilting laughter and bouncing of a ball have been heard in the corridors. She also fiddles with the volume on people's music players and knocks framed photographs off the walls, along with other irritating activity. Urban legend says she was the little sister of a former female resident. While the student's parents were helping the older sibling move into her room, the younger girl started playing with a ball outside. Depending on which story you hear, the ball rolled onto the road in front of the residence hall or the girl wandered over to a nearby stretch of railroad tracks. Either way, the child was struck and killed, and her apparition is now seen and heard in the two spots where she may have died as well as inside the dorm. In 2002, two male residents created an audiotape of giggling and a ball bouncing and played it as a gag during Quiet Hours to freak out others in the dorm. The wee wraith wasn't amused by their prank and disrupted electrical devices in their room to punish them. The story was featured on the "Collision Course/Deadly Dorm Games" episode of the Syfy series *School Spirits*.

The ghost of Mabel Silver, an esteemed alumna, haunts her namesake **Silver Hall,** a coed dormitory housing 142 students. Her hauntings are so well known that the name "Mabel" is on the "LVC Lingo" word list given to new students each year! The dorm was once a residence hall for females only, and Mabel is still protective of "her girls." Guys have felt her ghostly hands shoving them out the door, and the eyes in her portrait in the lobby follow people around the room.

North College Hall has seen its share of hauntings as well. The simple two-story house in the center of campus is home to representatives of the university's various Greek societies. It houses up to ten men on the ground floor and eleven women upstairs. Residents hear disembodied foot-steps, furniture is rearranged, and various letters or possibly initials are carved into wooden objects. Students also often have the feeling that invisible spirits are watching them.

MORAVIAN COLLEGE

1200 Main Street, Bethlehem, PA 18018; (610) 861-1300 www.moravian.edu

Moravian College is a private, coeducational liberal arts school founded by and affiliated with the Moravian Church in America. It was founded in 1954 when the Moravian Seminary and College for Women and the men's Moravian College & Theological Seminary (both of which date from 1742) merged. The college offers both undergraduate and graduate degrees.

Comenius Hall, built in 1892, was one of the first two structures on Moravian's North Campus, also known as the Main Street Campus. The phantom of a young serviceman who was killed in World War I has been spotted on the premises. It's believed that he left Moravian College to go to war and has returned from the Afterlife to complete his degree.

Brethren's House on South Campus was constructed in 1748 for single men in the Moravian community and later acted as a hospital for soldiers during the Revolutionary War. Today it houses Moravian's music department. Paranormal phenomena in the building include cold spots, icy drafts, and doors that open and shut themselves. Occasionally people see the spirits of Revolutionary-era soldiers there, but more often they run into a spectral nurse from the same period. She's still making the rounds, wearing an eighteenth-century dress and bonnet.

Main Hall is also on South Campus. The building opened in 1854 as a women's residence hall and is still a female dorm accommodating fifty-seven students. The apparitions of an elderly man and woman have been seen sitting together on a couch.

Finally, urban legend says that tunnels connect various campus buildings on South Campus. Supposedly they're haunted by a number of entities that love to make banging noises. The sounds carry aboveground to disrupt classrooms.

Muhlenberg College

2400 Chew Street, Allentown, PA 18104; (484) 664-3100
www.muhlenberg.edu

Muhlenberg College is a private liberal arts institution founded in 1848 affiliated with the Evangelical Lutheran Church in America.

Oscar Bernheim was at the college from 1907 to 1946 in a number of capacities, most sources say as registrar and possibly a trustee, and he willed his home to the university. Not long after Bernheim's death, his apparition began appearing in the attic, the basement, and the former third-floor bedroom where he allegedly died. His spirit also puttered around the garden out back. The building was leveled in 1998 to construct the Trexler Pavilion for Theatre and Dance as well as three residence halls in the southwest corner of campus.

It's commonly believed that one of those dormitories, **South Hall,** was built over Bernheim's beloved garden because the building's been haunted since it opened in January 2002. (In 2005, Muhlenberg president Randy Helm pointed out that it's actually Trexler, not South Hall, that's located where the garden used to be.) Personal objects move around in South Hall, TVs turn themselves on and off, and odd noises come from the walls and other strange places. According to an article in the campus newspaper, the *Muhlenberg Weekly*, the Office of Residential Services took the early reports of purported ghost activity seriously. In fact, after three girls who lived in South Hall complained about continual disturbances, the ORS went so far as to contact Chaplain Bredlau (the college's minister) and other religious authorities to see if anything could be done. The students also met with Rudy Ehrenberg, the dean of students. While they were in his office, one of the girls recognized a man in a photograph as being the spectre she had seen in her room. It was Bernheim!

The girls had a fourth roommate who was never bothered by the ghost, so they pondered why the spirit was leaving her alone. They remembered that the girl always had a rose-printed comforter on her bed, so when they went back to their dorm room they set out vases of roses. The hauntings stopped. The story soon spread that all a student had to do to prevent Bernheim's ghost from showing up was to keep a fresh plant of any kind in the room.

PENNSYLVANIA STATE UNIVERSITY

University Park, PA 16802; (814) 865-4700; www.psu.edu

The Pennsylvania State University, also known as Penn State or PSU, was founded in 1855. In addition to its main campus, Penn State has nineteen commonwealth campuses scattered throughout the state. In all, the university has about 98,000 students. The University Park campus in the town of State College is in the exact geographic center of the state.

By far, Penn State's most unusual ghost is a pack mule named Old Coaly, who assisted in the construction of several university buildings in the 1850s. After its death, the skeleton was mounted and put on display in the original Old Main. Following a roof fire in 1892, Coaly was warehoused in the basement of **Watts Hall.** The bones have been moved several times since, including stops in the attic of the old PSU veterinary school, the Agricultural Administration Building, the Ag Arena, and currently the HUB-Robeson Center. Old Coaly's spirit stayed at Watts, however, and the ghostly beast of burden walks the hallway outside the old downstairs storage room. Staff also sometimes hear its bray inside the locked room. The apparition has appeared on the first floor as well. Sightings have been slim since the basement was converted into a study area and game room, but Old Coaly's essence is still believed to be in the building.

Schwab Auditorium, which hosts many university special events, is haunted by at least two ghosts. One may be George W. Atherton, an early president of the university, who is buried beside the hall. The other is thought to be Charles Schwab, for whom the building is named.

Built in 1887 the **Old Botany Building,** across from Schwab, is the oldest academic building on campus. It houses the spectre of Francis Atherton, wife of George Atherton. She stares out of the attic windows, looking at the grave of her husband. The garret is normally locked, yet lights have been seen going on and off inside. In the 1860s Professor of Horticulture William Waring planted a patch of evergreens behind the building. The grove featured a secluded pathway that later became a lover's lane, but it's said that a student froze to death on the trail during a blizzard before the decade was out. The trees were removed in 1929, but people walking through the area still feel an unsettling presence there.

In 1969, female student Betsy Aardsma was knifed to death in **Pattee Library.** It's claimed that students passing through the stacks on the second floor sometimes feel the spectral repercussion from the attack. Air seems to leave the room, making it hard for them to breathe, and there's a general sense of uneasiness. A few have felt the touch of an unseen stranger.

Beam Business Administration Building, constructed in 1957, was once a residence hall. Most of its paranormal events have occurred in a second-floor men's bathroom.

Rumor has it that a man hanged himself from a pipe over a stall by the door. People still report impish, poltergeist-like activity in the room.

Finally, Room 318 in **Runkle Hall,** a dormitory, was the site of major ghost activity in 1992, then again in 1994. A resident assistant (or RA) reported loud banging noises, a bucking bed, lights flashing on and off, a self-locking door, and a babbling disembodied voice. Some phenomena continue today, and the supernatural activity has also spread to other locations in the building. Fans turn themselves on; items fall off the walls. The hazy phantom of an old woman in a rocking chair was spotted at the end of one of the halls. Furniture in the study lounge rearranges itself when no one's around, and loud noises come from inside the room when it's locked. One student decided that the spirit (or at least one of them) has to be Hispanic because her TV would turn itself on, but always to a Spanish-speaking channel. Also, some students playing with a Ouija board have received responses in Spanish. Urban legend says that the spirit may be a former student who hanged himself in a stairwell, but the nearest documented suicide took place in Leete Hall, where a resident was found hanging between the third and fourth floors.

Slippery Rock University of Pennsylvania

1 Morrow Way, Slippery Rock, PA 16057; (724) 738-9000
www.sru.edu

Slippery Rock University of Pennsylvania was founded in 1869. There are more than seven thousand students on its 661-acre campus located about forty miles north of Pittsburgh.

The campus's most famous ghost, Emma, visits two places: primarily **Miller Auditorium** but also **North Hall.** The spirit is believed to be Emma Guffey Miller, a former local politician, SRU booster, and onetime trustee who died in 1950. She haunts the playhouse because it bears her name, of course, but she also loved theater. "Emma the Ghost" makes herself known during rehearsals by flickering lights or making thumping noises, even from behind locked doors. Costumes previously not known to be in the theater's collection will suddenly turn up in Emma's Closet, which is the nickname for the wardrobe department. People also fleetingly catch Emma's apparition out of the corner of their eye, but never head-on. Actors are notoriously superstitious, and a tradition sprang up that a particular doll had to be hidden somewhere on the set to prevent Emma from disrupting performances. If the doll goes missing, it's thought, chaos will ensue. (After years of use, however, not much is left of "Baby" but its head.) An area ghost research team, Baelfire Paranormal Investigation, inspected the auditorium in 2009, and they "certified" the building as being haunted. As for Emma's activity in North Hall, the wraith materializes in students' rooms at night and watches over them. Her presence is thought to be lucky. Passersby have seen the apparition through the windows. Locked doors in the dorm also have a way of opening themselves.

A former off-campus fraternity house was haunted by the ghost of a Native American who hanged himself near the building in the mid-1800s. Footsteps paced the third floor, wiring short-circuited, doors slammed, paddles in the Chapter Room fell off the wall, and personal belongings disappeared. Residents named their spectral guest "Ted." The house, located on Keister Road, is now a private residence, and the owners would prefer not to be visited by ghost hunters. The fraternity's story (with its name changed) was documented for the "Frat House Phantom" episode of the Syfy series *School Spirits*.

University of Pittsburgh

4200 Fifth Avenue, Pittsburgh, PA 15260; (412) 624-4141
www.pitt.edu

The University of Pittsburgh, commonly referred to as Pitt, was founded as the Pittsburgh Academy in 1787 when the Steel City had only about fifteen hundred inhabitants and was still at the western edge of the American frontier. The school suffered devastating fires and underwent changes of venues, nomenclature, and curricula over the next century, but in 1908 it was finally able to take the name University of Pittsburgh.

The Late Gothic Revival **Cathedral of Learning** is the second-tallest university building in the world. Its ghost is thought to be Martha Jane Poe McDaniel, whose wedding quilt lies on a four-poster bed in one of the loft rooms. McDaniel's spirit rocks a small cradle in the corner of the room and turns down the bedding when no one's around. The ballroom and parlor were once part of a mansion built by William Croghan Jr. The ghost of Croghan's daughter Mary supposedly haunts a secret room behind a false fireplace.

Bruce Hall, formerly the Schenley Apartments, is on the Schenley Quadrangle. Residents hear footsteps in the halls and stairwells as well as a woman's voice and other noises. Objects big and small, from furniture to hand-size personal items, move themselves around the rooms. One urban legend says that elevators sometimes don't stop at the correct floors but instead continue to the twelfth story and stay there.

Depending on which rumor you hear, the hauntings in Bruce Hall are caused either by the wife of the former apartment building owner or his mistress. Or both. Some say the wife hanged herself in Suite 1201, while others claim that she leapt from its window to her death. A few think both women killed themselves. Whoever the spectre is, many students call her "Harriet."

Litchfield Towers is a complex of three coed residence halls, and one of them, **Tower B,** seems to have a very unhappy ghost. The shared shower rooms are haunted. While using the facilities, female residents have heard the unmistakable echo of a disembodied human voice crying or screaming. However, no apparition has ever made itself visible, and there's no accepted legend as to whose spirit is causing the upsetting sounds.

The **William Pitt Union** is haunted by the ghost of a Russian ballerina. The story is told that back when the building was the Schenley Hotel, the prima ballerina slept through one of her performances. Her director was furious and demoted her to the corps. Humiliated, the dancer went back to the hotel and killed herself. These days if she catches people napping in the Red Room, she wakes them up so they don't miss class.

RHODE ISLAND

SALVE REGINA UNIVERSITY

100 Ochre Point Avenue, Newport, RI 02840; (401) 847-6650
www.salve.edu

Salve Regina was chartered by the Sisters of Mercy in 1934. The college became coed in 1973, added graduate programs two years later, and became a university in 1991.

Three of the school's current and former properties have ghosts. From 1974 to 2009, Salve Regina University leased the former **Carey Mansion.** Spookmeisters recognize it because its exterior was used as Collinwood Mansion on television's *Dark Shadows*. The spirit or spirits inside are unidentified. According to rumors—all of them unsubstantiated—back in the 1940s a woman named Nina was having an affair with someone named William in the "circle room." His wife, Amber, caught them and set the house on fire. The blaze was extinguished, but the adulterers perished. Amber hanged herself in the same room. Another tale says that the woman who hanged herself was a nun, made pregnant by a priest.

The problem with all of the stories is the room was unfinished and blocked off when the events supposedly occurred. The building experienced general spirit disturbances during Salve Regina's lease, but one of the most unsettling was when the image of a ghostly woman showed up on a paper in the tray of a printer kept in the circle room.

Wakehurst was built for James J. Van Alen in 1884. The university acquired the mansion in 1969, and it now holds classrooms, faculty offices, and the student center. Spectral noises, including the sounds of a dinner party, are heard on the main staircase. Staff members hear thumping overhead, even when the rooms are vacant. A man dressed in equestrian riding gear makes his home on the third floor. People walking outside at night see the ghost of a man through the windows on the top floor. Also, it's said that on the night of the year's first snowfall the apparition of an unknown young woman appears outside the building, pushing an antique baby carriage.

The most active ghosts on campus are in the **William Watts Sherman House,** built by the New York City businessman in 1875–1876 and acquired by the university in 1982. Sherman never had a son, but one of the spectres in the house is a little boy, who has been nicknamed Adam. Folklore says he was chasing a ball on the second floor when he fell down the stairs, killing himself. His ball is heard bouncing throughout the building, especially near the second-story staircase and, oddly, in the basement. Some residents have reported seeing his mother, a Woman in White who hanged herself in despair. Other hauntings include the sound of furniture being dragged about in the attic, beds that shake, and rapping on the third-floor windows. Lastly, for several weeks in the early part of this century, all the girls in Room 308 would inexplicably wake up every morning at the stroke of 4:00 a.m.

VERMONT

Champlain College

163 South Willard Street, Burlington, VT 05401; (802) 860-2700
www.champlain.edu

Champlain College started out as Burlington Collegiate Institute in 1878. It took its present name when it moved to its current campus in the Hill Section of Burlington in 1958. Its first bachelor's degree programs were offered in 1991. The first master's degree program was added in 2001.

Jensen Hall, one of the school's most popular residence halls, was bought by the university for use as a dorm in 1965. Crowned with a two-story tower, the whole building is said to be haunted by a sea captain who was supposedly one of its first owners. According to legend, his wife used to climb to the top level of the tower to watch for her husband's ship to return. The captain's spirit is almost never seen.

The ghost story is acknowledged on a link found on the college website, but no one has been able to prove that a ship captain or his wife ever lived in (much less owned) the house before it became Jensen Hall.

UNIVERSITY OF VERMONT

85 South Prospect Street, Burlington, VT 05405; (802) 656-3131
www.uvm.edu

The University of Vermont was founded in 1791. It's located forty-five miles south of the Canadian border on a 451-acre campus just blocks from Lake Champlain.

Several spirits "live" on the grounds. Henry, a former medical student, has been known to haunt **Converse Hall,** a six-story, 164-student coed dormitory. The young man supposedly committed suicide in the attic in the 1920s, perhaps because he was distraught about flunking a major exam. Though never seen, he would turn lights on and off, open or slam doors, rock a rocking chair, toss around beer cans, and move other furniture. It's uncertain whether he's still present. A psychic claimed to have eased his spirit on to the Other Side in 1986.

Interestingly, staffers have reported similar activity in the UVM **Office of Admissions** building, and legend suggests that the phenomena also stem from a suicide.

The shimmering spectre of an elderly gentleman with a bulbous nose floats down the halls of the **Counseling and Testing Center.** Though the phantom is benign, a custodian reported that it turns lights on and off and has spilled the bucket he uses to mop floors.

The **Public Relations office** is still occupied by the phantom of a former owner of the building, and ghosts make the floors shake in the **Continuing Education** building. In the **Alumni Relations office** a poltergeist-like spirit makes a racket slamming drawers and doors and stomping on the floor.

Then there's **Bittersweet House,** which was built in 1809 and is now home to UVM's environmental studies program. From 1928 to 1940 it was owned by Margaret Smith, a widow who dubbed her home "Bittersweet" after the vines that grew on the grounds. She sold the property to the university with the understanding she could reside there until she died. She lived another twenty-one years, passing away in 1961 at the age of ninety-four. But she's still in the house. Lights turn themselves on in the empty, locked structure in the middle of the night, and passersby might see her silhouette in the windows. But her apparition shows up during the day as well. She chooses to materialize as a middle-aged woman, always wearing a period ankle-length dress and high-collared blouse.

Part Two

SOUTHERN SPIRITS

It's easy to get lost in the folklore of the Old South. The fables feed contemporary tales where myth and mood merge in such novels as *Midnight in the Garden of Good and Evil* and *Interview with the Vampire*. But perhaps the regional legends aren't all just baseless superstitions.

The South, the Deep South, and Dixie have always been relative terms. In this section of the book you'll find the states located below the old Mason-Dixon Line, all of the states from the Confederacy, and a couple of border states such as Delaware, Kentucky, and West Virginia.

ALABAMA

Athens State University

300 North Beaty Street, Athens, AL 35611; (256) 233-8100
www.athens.edu

The Athens Female Academy, founded in 1822, became a state college in June 1975. The school took its university title in 1998. It is the only two-year upper-level university in Alabama.

Its main structure, **Founders Hall,** was constructed in 1842. Four massive Corinthian columns, named Matthew, Mark, Luke, and John, front the edifice. During the Civil War, the building narrowly missed being torched by Union troops invading the city. At some point after the war, however, two female students who lived on the top floor tried to sneak out at night to meet their beaus. As they descended the grand staircase, a gust of wind blew sparks from the candle one girl was holding into her hair. She was soon fatally engulfed in flames.

Founders Hall is no longer used for housing, but the ghost of the fire victim, whose name has been lost to time, still resides there. Students and faculty have reported hearing her disembodied footsteps, especially on the main staircase, as well as rattling doorknobs, keys, and chains. There are cold spots and inexplicable breezes throughout the building, and the spirit also likes to turn on light switches—perhaps so she doesn't have to use a candle! Occasionally she'll materialize as a hazy human form, and sometimes passersby see her through a third-story window.

A typhoid epidemic passed through Athens in 1909. One teacher, Florence Brown, chose to stay behind and tend to the female students who had already been stricken and could not be moved. Unfortunately, Brown and all the girls died. Brown's parents pledged funds to the school to build a new women's dormitory, **Brown Hall,** in her honor. It was completed in 1912.

Today the building primarily houses administrative offices, and it's haunted, perhaps by Brown herself or one (or more) of the students that had been in her care. The paranormal activity reported most often concerns objects that move overnight while everyone is away. On at least one occasion, though, an entire continuing education class saw a chain reaction of poltergeist-like effects, including a picture falling from a wall and a pounding noise emanating from a waste can.

The university's most famous resident spirit can be found in **McCandless Hall,** where she began to appear shortly after the auditorium was dedicated in 1914. The ghost is a young blonde woman dressed in a white formal gown and holding flowers. She emits an eerie light and shows up in an upper-story window and elsewhere throughout the building, including the dressing rooms. Even when she doesn't materialize, students smell her flowers and hear her footsteps.

For many years it was thought that the ghost was Abigail Lylia Burns, an operatic soprano who supposedly appeared in the auditorium's opening-night concert. (Although Burns did sing in the hall, recent research suggests she didn't appear on the first night's program.) She got a standing ovation and vowed to return one day. Unfortunately, she died on her way home when her horses shied in a storm and the carriage overturned. Legend has it that Burns's phantom has returned to make good on her promise.

Auburn University

Auburn, AL 36849; (334) 844-4000; www.auburn.edu

Auburn University opened its doors in 1856 as the East Alabama Male College. The institution took its current name in 1960.

During the Civil War, the **University Chapel** (then the Auburn Presbyterian Church) was turned into a hospital. In 1926 the Department of Theatre moved in, and for whatever reason the new activity woke the spirit of Confederate soldier Captain Sydney Grimlett, who had died there.

Before long, props were breaking, scenery was being shifted overnight, and the sounds of whistling and foot tapping could be heard coming from the attic. A light orb would appear and float over the stage, and a few students thought they perceived the apparition of a male figure. It was a visit to a Ouija board that first identified the phantom prankster as Grimlett.

Over the years, theater students not only came to accept their ghost's presence, they welcomed it and named their highest annual honor the Sydney Award. In 1972, when the theater department moved to a new state-of-the-art playhouse, the **Telfair B. Peet Theatre,** a few students left behind handwritten notes giving Grimlett directions to the building.

He took them up on their offer! The phantom fighter has adapted well to his new surroundings and takes it upon himself to fiddle with the lights, reposition props and small personal items (especially shoes in the costume department), get into drawers and lockers, open and shut doors, and play with technical equipment. There have been knocks from inside the walls, rattling noises in the air conditioner even when it was turned off, the sound of coins rolling in the halls, disembodied footsteps, and the echo of a piano playing itself.

The soldier's spectre, which is about five and a half feet tall, has been seen on the stairs heading to the costume shop, in the shop itself, in dressing rooms, and in the adjacent hallway. He most often appears on the catwalk above the stage—during both rehearsals and opening-night performances. Cast members and crew leave chocolate candy for him on the fly gallery walkways, and it's always gone the next time anyone checks. He seems to be partial to peanut M&Ms.

HUNTINGDON COLLEGE

1500 East Fairview Avenue, Montgomery, AL 36106; (334) 833-4497 or (800) 763-0313; www.huntingdon.edu

Founded in 1854, Huntingdon College is a coeducational liberal arts college affiliated with the United Methodist Church. Two ghosts haunt the school.

The Red Lady, who appears in **Pratt Hall,** is the revenant of a former student from New York. She disliked being at the school and spent hours upon hours by herself. She loved the color red; everything in her fourth-floor dorm room was decorated in the shade, and all her clothing was red as well. In fact, she was wearing her red robe and was under a red blanket when she was discovered dead in her bed, covered in red blood from slashing her wrists.

Despite her contempt for the campus when she was alive, she's still there, wandering Pratt Hall, especially its fourth floor. Red bolts of light supposedly flash in her old room, and her spirit is sometimes seen staring out of a front window.

The other spook at Huntingdon College is male, a former student who shot himself on the centrally located **campus green.** The Ghost on the Green, as he's called, roams the area at night, grabbing at people's clothing, ruffling their hair, or blowing into their faces.

UNIVERSITY OF ALABAMA

Tuscaloosa, AL 35487; (205) 348-6010; www.ua.edu

Established in 1831, The University of Alabama is the oldest and largest university in the state. Its campus was burned during the Civil War just five days before General Lee's surrender, with only four buildings surviving the inferno. One of the structures that made it through the 1865 torching was a tiny building called the **Little Round House,** which is actually octagonal and used today as a clubhouse for campus honor societies.

When the Northern troops invaded, three Union soldiers were shot to death by one of the student guards in the Round House. Their spirits rested in peace for years, but it's thought that all the activity surrounding initiation rituals for new members of the Jasons honor society roused the soldiers from their Eternal Slumber. No spectral sightings have been reported since Jasons Shrine was renamed the University Honor Societies Memorial in 1990.

Smith Hall, constructed in 1910, houses the Alabama Museum of Natural History. The Beaux-Arts building also holds classrooms, a lecture hall, and offices. Apparently some of the schoolchildren who toured the museum in its early years passed on to the Other Side and have returned. Since the 1950s, students and professors alike have heard the disembodied voices and footsteps of youngsters on the second floor. There was a surge of paranormal activity in 1955 and the early 1970s, and the spectral phenomena have never completely stopped.

UNIVERSITY OF MONTEVALLO

75 College Drive, Montevallo, AL 35115; (205) 665-6000
www.montevallo.edu

Founded in 1896 as the Alabama Girls' Industrial School, the institution became the University of Montevallo in 1969. The central core of the 160-acre campus is on the National Register of Historic Places.

The university's best known ghost, Condie Cunningham, haunts a women's dormitory, **Main Hall,** which is the oldest and largest residence hall on campus. On February 2, 1908, Cunningham and several friends were cooking fudge when they accidentally spilled some cleaning oil, which caught fire. The flames jumped to Cunningham's housecoat, and she was badly burned. She died in a nearby hospital after an agonizing two days.

Her terrified, shrieking ghost is still heard all over Main Hall. At some point, what some people perceived to be the upside-down silhouette of a girl, her long hair streaming below her, was discovered in the wood grain of a door to a dorm room on the fourth floor. The university eventually removed the door and placed it in storage, but that didn't stop the whispers. Neither did the fact that the door wasn't original to the building and wouldn't have been there when Condie was alive.

The ninety-room, three-story **Hanson Hall** was constructed in the 1920s. The resident spectre is never seen, but people feel its presence. The phantom also steals small objects when no one is looking, but it always returns them.

Two of the university's theater facilities are haunted. **Palmer Auditorium,** inside Palmer Hall, was built around 1930. The building has several ghosts, including former drama professor Walter H. "Trummy" Trumbauer. Although Trummy's been on the Other Side for years, he's thought to return for College Night, a competition in which students perform plays they've written and produced. If he likes something during rehearsals, one of the seats in the auditorium will drop—a sign that the beloved teacher is sitting down to watch. Before the awards are announced at the end of the evening, Trumbauer—or something—makes the lights sway above the actors who will win. His apparition has never materialized, but other spectres have. Their reflections have shown up in the mirrors of a large dressing room backstage. Also, phantom fingers play the keyboard of an organ whose music can be heard after everyone has left the building.

Reynolds Hall, dating from the 1850s, is named for Captain Henry Clay Reynolds, the university's first president. No one knows whether Reynolds is the visitant causing all the hijinks in the building because the ghost has never been seen. Windows rise and slam on their own, doors open, indecipherable sounds come from the attic, and there are unaccountable gusts of wind in the halls. One female student claimed to have been kicked. Much of the activity takes place in and around the building's **Reynolds Studio Theatre,** a 160-seat playhouse that's been in operation since 1923.

King House is one of the campus's most historic structures. The Georgian two-story brick mansion was built by Edmund King Jr., a well-to-do Georgia planter who moved to Montevallo around 1815. Today the sound of clinking coins can be heard coming from the second story, as can King's phantom footsteps pacing the floor. A dim, moving light is sometimes spied through the upstairs windows late at night, and on occasion a curtain is pulled back for a few moments as if someone is peeking around it. King's ghost doesn't appear in the house, although it has been spotted outside in what used to be his orchard. His elderly, bent figure is seen holding an oil lantern and carrying a shovel. People say King buried his treasure, a cache of coins, in what used to be the peach grove—close to where Harman Hall now stands.

Finally, the phantom of a woman wearing a yellow dress has been spied sitting on a rock in the **Quad.** "The Lady of the Rock" isn't seen often, and when she is she's usually crying, perhaps because of a broken heart. Some believe she's Edmund King's first wife, who had a difficult life. (A few sources say the Lady appears instead near the Alpha Tau Omega fraternity house on Bloch Street.)

ARKANSAS

Harding University

915 East Market Avenue, Searcy, AR 72143; (501) 279-4000
www.harding.edu

Harding College, a private Christian liberal arts school, was founded in 1924 when two junior colleges merged. The resultant institution received university status in 1979.

Almost all Department of Music activities take place inside the **Donald W. Reynolds Center for Music and Communication,** which was completed in 1998. The Reynolds Center replaced an older music building on campus. According to a popular myth, back in the 1930s the boyfriend of a female music student at the school died in a car crash. The girl mourned her lost love for hours on end by playing the piano in a third-story practice room. She died—perhaps of a broken heart?—before the school year was through. Before long, students and staff began to hear piano music coming from the third story of the empty hall, long after it had been locked up for the evening.

The young lady and even the building are long gone, but to this day, students on the second story of Reynolds Center say they can occasionally hear spectral piano music coming from overhead—from a nonexistent third floor.

HENDERSON STATE UNIVERSITY

1100 Henderson Street, Arkadelphia, AR 71999; (870) 230-5000
www.hsu.edu

Established in 1890 as Arkadelphia Methodist College, **Henderson State University** is a four-year public liberal arts institution. It became Henderson State College in 1967, then Henderson State University in 1975.

The school's ghost dates from Henderson's time as a Methodist college. It's a tale of star-crossed lovers. A boy from Arkadelphia Methodist fell in love with a female student from rival school Ouachita Baptist University, located literally across the street. The young man's friend persuaded him that the girl was wrong for him because they were from different religious denominations. The boy stopped dating her and asked someone else to his college's homecoming dance. Humiliated and brokenhearted, the girl committed suicide.

Since her death she's returned to the Henderson State campus on the eve of the university's homecoming football matchup with Ouachita. Dressed all in black, the spurned student roams the campus looking for her former boyfriend. Those who see the spectre refer to her as the "Black Lady."

As with many good ghost stories, there's an alternate version of the tale. Some say that instead of killing herself, the girl was so unhappy she simply gave up on life and pined away. And it's been suggested that her ghost is actually out for revenge and looking for the girl who stole her beau.

LYON COLLEGE

2300 Highland Road, Batesville, AR 72503; (800) 423-2542 www.lyon.edu

Several Presbyterian ministers in Batesville, most notably the Rev. Isaac J. Long, founded Arkansas College in 1872. The school was rechristened Lyon College in 1994 to honor former president of the board of trustees Frank Lyon Sr.

The hauntings on campus began to take place between 1969 and 1972 in the **Brown Chapel and Fine Arts Building.** The earliest phenomenon was a cloudy blue-green haze with a stale, dank odor that materialized in the hall's five-hundred-seat auditorium. The rumor began to spread that a tapestry in the Bevens Music Room was causing the manifestation.

Legend had it that the wall hanging was originally a rug, and a Confederate soldier had bled to death on it during the Civil War. The tapestry supposedly went through several owners before it arrived at Arkansas College, and wherever it went the misty figure and scent went with it. Supposedly when it first arrived at the college, students could make out the bloodstains on the carpet. In 1985 Stan Fowler, a student in a folklore class, checked out the fable and was able to locate the tapestry's donor, Mary Barton. The story of a soldier dying on the rug wasn't true; in fact, the weaving had never been used as a carpet. It had always hung on a wall in Barton's home in New Jersey before being sent to the college. The tapestry's origin was debunked, but not its ghost.

There are other spectral activities in the auditorium not attributed to the cloth. Seats drop on their own as if someone were sitting in them, and there are disembodied footsteps on the catwalks. Objects move or rearrange themselves in the prop and costume rooms backstage. There are unexpected cold spots in the building's playhouse and the chapel, and doors mysteriously become locked or unlocked. Even when no physical phenomena are taking place, some students feel invisible spirits watching them in the auditorium.

University of Central Arkansas

201 Donaghey Avenue, Conway, AR 72035; (501) 450-5000
www.uca.edu

The University of Central Arkansas was founded by the state legislature as the Arkansas State Normal School in 1908. After several name changes and alterations in the school's offerings, it became the State College of Arkansas in 1967. Just eight years later the institution became the University of Central Arkansas.

Constructed in less than five months in 1934, **Wingo Hall** was originally an apartment-style residence hall, but today it houses the administration. No one knows who the female spirit in Wingo Hall might have been in life. She's been spotted throughout the building, including the attic. Though not particularly menacing, the spectre does seem to have a bit of the poltergeist in her. She knocks things off bookshelves and tables, moves objects from one end of the room to the other, raises window shades, and opens doors or slams them shut.

DELAWARE

UNIVERSITY OF DELAWARE

401 Academy Street, Newark, DE 19716; (302) 831-2791
www.udel.edu

The University of Delaware had its start in 1743 when Dr. Francis Alison founded the New London Academy in his own New London, Pennsylvania, home. The school moved briefly to Maryland, then in 1765 to Newark, Delaware. In 1843 the school was rechristened Delaware College. It merged with a sister school, Women's College, in 1921, creating the University of Delaware.

According to legend, the cupola of the **Academy Building,** currently used by the Office of Communications and Marketing, is haunted by the spectre of an unidentified student from the eighteenth century. Supposedly the young man left school to join the Continental forces in 1777. He linked up with a group of volunteers in a camp on Iron Hill. It's unknown whether the boy's father didn't agree with the Revolutionary cause or simply wanted his son to continue his studies, but he personally went to Iron Hill and forced the boy to return to school. Furious and mortified, the lad went up to the tower atop the Academy Building and hanged himself.

FLORIDA

BROWARD COLLEGE

Central Campus, 3305 Davie Road, Davie, FL 33314
(954) 201-6700; www.broward.edu

Broward College was founded in 1959 as the Junior College of Broward County. The college's first permanent campus was the A. Hugh Adams Central Campus in Davie. Its **Fine Arts Theatre** is home to a playful spirit that students have nicknamed Omar. He never appears, but he plays the customary backstage tricks common among all theater ghosts. When he's there people can feel the unexpected cold spots, or they might simply sense his presence. Omar always stays behind the scenes, though. He never wanders out into the house or the lobby.

The campus's other haunting dates from a tragic murder-suicide that took place in January 2002. Twenty-three-year-old Michael Holness walked up behind his ex-girlfriend, twenty-year-old Moriah Ann Pierce, and shot her in the back of the head with a .357 Magnum. He then turned the gun and shot himself. Both died later at Broward General Medical Center. The incident took place between the performing arts building and the English department building. It's said that, at night, people sometimes see hazy white figures and smell odd odors at the spot where the couple fell. Allegedly there are also bloodstains on the ground that can't be washed away.

Flagler College

74 King Street, St. Augustine, FL 32084; (904) 829-6481 or (800) 304-4208; www.flagler.edu

Flagler College opened as a women's college in 1968 and went coeducational in 1971. The showpiece of the school is the former Ponce de Leon Hotel, a National Historic Landmark. It's now **Ponce de Leon Hall,** a dormitory for up to 480 female students. The residence hall also contains a dining room.

When railroad and oil baron Henry Morrison Flagler built the four-story Ponce de Leon Hotel in 1888, it was the first of the grand hotels that would eventually line Florida's eastern seaboard. In 1913, eighty-three-year-old Flagler fell on a marble staircase in Whitehall, the Palm Beach mansion he had built for his third wife, Mary Lily. His health quickly declined, and he soon died. Prior to his burial, a memorial service was held in the rotunda of the Ponce de Leon Hotel. Midway through the service, mourners were stunned when the rotunda doors suddenly slammed shut. To this day, Flagler's ghost has been seen throughout the building. Some students have also seen a female spirit that they believe to be Ida, his second wife. Others think that it's Mary Lily, who remarried in 1916 and died just eight months later of edema and a heart condition.

The spectres of three people who died inside Ponce de Leon Hall still reside there, but none of their identities is known. The first is a woman dressed in blue. Legend has it that she was the mistress of a man staying at the old hotel. She became pregnant and expected her lover to leave his wife for her, but he refused. As the mystery woman fled in despair, she tripped on her dress on the stairs and broke her neck in the fall. There has been a rumor that the other ghost, who haunts the top floor where she hanged herself, was a mistress of Henry Flagler. The third apparition is a little boy who either passed away at the hotel from disease in the early 1900s or fell to his death from one of the balconies.

It should be noted that there are no records of any of these deaths at the hotel, nor is there any evidence that Flagler had a secret mistress tucked away. Furthermore, the college categorically denies that Ponce de Leon Hall is haunted. But why let facts get in the way of a good ghost story?

FLORIDA ATLANTIC UNIVERSITY

777 Glades Road, Boca Raton, FL 33431; (561) 297-3000
www.fau.edu

Florida Atlantic University, chartered in 1961, now has ten colleges, including an Honors and a Graduate College. The Dorothy F. Schmidt College of Arts and Letters is located on the east side of campus. Its **University Theatre,** built in 1966 and formerly known as the Esther B. Griswold Theatre, can seat upward of five hundred audience members.

Like so many other theaters throughout the world, the University Theatre is haunted, but nobody has a clue who the ghost might be. It's believed she's female, but that's all anyone knows.

The first reports concerning the spirit date from around 1993. Everyone from actors and stagehands to custodians and security guards has heard her voice throughout the building. There's also the sound of footsteps running and the slamming of doors, even if the building is empty and locked up tight. At night, people working near the hydraulic machinery beneath the stage feel her nonthreatening presence, but no apparition has ever been seen.

FLORIDA STATE UNIVERSITY

600 West College Avenue, Tallahassee, FL 32306; (850) 644-2525
www.fsu.edu

Florida State University traces its origins from the East Florida Seminary, which opened in 1851. The main campus of the research university, composed of sixteen colleges offering more than three hundred programs, is located on 489 acres in the state capital.

The ghost stories told most often about FSU concern **Cawthon Hall,** a residence housing 297 men and women. Over the years a few people have seen the misty apparition of a woman clad in green floating through the halls. She acquired the sobriquet "Tissie" at some point, but the consensus is that the otherworldly visitor is actually Sarah Landrum Cawthon, for whom the building is named. Other spooky activity in the dorm revolves around an unseen spirit thought to be a female student who was killed by a freak lightning strike while she was sunbathing on the roof. Books and photos move, lights turn on, and televisions change channels—all without human hands. Also, the late student's room is supposed to be especially active. (There's no record of such a death, by the way, but a student *was* injured by lightning, though not fatally, while tanning on the roof in 1958.)

Another dormitory, **Gilchrist Hall,** houses 229 men and women in two-bedroom suites. The dulcet sounds of a flute being played by a spectral music student float though the residence hall.

The **Chi Omega sorority house** was the scene of a murderous assault by serial-killer Ted Bundy in the wee hours of January 15, 1978. Four women were attacked; two of them died. It's believed that the spirits of the two victims who perished are still in the house, even though their apparitions have never been seen. Ever since the horrendous events took place, many sorority sisters have felt the pair's uneasy presence, although the sensation has lessened with each new generation of students.

Nova Southeastern University

3301 College Avenue, Fort Lauderdale, FL 33314; (800) 541-6682
www.nova.edu

Nova Southeastern University was founded in 1964 as the Nova University of Advanced Technology. It became Nova University a decade later. The private, coeducational institution took its current name after merging with Southeastern University for Health Services in 1994.

The Leo Goodwin Sr. Residence Hall, or **Goodwin Hall,** is the principal dormitory for first-year students on the main campus in Fort Lauderdale. The coed facility was opened during the 1992–1993 academic year and can house 320 students. The building is named for a major donor to the university—and it's known to be haunted.

The phantom doesn't materialize often, but the shadowy apparition will sometimes show up in students' rooms, standing silently by the bedside. More often, it will rearrange furniture when the resident is gone. It also likes to steal perfume. So far, the spirit's identity remains a mystery.

Ringling College of Art and Design

2700 North Tamiami Trail, Sarasota, FL 34234; (941) 351-5100
www.ringling.edu

The Ringling College of Art and Design, a four-year private school, was established in 1931 as a branch of Florida Southern College. Dr. Ludd M. Spivey, Florida Southern's president, located the institute in Sarasota to associate it with circus magnate John Ringling, who had a world-renowned art collection. In 1933 the art institute became independent and was named the Ringling School of Art. Offering only associate degrees at first, the academy added four-year programs in the 1980s and took its current name in 2007.

The college's ghost, "Mary," resides in **Keating Center,** which is the fully transformed former Bay Haven Hotel. Her apparition is spotted walking down hallways, and it's said that students staying in Mary's old room will come in to find paintbrushes swirling in their cups of rinse water.

It *is* possible that Mary may have been a student at the college at one time, but popular legend says she was a "working girl" who visited the hotel to provide "horizontal refreshment" for men staying there. It's said she died in the 1920s, most probably by hanging herself in the stairwell between the second and third floors. (Those stairs are no longer in use. They're now for emergency exit only.)

UNIVERSITY OF FLORIDA

2500 Southwest Second Avenue, Gainesville, FL 32607
(352) 392-326; www.ufl.edu

The University of Florida is located on two thousand acres in Gainesville. The school considers the now-defunct East Florida Seminary its direct predecessor and 1853 as its founding date. It has operated on its current campus since 1906.

The thirteen-story dormitories known as the **Beaty Towers** are the only high-rise buildings on campus. Legend has it that in the late 1960s or early 1970s, an unknown female student at the university committed suicide by leaping from the top floor of one of the two Towers. In one version of the story, she did it because her boyfriend dumped her after he found out she was pregnant. In another variation, the young woman was high on LSD or some other hallucinogen and thought she could fly. Regardless, her silent apparition is now seen walking calmly through the corridors in both residence halls. She's also been known to enter students' rooms and move stuff around.

Some dismiss the tale as a complete myth. However, according to UF historian Carl Van Ness (quoted in a 2007 article in the student newspaper, the *Independent Florida Alligator*), there *have* been suicides on campus, and at least one involved a leap from Beaty Towers.

Norman Hall holds classrooms, labs, a library, and more, but it started in 1932 as the P. K. Yonge Laboratory School for elementary through high school students. The university acquired the building in 1958. Rumor has it that the ghosts of former grade school students have been seen in the building. There's also a story of an old hospital bed on the top floor that somehow unmakes itself during the night, even though it's never used.

At least one tale can be dismissed out of hand. Gossip still circulates that Thomas Hall, one of UF's two original buildings, is haunted. Though it's now a residence hall, it once held offices, a library, classrooms, an auditorium, the infirmary, the dining room, and the kitchen. The phantom of Thomas Hall is alleged to be a rowdy former cook named Steve. The enduring ghost story—that the sound of old pipes banging throughout the building is actually Steve rattling his pots and pans—was made up as a joke, but the tale unexpectedly gained traction. Unfortunately, it's hard to debunk even an admitted fabrication once it's become folklore.

UNIVERSITY OF TAMPA

401 West Kennedy Boulevard, Tampa, FL 33606; (813) 253-3333
www.ut.edu

The University of Tampa, established in 1931, is a private college with a hundred-acre downtown campus. It has more than seven thousand students and offers both undergraduate and graduate degrees. The university's main building is **Plant Hall,** a National Historic Landmark constructed by Henry B. Plant in 1891 as the 511-room Tampa Bay Hotel. The school acquired the building in 1933. Several apparitions reside in the five-story Moorish Revival structure, the most famous being the "Brown Man"—so called because he's usually seen wearing a brown three-piece suit. He primarily manifests on or near the grand staircase. It's also thought that there are spirits in the tall minarets that tower over the former hotel. Other phenomena in the building have included objects moving on their own, doors being held closed, and a flashlight getting knocked out of a security guard's hand.

One of the most active parts of Plant Hall is the science wing, which used to be the hotel's staff quarters. At night the spectral sound of the rattling wheels of old serving carts is heard in the hallway leading from the science wing to the rest of the building. Students have spotted the spectre of a man with a dark complexion wearing boots and a straw hat. He's thought to have been a resident caretaker. In addition, the invisible presence of another man—believed to be Teddy Roosevelt!—is sometimes felt.

More widely reported than any of the Plant Hall phantoms is the ghost that lives in the thousand-seat **David Falk Theatre.** The playhouse opened in 1928 as the Park Theatre, a vaudeville and movie house that also catered to touring companies. The University of Tampa took over the Park Theatre in 1962 and renamed it to honor a member of the board of trustees.

The theater is haunted by the spirit of actress Bessie Snavely. After her husband left her for another member of the troupe, Bessie went to her dressing room and hanged herself. Some people say the suicide occurred in a stairwell. Regardless, the third-floor dressing room thought to have been Bessie's now feels several degrees colder than the rest of the building, and there are random cold spots throughout the theater. People hear Bessie's footsteps as well as her voice talking or singing. She'll clean up after other people and close doors that have been left ajar. One technician credits her with preventing his fall from a scaffold. Bessie's apparition is seen in the tech booth and elsewhere around the theater as she watches rehearsals and performances. Sometimes she manifests in human form and other times as a diaphanous cloud that evaporates into the walls.

Bessie has one idiosyncrasy: She doesn't seem to like the color red. Pieces of wardrobe in that shade have been inexplicably torn or damaged, and an actress in a red costume once felt herself being physically held back by invisible hands as she tried to make her stage entrance.

The third haunted building on the University of Tampa campus is the student union, the nine-story Vaughn Center. The multipurpose facility was constructed on the site of a hotel gaming hall that was destroyed by fire in 1941. Late in the evening, students and staff who happen to be passing by or through the large, two-story cafeteria (**"the Caf"**) hear odd, casino-esque noises such as the sound of dice being tossed.

GEORGIA

BERRY COLLEGE

*2277 Martha Berry Highway, Mount Berry, GA 30149
(706) 232 5374 or (800) 237-7942; www.berry.edu*

In 1902, Martha McChesney Berry opened a rural school to educate elementary- and high school–age boys in today's Mount Berry, just outside Rome, Georgia. Today, Berry College is a post-secondary school with two campuses.

The **Ford Complex** on the Main Campus consists of seven Gothic buildings, including Ford Auditorium and a majestic dining room modeled after the dining hall of Christ College at England's Oxford University. A female spectre appears in all the structures, but most of her activity takes place in an empty room high up in the central tower between the east and west wings of Mary Hall, a female dormitory. Supposedly the phantom was a student who hanged herself after her boyfriend was killed in World War II. Residents hear her cries in the distance and feel a cold rush when the girl's invisible spirit unexpectedly walks through them.

Blackstone Hall, the first brick building at Berry College, was constructed in 1915. It's served many functions but in 1982 was transformed into the **E. H. Young Theatre.** Little is known about the playhouse's prankster. Even the story behind his long-standing nickname, the "Sepia Boy," is shrouded in mystery.

Lemley Hall, the oldest brick residence building, was built in 1921. **Morton Hall** opened in 1953. Both originally served as male dormitories. Today they are for women only and collectively hold about two hundred students. The buildings, referred to as Morton-Lemley Hall, share several common rooms. They also share a ghost named Ruth, a housemother from back when the halls housed young men.

Martha Berry's office was in the two-story **Hoge Building,** constructed in 1905. The room has been the site of cold spots and dark shadows. Also, a bright yellow light has been seen exiting the frame structure. People say the spectres are a former professor and one of Berry College's presidents.

Oak Hill at the edge of Main Campus is Martha Berry's former home. Opened as the Martha Berry Museum in 1972, the Greek Revival, six-columned mansion and the recently attached exhibition hall showcase the story of the educator and the history of the college that bears her name. Windows open and close on their own, objects move from one part of the house to another, and security alarms go off without anyone tripping them. There may be as many as three spooks in Oak Hill. One is thought to be a child who frequently moves around the dolls in the nursery. He or she also plays pranks, throwing small objects from the second floor onto people walking below. The second apparition, the "White Lady," is probably Frances Rhea Berry, Martha's sister. Dressed all in white, she materializes in Frances's former bedroom as well as on the staircase. Some people think Martha visits her own bedroom because visitors sometimes feel an invisible form brush against them there, but she's never been seen. Also, the adjacent bathroom door slams on its own, and the knob sometimes rattles.

A spectral female appears on **Stretch Road,** the three-mile byway that connects the two campuses of Berry College. One legend says the apparition can be summoned by stopping on the road and honking the car horn three times. Sometimes the spectre appears as nothing more than a green haze. More often a human figure takes shape, especially near a short bridge on the route. The phantom is slender and wears a dress from the early twentieth century. Some who have gotten close enough to get a good look said she has no eyes, while others report that her skin is tinged green—which is why she's sometimes called the Green Lady. The first written records of the ghost date from 1985, although there may have been oral accounts before that. There are multiple candidates for her identity, but the Green Lady could be someone else entirely.

The Mountain Campus has one or two otherworldly entities as well. In 1922, students and staff built the **House o' Dreams** to commemorate the school's twentieth anniversary. Martha Berry used it as a private getaway and to entertain guests. Today, people associated with the college can visit it by making a reservation. Other visitors can see it as part of a campus tour. Strange lights as well as the apparition of a toothless woman have been spotted during the off hours. The ghostly woman is thought to have died—and to have lost her teeth—when the plane she was in crashed into the mountainside.

Also, back in the early days of the school, older boys used to scare the younger students by telling them that a mysterious mountain man named Swafford lived in the high forests. As a rite of passage, freshmen had to walk into the woods to show their courage, and according to legend some of the boys never made it back out. The story has persisted to modern times, and it's said that Swafford's ghost now tries to scare away those who venture up the mountain. (Apparently there actually was a hermit up there at one time, and he liked to shoo outsiders off "his" property, but there were never any disappearances.)

Georgia Regents University Augusta

1120 Fifteenth Street, Augusta, GA 30912; (706) 721-0211
www.gru.edu

Georgia Regents University came into being in 2012 when Augusta State University merged with Georgia Health Sciences University. Later that same year the new institution added the city's name for official and marketing purposes, technically making the school Georgia Regents University Augusta. The hauntings at GRU take place in sites that were all part of Augusta State University, which had begun as a high school in 1783 (though college-level courses were being offered by 1785).

Bellevue Hall, built in 1815, was US Senator Freeman Walker's summer home. Emily Galt was twenty-one and living in the house with her family in 1861 when she used her diamond ring to scratch Emily Galt into one of the windows. (Her younger sister Lucy also etched her name into the pane. The glass is now kept safely in storage.) Supposedly Emily argued with her fiancé about his intention to join the Rebel army during the Civil War. When she heard he had been killed in battle, she flung herself from a second-story window.

Emily's ghost (and perhaps her beau) returned and is apparently still in Bellevue Hall today. People in the building have heard the voices of a man and a woman fighting late at night, although further investigation turned up no one. The phones sometimes ring like crazy, doors open and close themselves, and the television in the lounge turns itself on.

Next door, **Benet House** is also haunted. Built between 1827 and 1828, the white-columned building eventually became the admissions office for ASU. Paranormal activity includes disembodied footsteps, the creaking sound of a rocking chair in motion, and doors that slam shut. Staff members come in to discover objects have rearranged themselves overnight, and on at least one occasion construction workers briefly saw an apparition.

As part of Walker's deal to sell his estate to the school, he demanded that his family cemetery be allowed to remain on the property. The tiny **graveyard on Arsenal Avenue** is still there. The spectre of a Confederate soldier in a long gray coat with a yellow sash has been spotted on the burial grounds, and visitors have experienced cold spots there even in broad daylight.

LaGrange College

601 Broad Street, LaGrange, GA 30240; (706) 880-8000
www.lagrange.edu

LaGrange College, founded as LaGrange Female Academy in 1831, is the oldest private college in Georgia. The school's ghost resides in **Smith Hall,** the first structure built on the campus. Now containing mostly classrooms and offices, the edifice has undergone a variety of uses since it was constructed of local handmade bricks in 1842. The building is on the National Register of Historic Places.

Its apparition is historic, too: He's a Confederate officer in full dress regalia, and his name is Lieutenant John Griffin. After being wounded in battle, Griffin ordered that he and his men be taken to the hospital in LaGrange thirty-six miles away. The facility was better than a closer hospital, plus his sister Indiana was enrolled in LaGrange College. After surgery, Griffin was moved to Smith Hall, which had been turned into a makeshift hospital. Some say he never recovered, so his spirit never left the building. A more romantic version of the tale says that Griffin woke up expecting to see his sister's face, but the nurse who had attended him on the trek to LaGrange, Lorena, was hovering over him instead. Unfortunately, the lieutenant took a turn for the worse and died. The soldier's ethereal essence either stayed or went back to Smith Hall, where he is spending eternity looking for his personal Nightingale.

University of Georgia

212 Carlton Street, Athens, GA 30602; (706) 542-3000 www.uga.edu

The University of Georgia was chartered in 1785. The first classes of what was then called Franklin College (after Benjamin Franklin) were held in 1801. The university now offers more than 140 degree programs within 18 colleges. At one time or another, all of the haunted buildings at UGA have housed students or faculty, and the ghosts seem to be former residents.

Lustrat House was built in 1847. Today it's home to the university's Office of Legal Affairs. The two-story, eight-room antebellum home originally sat a few yards north, but it was moved to make room for a new library. Its spectre sits by the fireplace reading and working on papers in a Confederate uniform. As a result of his attire, many people believe the spectre to be Professor Charles Morris, a former chairman of the English department who died in 1893. He had been a major in the CSA army.

The Department for Germanic and Slavic Studies is housed in **Joseph E. Brown Hall.** At one time the building was used as a dormitory, and it's said that a student committed suicide there. Now the young man's spirit is seen at the windows, sometimes peeking in, sometimes peeking out.

The **Alpha Gamma Delta sorority house** was built in 1896, predating the founding of the local chapter in 1923. Its otherworldly resident was a woman who lived in the building before the sisters of Alpha Gams took it over. The young lady was to be married in the Southern mansion, but when her fiancé failed to show on the wedding day, she killed herself. Perhaps he'll turn up one day. If so, his bride-to-be is still there waiting for him.

Young Harris College

1 College Street, Young Harris, GA 30582; (706) 379-5032 or (800) 241-3754; www.yhc.edu

Affiliated with the United Methodist Church, Young Harris College is a small private liberal arts school nestled in the Blue Ridge Mountains, very close to the state border with Tennessee. Founded as McTyeire Institute in 1886, the institution of higher learning settled into its role as a junior college in the second half of the twentieth century. Its first class of four-year students enrolled in 2008.

The **Clegg Fine Arts Building** on campus was completed in 1965. Its revenant is Charles H. Clegg, the building's namesake, but everyone calls him "Charlie." In fact, students and teachers often call out "Goodnight, Charlie" on their way out. People see his apparition from time to time, usually after dark, sometimes walking across the auditorium stage or standing in a hallway. More often than not they just hear him. He'll softly call out to someone by name or whisper a forgotten line into an actor's ear. He's also been known to play an organ down in the basement. Charlie sometimes messes around with props, but he also returns them if they go missing. Most of Charlie's antics are in good fun, but people find it a bit unnerving when his disembodied hands reach out and touch them.

The 175-seat **Dobbs Black Box Theatre** has a ghost as well. His name is Jesse, and he was a custodian at the college in the 1990s. He apparently loved the playhouse so much that after he was killed in a car accident he decided to return to it in spirit form. Jesse shows up at all hours. Even when he's not seen, he'll set off motion detector security alarms, move stuff in the storerooms, or walk around—even overhead on the catwalks.

Three-story **Enotah Hall** is a relatively new dormitory on campus. Its resident phantom is spotted in two places, day or night: sitting on the grass outside the building reading a book of poetry or hanging from a noose on the third (or sometimes the second) floor. He's also been known to rattle window blinds, make a racket in the restrooms, switch computer monitors on and off, and knock on doors. One story says that the apparition was a student who hanged himself in whatever building was on the site before Enotah Hall was constructed. Another variation of the tale identifies the spook as Byron Herbert Reece, a former professor and Pulitzer Prize–nominated poet who shot himself on June 3, 1953, after learning he had contracted tuberculosis. But if the ghost is Reece, why would he appear hanging from a rope?

KENTUCKY

ALICE LLOYD COLLEGE

100 Purpose Road, Pippa Passes, KY 41844; (606) 368-6000
www.alc.edu

Alice Lloyd College was cofounded by Alice Spencer Geddes Lloyd and June Buchanan in 1923 as Caney Junior College. It has been a four-year liberal arts college since the 1980s.

There have been generalized rumors for years about several buildings on campus being haunted. Students and faculty have heard disembodied voices and the sounds of throbbing heartbeats through shower vents. Doors of bathroom stalls swing on their own, bedsheets get torn, books tumble from shelves, and rooms unlock themselves. Some folks have seen the spectre of an elderly woman. Among the spots rumored to harbor ghosts are the **Alice Lloyd Radio Station, Anderson Science Center, Cushing Hall,** and **Grady Nutt Athletic Center.**

There's probably more paranormal phenomena in **Lilly Memorial Hall,** a three-story women's dorm built in 1981, than at any other place on campus. The second floor seems to be particularly active. Small objects disappear, only to reappear elsewhere. Residents get locked out of their rooms. Scratching, wailing, and other odd noises are heard in the depths of night. And, yes, there's an apparition, but it's always seen as a drifting shadow rather than a human form.

BEREA COLLEGE

101 Chestnut Street, Berea, KY 40403; (859) 985-3000 www.berea.edu

Berea College, a private liberal arts school, was founded by abolitionist John Gregg Fee in 1855. It was the first coeducational, nonsegregated college in the South. The school is a work-study institution. Admission is reserved for those in need, and full tuition is provided free in exchange for service to the university.

Fairchild Residence Hall was built in 1872 and is the oldest building on campus. The dorm's spectre is Abigail, a student from the late 1800s. She hanged herself after becoming pregnant by her boyfriend, a local lad who brought chopped wood to the college. (In some variations of the tale, she delivered the baby and gave it up for adoption before killing herself.) Students have seen Abigail leaning against a second-story railing wearing the college uniform of her day—a white blouse and long, dark skirt. Others have spotted a candle in the attic window or heard the sounds of footsteps and a rocking chair coming from the garret. At least one person has reported creeping up to the attic and seeing the apparition of a woman in a shawl rocking in the chair.

The five-story **James Residence Hall** was completed in 1918. Since 2001 it's been a men's dormitory, housing up to ninety-nine students. At some point in the far past, a young woman named Carol living in the hall was "led astray" by an area farmer. Rather than live with the shame of having lost her innocence, she hanged herself in a second-story elevator that's since been converted to a custodial closet. People hear Carol's disembodied footsteps entering the small room between 11:00 p.m. and 3:00 a.m., but no one ever hears her leave. Sometimes wet footprints heading toward the closet door also appear. Once, the cleaning staff came in just before fall orientation and found the dorm already spotless. Carol had left them a note saying that she had tidied up because she wanted to help.

Pearsons Residence Hall was constructed between 1909 and 1910 as a men's dormitory, with bricks handmade by the students. The fourth floor is haunted by the Phantom Runner, whose footsteps can be heard racing down the hall. Students standing in the corridor can feel a breeze as the spirit shoots by. The activity usually takes place in the early morning or late at night between midnight and 3:00 a.m., and it occurs most often during the fall semester when new students are just settling into the dorm. The footsteps are loud enough that kids living on the third floor, not realizing they were dealing with a ghost, have gone up to the fourth floor to complain. The apparition is believed to be Charles Seabury Jr., a student in the 1920s who broke his neck while playing football and died.

The **Jelkyl Drama Center,** built in 1980, is a polygonal building. An unknown but benign spirit has been sensed in a stairwell, and a few students have seen a spectre drift across the stage of the three-hundred-seat McGraw Theater—even though the ghost is sometimes nothing more than a glowing speck of light. Folks have posited that the apparition was "released" when a collection of nineteenth-century costumes stored in a barnlike pavilion nicknamed "the Tab" was destroyed by fire in the late 1970s. (The building acquired its odd sobriquet because students thought it resembled the Tabernacle described in the book of Exodus.)

Presser Hall was constructed in 1931 and houses the offices of the music department, classrooms, and the five-hundred-seat **Gray Auditorium.** The recital hall's organ has a habit of playing itself when no one—at least no one living—is in the room. Students and faculty are sure that either Margaret Allen, who donated the funds to buy the instrument, or former music professor Harold Rigby is at the keyboard.

Finally, there's **Boone Tavern,** a Colonial Revival inn built by Berea College in 1909 to act as a guesthouse for visitors. The apparition of a little boy dressed in clothing from the turn of the twentieth century, including short pants, famously haunts the tavern. He most often materializes in Room 312—sometimes accompanied by a woman from the same era wearing a white blouse with a starched collar—and they've both been seen leaving the room by walking through the wall. Even when he's not visible, the boy giggles, and his laugh has been heard all over the building, especially in the basement. Staff and guests have also heard spectral footsteps as well as the sound of papers rustling. Now and then, they see objects move on their own.

Campbellsville University

1 University Drive, Campbellsville, KY 42718; (270) 789-5000
www.campbellsville.edu

Campbellsville University was founded in 1906 as Russell Creek Academy. The private school is affiliated with the Kentucky Baptist Convention and sits on an eighty-acre campus. The university has more than three thousand students and offers associate, baccalaureate, and master's degrees.

The **Gosser Fine Arts Center** is home to the School of Music. The facility contains classrooms, practice and rehearsal rooms, offices, and the Gheens Recital Hall. The place is haunted. Inexplicable cold spots, thought to be evidence of spectral presences, dot the premises. Visitors have heard the sound of babies crying in the area where the nursery used to be, and art students have seen pottery wheels start to spin on their own. Shades of the Patrick Swayze/Demi Moore movie, *Ghost*!

Eastern Kentucky University

521 Lancaster Avenue, Richmond, KY 40475; (859) 622-1000
www.eku.edu

Eastern Kentucky University was founded as a teachers preparatory institution in 1906. EKU remained a teachers college under a variety of names through the first half of the twentieth century, finally becoming a full university and taking its current appellation in 1966.

The most famous ghost on campus is the Blue Lady, who haunts the **Keen Johnson Building.** Her identity is unknown, but she got her sobriquet because she's often seen surrounded by a blue mist. Sometimes she appears simply as the cloud itself. Occasionally the haze envelops the entire exterior of the building, usually starting at the bell tower and spreading downward. Sightings of the Blue Lady began in the 1950s, and plenty of tales about her exist. She's said to be a young woman, probably a former student, dressed in a ball gown. Supposedly she committed suicide in Keen Johnson by hanging herself either on the sixteenth floor or in the Pearl Buchanan Theatre on the ground level. (It's worth nothing that no suicide on campus has ever been documented.)

The Blue Lady has been heard singing, especially backstage in the theater and in the bell tower. She also roams the ballroom and the sixteenth floor. Doors open and shut on their own, or the knobs will move or rattle. Elevators operate without being called, and ethereal piano music has floated through the air. A few people have reported hearing loud music from inside the walls.

Male students are especially intrigued by the spirit that strolls through the **Moore Building,** which was constructed in 1968. The female phantom is pretty, of average height and weight, and completely naked! She must think she's alone in the building, because she seems to be even more shocked than the students when they see each other. She doesn't stick around very long; once discovered, she instantly disappears.

Dedicated in 1909 and expanded four years later, **Sullivan Hall** is a coed dorm. Supposedly a female shade named Victoria haunts the residence hall, in particular Room 419. Objects fly across the room, poltergeist-like, and the closet door opens and slams shut throughout the night. Rumor has it that the visitant was a nurse who hanged herself in the room in the 1970s. At one time the school infirmary was in the basement, which gives part of the tale some credibility, but there's also a version of the story that says Victoria dates from when Sullivan Hall was a field hospital during the Civil War—impossible since the place wasn't built until forty years after the war ended.

TAPS, the Atlantic Paranormal Society featured on Syfy's *Ghost Hunters* series, investigated **Commonwealth Hall** in 2010 with mixed results. The producers of *School Spirits*, a short-lived ghost series on the same network, featured Eastern Kentucky University on its "Campus Warning Signs" episode.

LINDSEY WILSON COLLEGE

210 Lindsey Wilson Street, Columbia, KY 42728; (270) 384-2126
www.lindsey.edu

Founded in 1903 and affiliated with the United Methodist Church, Lindsey Wilson College started out as a K–12 training school. By the 1990s the school was offering master's degrees.

Horton Hall dates from the 1950s and is now part of the three-building Horton Hall Complex, which also includes Parrott and Weldon Halls. The hauntings all occur in Horton itself and take place primarily in rooms on the second floor. The ghosts have been described as "Dark Figures," shadowy forms that shake the ceiling tiles or lift them up and slowly ease themselves down into the students' rooms. The wraiths appear at any time of the year, but usually on weekends and always late in the evening. It's said that if one of the spooks is surprised, it will scream before disappearing into the night air.

MOREHEAD STATE UNIVERSITY

150 University Boulevard, Morehead, KY 40351; (606) 783-2205 or (800) 585-6781; www.moreheadstate.edu

Morehead State University originally opened as a teachers school in 1887. After several changes in name, curricula, and departments, it emerged as a full university in 1996.

Baird Music Hall is home to the school's music department. A rumor has spread that during one of the hall's expansions, a homeless man who sought shelter in the construction area after dark was accidentally buried by concrete. That section of the building, now a rehearsal hall and classroom used by percussionists, is dubbed "Drum World." The stranger has been known to wander through it at night.

The ghost who's most frequently seen in the building, though, is its namesake, former university president William Jesse Baird, who usually turns up on the third floor. When paranormal activity first started to occur there, people who knew Baird recognized certain sounds and scents they associated with the educator, convincing them that he had, indeed, come back. It took only a few people to identify his apparition for the legend to take hold.

Built in 1928 and named for the university's first president, the three-story **Button Auditorium** houses the Department of Military Science, offices for the ROTC program, an indoor rifle range, and a twelve-hundred-seat auditorium. The building was once home to the theater department, where a unique hazing purportedly took place. First-year acting students were suspended from the flies by two ropes, a sturdy one around the waist and, to terrify them, an unattached one around the neck. On one occasion the ropes accidentally got tangled or switched, and a female student was killed. People standing on stage sometimes hear the ghostly, horrific sounds of her choking to death. The structure is also haunted by the phantom of a female custodian who fell while cleaning the bell tower and broke her neck. Her spectre, still in her work uniform, has been seen and even photographed throughout Button Auditorium.

Cartmell Hall, a residence facility, is haunted by the spirit of a student who died trying to ride an exposed cable that stretched from the sixteenth to the ninth floor while the dorm was still under construction. He now pulls pranks on the ninth floor, moving around students' personal items and television sets. The other haunting is outside Cartmell, and it stems from an accident that took place in the 1980s. A music student was supporting himself by selling hot dogs out of his van—that is, until he was killed when his propane tank exploded. Allegedly people can still smell frankfurters at the spot where the vehicle was parked.

It's claimed that a former student named Penelope has returned to **Nunn Hall.** She leapt to her death from the ninth floor after becoming pregnant by a young man her parents didn't like. The spectre is most often seen early in the morning or very late at night. She flicks lights, runs water in the showers, shakes beds to wake students who oversleep, and turns TVs on and off.

Students in **Butler Hall** hear disembodied footsteps and unrecognizable sounds at night, and computers and televisions turn themselves on. The commotion may be caused by any or all of three former residents who allegedly died in the dorm. One is said to be a female student who was taunted and bullied to the point of hanging herself on the second floor during spring break.

Lastly, a female student, whose name is unknown, died by drowning herself in **Eagle Lake,** which adjoins campus. Her screams and calls for help drift across the surface of the water on still, misty nights.

MURRAY STATE UNIVERSITY

102 Curris Center, Murray, KY 42071; (270) 809-3011 www.murraystate.edu

Murray State opened in 1923 to provide training for teachers. As liberal arts classes and other programs were added, the institution underwent several name changes and became Murray State University in 1966.

The eleven-story **Price Doyle Fine Arts Center,** located on the east side of the Quad, is the tallest building on campus. Its elevators may be haunted: They go to the wrong floors, they get stuck between stories, or their doors won't open. Even when they operate correctly, they tremble and sound like they're about to break down. They also have a tendency to stop on the fourth floor, even when no one has called for that level.

The ghost causing all this trouble is a female student who plummeted to her death after falling down the empty elevator shaft. When the door opened, she stepped forward, not noticing that somehow the car hadn't arrived. Other folks say the ghost is "Vincent," a construction worker who accidentally tumbled down the shaft. A more grisly version has poor Vincent being decapitated by snapped cables.

According to one legend, at some nebulous time in the past, a despondent male student leapt to his death from the sixth floor of the adjacent **Old Fine Arts Building.** He's been credited with the sound of piano music coming from an unoccupied practice room on the third floor. Some say his ghost has been seen wandering the aisles of the 2,500-seat **Lovett Auditorium** next door.

In 1998 there was a fire in **Hester Hall,** and a male student in Room 402 died from smoke inhalation before he could escape. The following year the room was left empty and locked, but the door would sometimes open on its own. Students standing outside the room reported that they felt they were being watched. Residents in Room 406 would hear scratching at their door at night, but whenever they checked there was never anyone in the corridor.

When the Sig Ep frat house burned down in the 1970s, the brothers rented rooms in the home of an elderly lady they nicknamed "Ma" Crawford. When she died she willed her property to the fraternity, and they turned it into their new **Sigma Phi Epsilon fraternity house.** Well, she's still there looking out for the boys. They hear her disembodied footsteps on the stairs, and the light in her old bedroom turns itself on and off. Sometimes one of the doors will open a crack, as if Ma is making rounds. And apparently she's not the only spectre in the house: At times when the guys are all upstairs, they'll hear the sound of several people in conversation in the empty living room downstairs.

UNION COLLEGE

310 College Street, Barbourville, KY 40906; (606) 546-4151
www.unionky.edu

Union College was founded in 1879 in affiliation with the United Methodist Church. The private liberal arts school has about 825 undergraduate students on its hundred-acre campus.

Most of the paranormal ruckus on campus takes place in **Pfeiffer Hall,** built in the 1940s. So here's its ghost story: In the early 1960s a student named James Garner lived in Room 245. Standing 6'4" and weighing 250 pounds, he was a star athlete on campus, playing both football and basketball. While trying to close his dorm window on the chilly evening of October 30, 1963, he somehow fell out and dropped to his death. If you go into that room at midnight now and open the window, Garner's spirit will slam it shut. He also turns on lights and opens doors. Usually his apparition remains invisible, but some students have said that they've seen it.

Although the tale of Garner's ghost is the most popular spook legend at Union College, it's not the only one. In fact, it's not even the only one about Pfeiffer Hall. There's a story circulating that Room 131 is haunted as well. Its spectre moves clothing in the closet and throws things on the floor.

Also, there's supposedly a female phantom skulking around the **Office of Financial Aid.** The most frequently repeated version of the story says the department is housed in a building that was once someone's home. It goes on to claim that the ghost, a former resident, died there under mysterious circumstances. The apparition of the unknown woman closes and opens doors, or she'll lock or unlock them. She even materializes from time to time. The only trouble with the tale is that the building was never a private residence. The Financial Aid Office is located in Speed Hall, which was constructed by the college and completed in 1905.

UNIVERSITY OF KENTUCKY

Lexington, KY 40506; (859) 257-9000; www.uky.edu

With almost 29,000 students, the University of Kentucky is one of the largest institutions of higher learning in the state. It traces its origins from the Agricultural and Mechanical College of Kentucky, which was founded as a department of Kentucky University in 1865. The college broke away in 1878 and eventually became the University of Kentucky in 1916.

The 288-seat **Guignol Theatre,** built in 1927, acts as the main playhouse for the university's Department of Theatre. It was completely refurbished in 2000. The performance space has an otherworldly presence, the ghost of a man who roams through the theater at night after it's closed. The spectral image has never been distinct enough for anyone to recognize him or even identify in what era he lived. He's shown up all over the playhouse, including the tech booth and the catwalk over the stage. Even when students can't see him, they know he's around. They sense his invisible spirit watching them, or they'll hear strange noises, such as the inexplicable banging of pipes.

University of the Cumberlands

6178 College Station Drive, Williamsburg, KY 40769
(800) 343-1609; www.ucumberlands.edu

The Williams Institute was founded in 1889 after eighteen Baptist churches in eastern Kentucky sought higher education in the region. With the acquisition of Highland College and its three buildings, the school became Cumberland College in 1913. It was renamed the University of the Cumberlands in 2005.

Paranormal activity has been reported inside two of the women's dormitories. **Gillespie Hall,** a three-story brick building formerly named Johnson Hall, houses up to 129 female students. The longtime phantom of the residence hall is a girl whose identity is unknown, but it's believed she was never a student at the university. Sometimes people see her standing stock-still, silently staring ahead; other times she's crying. After a while, she simply vanishes. There are nonapparitional hauntings in Gillespie Hall as well. Computers, TVs, stereos, and radios turn themselves on and off. Doors open and shut even when they are locked, and occasionally at night a light can be seen seeping out from under the closed door of the empty attic.

The **Ruby Gatliff Archer Hall** opened its doors in 1966 and houses 172 women. About a third of the residents are first-year students. It's said that one particular room on the first floor is haunted. Personal belongings move around, and CD players turn on without being touched. Alarm clocks go off at midnight no matter what hour has been set. Posters also drop mysteriously from the walls.

WESTERN KENTUCKY UNIVERSITY

1906 College Heights Boulevard, Bowling Green, KY 42101
(270) 745-0111; www.wku.edu

Western Kentucky University was founded in 1906. Its two-hundred-acre campus sits on a rise known as College Heights or the Hill, high above the Barren River. There are so many haunted sites on campus—many of them detailed on the university's website—that it's hard to know where to begin.

Van Meter Hall, opened in 1911, was the first building on campus. A ghost face appears in a dressing-room mirror. Furniture and music stands rearrange themselves, and computers malfunction. And there's a phantom: a man in his fifties, dressed all in white. There's a difference of opinion as to who the spectre might be. He's often identified as a worker who fell through a skylight over the lobby during the building's construction and crashed to the floor below. An alternate version of the story says he was distracted by an airplane flying overhead—still a novelty at the turn of the twentieth century—and he dropped to the stage. Over time these two variations have intermingled, so some say the worker fell through a skylight onto the stage—even though there obviously wouldn't have been a skylight above the performing area. In yet another tale, the ghost is a student who supposedly fell to the stage while hanging lights. In all the accounts, the victim left behind a bloodstain on the floor that was impossible to remove. In some tellings, it glowed. Eventually the floorboards had to be replaced. There's even a story that the ghosts of the construction worker's wife and daughter now wander the building as well, singing and conversing in a strange language. An entirely different piece of folklore suggests there are natural tunnels deep beneath the hall, and the apparition of a hermit who lived down there sometimes makes his way into the theater carrying a lantern that emits a strange blue light.

Potter Hall, built in 1921 and now housing administrative offices, was originally a women's dorm. Its ethereal presence was most active in the 1980s and 1990s. Furniture would be moved, lights went on and off, desk drawers rattled, cold winds blew through the rooms, and doors opened and closed (sometimes becoming locked or unlocked in the process). There was also the sound of loud, disembodied footsteps, coins dropping into the snack machine, and pipes clanking in the basement. Some students even heard their names being whispered. People began to call the phantom Allison, even though many believed the spirit to be Theresa Watkins, a student who lived in Room 7 on the basement level. On April 29, 1979, she used a belt to hang herself from heating pipes in the room. Students contacted her by a Ouija board, and she said she now goes by the name Casparella. She claimed she was happy only when she pranked people. The apparition's antics seem to have died down, but has she gone away? Sometimes staff members come into their offices in the morning to find loose pennies lying around. They've nicknamed their beneficent nighttime caller "Penny," but is the spectral visitor really Casparella by another name?

Schneider Hall now houses the Academy of Mathematics and Science, but it was a girls' dorm when it opened as West Hall in 1929. During the building's years as Whitestone Hall, a lunatic who had escaped from an asylum climbed the walls and crawled through an upper-story window. The place was almost empty because it was spring break, but he broke into the room of one of the resident assistants (called Judy in some versions of the tale). He woke the girl before striking her in the head with an ax. As the man ran off, Judy dragged herself down to the far end of the hall to the other RA's room. Too weak to call out, she clawed at the door for help with her last ounce of strength. The girl inside awoke but was too terrified to answer. In the morning she found Judy's body lying on the floor outside her room, the blade of the ax still embedded in her skull and bloody scratch marks from her fingers on the door. Judy's ghost now returns each spring to seek her assailant, who was never captured.

Barnes-Campbell Hall is a nine-story dormitory built in 1967 that houses 392 men. There are few details about the hauntings that take place there, but the ghost is well known. He was a twenty-year-old RA, a junior named James Wilbur Duvall who lived on the fifth floor. There are two stories surrounding his death. In one, he plummeted down an empty elevator shaft. In the other, the elevator became stuck and he entered the empty shaft to reset the switch. He forgot to look up first, however: The elevator was already rapidly descending. It crushed him between a steel beam and the wall of the shaft.

Opened in 1970, the twenty-seven-story **Pearce Ford Tower** is the tallest building on campus. There are two different ghost sagas about the building, and both have to do with the elevators. Some say a repairman died when he fell down the empty elevator shaft. When his ghost comes around—always during the summer—he likes to pester people by pressing all of the call buttons. The other legend claims that, back when Pearce Ford was a men's dorm, there was a student who, for some reason, would never shower on his own floor. Instead he would take the lift up or down to one of the other levels. One day, wearing only a towel, he stepped forward when the elevator doors opened, but tragically the car hadn't arrived. He fell twenty stories. His damp footprints are now sometimes seen in front of the elevators, especially on the anniversary of his death.

Rhodes-Harlin Hall, built in 1966, is a nine-story women's dorm housing 368 students. Its spectre's story is short and sweet: A girl killed herself by jumping off the roof of the building, and she now appears on the anniversary of her death to frighten new students living in the hall. She loves to tap on doors, especially the rooms next to where she used to live. She always disappears before anyone can get to the door.

McLean Hall is a three-story coed dorm for honors-program students. The building's phantom is Mattie McLean, the secretary for the first two university presidents. She died in 1954, but she never appeared in her namesake hall until three girls started playing around with a Ouija board. Mattie came through, giving answers to questions about herself that the students were later able to verify. At the girls' insistence Mattie became visible for them, first as a bright glow, then taking human form—a Gray Lady: gray hair, gray attire, and even a gray face. Students say they can still feel her protective, almost motherly, aura in the building.

There's an active Greek life on campus, and there are spirits in several of the fraternity houses. Epsilon Xi, the WKU chapter of the **Delta Tau Delta** fraternity, was established in 1967. The Delts share their house with the ghost of Billy Lester, a former brother who died there in the 1980s. His old quarters are still referred to as "Billy's room." Its door opens and shuts on its own, and the stereo turns on by itself.

Kappa Sig fraternity came to Western Kentucky in 1965. The Theta Theta chapter can't seem to shake itself of a phantom nicknamed Cowboy Jim. A Ouija board originally revealed his identity, and he isn't happy about being trapped on Earth. The spectre is predictable, though: He visits each room at a specific time every day, always in the same order.

A young girl was killed in the **Lambda Chi Alpha house** on Chestnut Street before the fraternity bought it, and she's been seen running on the grass outside the English Tudor–style building. She, or some other entity, has been known to turn the chandelier on and off, light up the fireplace, and shift objects in the rooms. (One brother claimed that during the night while he was sleeping, she lit a candle on his nightstand and moved it to the foot of his bed.) The sound of a typewriter has also been heard clacking away in an unoccupied room.

The pipes in the **Phi Delta Theta house** may just be old, but the fraternity brothers are sure something surreal is making them rattle instead. Also, some of the posts on the staircase banister are missing, and the remaining ones seem to keep switching around on their own.

Sigma Alpha Epsilon house on College Street was supposedly pressed into service as a hospital during the Civil War. A soldier named Kevin—also identified through a Ouija board—died there of his wounds but has come back to stay. He's tall, slender, and dressed in his military overcoat and hat. He's thought to be responsible for most if not all of the ghostly activity that takes place in the building. Weird things regularly occur in Room 7. (Seven was Kevin's favorite number.) One year during finals, back when there was an answering machine connected to the house phone, the system would click on without the phone ringing, but no one ever left a message. Sometimes the phone would ring and no one would be on the line if anyone picked it up. In one of the rooms, a fan would turn itself on repeatedly, no matter how many times its owner shut it off. One night while a brother was getting food in the kitchen, the bulb snapped off in the refrigerator; then the room light went out, followed by the sound of the fridge door slamming shut.

LOUISIANA

Loyola University New Orleans

6363 St. Charles Avenue, New Orleans, LA 70118 (504) 865-3240 (admissions); www.loyno.edu

Loyola University New Orleans is a private Jesuit school in the Uptown area. Loyola College, as it was first known, opened in 1904. In 1912 the Louisiana Senate gave Loyola university status. It officially became Loyola University New Orleans in 1996 to differentiate itself from institutions with similar names.

Marquette Hall is Loyola's centerpiece and the oldest permanent building on campus. The edifice was constructed between 1907 and 1910. From around 1916 to late 1966, students taking anatomy classes dissected cadavers in the building. To lift the corpses to the fourth floor where the morgue and laboratories were located, the university erected a crane behind Marquette Hall. (This prevented having to carry the bodies up the stairs.) Reportedly, spirits from those days walk the building's halls.

Monroe Hall is one of the newer buildings on campus, having been completed in 1969. **Nunemaker Auditorium,** used for concerts, classes, and lectures, is on the third floor. Students and staff have heard piano and organ music coming from inside the room on several occasions when it was locked and supposedly empty.

Greenville Hall, located on Loyola's Broadway campus, has also seen its share of ghosts. The building was constructed in 1892 and placed on the US Register of Historic Places a century later. Most of the ghostly tales surround the cupola, which holds a statue of the Blessed Virgin atop the building. Supposedly, a pregnant nun hanged herself there long ago, and she now revisits Greenville Hall. The most credible accounts of paranormal activity have come from security guards who have reported hearing disembodied footsteps on the stairs.

MARYLAND

COMMUNITY COLLEGE OF BALTIMORE COUNTY–CATONSVILLE

800 South Rolling Road, Baltimore, MD 21228; (443) 840-2222
www.ccbcmd.edu

The Community College of Baltimore County offers associate degrees at its three main campuses and three extension centers. The Catonsville Campus opened as the Catonsville Community College in 1957. The institution originally operated out of Catonsville High School, but in 1962 it moved to what was once a dairy farm, the Knapp Estate.

The main building on the property was a former stone farmhouse that over time was transformed into a grand manor. One of its owners, Dr. Lennox Birkhead, named the place **Hilton** because of its relatively high elevation. There have been whispers for years that the place is haunted. The ghost that's seen most often is a woman wearing a nightgown and carrying a candle. Her identity is unknown, as is the era during which she may have lived in the house. The onetime mansion also has a troublesome spirit that moves objects around and plays pranks on people without causing any harm.

HOOD COLLEGE

401 Rosemont Avenue, Frederick, MD 21701; (301) 663-3131
www.hood.edu

Hood College was established in 1893 as the Woman's College of Frederick by the Potomac Synod of the Reformed Church of the United States. **Brodbeck Music Hall,** built in 1868, is the oldest building on campus. Today the structure is home to the music department and houses an auditorium, rehearsal studios, practice halls, dressing rooms, the costume shop, and offices. Brodbeck, along with much of the core campus, is listed on the National Register of Historic Places.

No one knows who the ghosts in Brodbeck Music Hall are. Doors unlock themselves. The sound of footsteps (and sometimes stomping) is heard in the auditorium. Lights go on and off by themselves, and glowing orbs float around the theater. Lights are also seen through the third-story windows, and the sound of loud talking and laughter is heard coming from the top floor—which is always closed off. The basement is also active, with workmen's items being moved around. At least two apparitions have been reported: an elderly woman holding a candle who peers from the upper-story windows and a girl walking from the music hall to the chapel. The latter spirit may be a student who, according to one legend, had her throat slit in the building and died in the 1970s.

Mount Saint Mary's University

16300 Old Emmitsburg Road, Emmitsburg, MD 21727
(301) 447-6122; www.msmary.edu

Mount Saint Mary's University, commonly referred to as the Mount, was established in 1808 as a private Catholic institution of higher learning. In 1809, Elizabeth Ann Seton started an academy for girls nearby, which evolved into the Saint Joseph College for women. St. Joseph closed its campus and merged its student body with Mount St. Mary's in 1973.

Perhaps the best-known ghost tale at Mount St. Mary's University involves the phantom of Father Simon Gabriel Brute (or Bruté). The priest emigrated from France and joined the staff in Emmitsburg in 1812. The pastor was called on mission to the Northwest Territory in 1815, but he made a major impression during his brief stay. He died in Indiana in 1839.

But has he returned? It's said his spirit plays tricks in **Brute Hall.** The building, whose cornerstone was laid in 1843, was originally known as Doric Hall, but it was rechristened to honor the revered father in 1908. In 1973, a priest residing in Room 252 began to experience strange phenomena. His lights and television would go on or off by themselves. He'd return to his room to find the bedding torn apart and his clothing, books, and papers thrown about. The next priest to stay in the room had a pet cat that would suddenly start to hiss and yowl at the empty air and then run under the bed. The room sat unoccupied for about twenty years. Then, in 1997, three female students moved in. They reported the toilet flushing itself and a mirror falling off the wall. Others claim to have experienced spectral activity in the room as well. Even though people usually blame

Father Brute for the tricks, his apparition has never been seen there. It has, however, been spotted around campus, following groups of people.

Another night creature that stalks the grounds is the phantom of a seventeen-year-old boy from South Carolina, a Confederate soldier who died at Gettysburg and whose body (along with two other corpses) was dumped down a dry well by a farmer. The problem was that he landed facedown under the other two men. Within weeks of his unseemly disposal, the boy's sad, barefoot ghost began to roam the campus at night. He's still there. He'll walk up behind people, tap them on the shoulder, and say, "Turn me over." As soon as people spin to face the lad, he disappears.

Every Christmas Eve for several years in the late nineteenth century, a professor of music named Henry Dealman performed an organ concert in a church on campus. His son Larry, a talented flautist, joined him for several years until an argument caused them to stop speaking to each other. Apparently the son wants to make up in the Afterlife. Every Christmas Eve around midnight, people from Emmitsburg can hear the sound of a flute playing yuletide carols as the music wafts down the slope from the graveyard.

Sheridan Hall was constructed in 1962. One urban legend on campus says that a student died in the dorm while listening to Led Zeppelin on his stereo. No one knows if the story is true, but it *would* explain the mysterious strains of the band's music that are heard in the halls from time to time.

There's a campus legend about a professor named Father Dan, who moved into a dormitory room where another priest had allegedly died thirty years earlier. Objects in the room—including his bed—would move in the middle of the night. The spirit, whoever it was, didn't materialize, but it would whisper into Father Dan's ear. One night the priest was play-ing cards with a student and confessed that a ghost was helping him win. Naturally the young man didn't believe him, so Father Dan told the student that the spirit was tell-ing him that the cat lying on the bed would wake up in thirty seconds, stare at an empty corner of the room, and dart out into the hall. The kid freaked out when it happened just as the priest had foretold.

Finally there's the tale of Leander, a male slave who had been "deeded" to the Mount in the 1800s. (In the first half of the nineteenth century it was common for the univer-sity to accept ownership of students' slaves in exchange for tuition.) Leander, one of the "indentured workers" at the university, was often caught stealing. At some point after being convicted of a major theft, his left hand was cut off as punishment and was buried as a warning outside McCaf-frey Hall, where most of the slaves-for-trade were housed. Leander was later set free and eventually became a popular figure at the school. When he died he was buried in the uni-versity cemetery on the hill, but his hand stayed in its grave outside McCaffrey. Or did it? The hand has been heard—and then seen—tapping on windows. It's sometimes spotted crawling down a hallway or discovered in a student's bed-room. This leaves one to wonder: Where might the frighten-ing fingers turn up next?

TOWSON UNIVERSITY

8000 York Road, Towson, MD 21252; (410) 704-2000
www.towson.edu

Towson University, founded in 1866 as the Maryland State Nor-mal School, was the state's first teachers training institution.

After expansion, a new location, and a few name changes, it eventually took the name Towson University in 1997.

The university acquired the **Auburn House** in 1971. Four years later the building was added to the National Register of Historic Places. Captain Charles Ridgely built it as a dower house for his wife, Rebecca Dorsey, in 1799. After Rebecca's death in 1812, the house went through several owners. It caught fire during a storm in 1849 and burned nearly to its foundations. Henry Chrystie Turnbull, the owner at the time, rebuilt the house the following year.

According to legend, a woman known only as Martha died in the 1849 fire. She wasn't family, and her reason for being in the house is unknown. She may have been a guest, a servant, or nanny, but there were evil rumors that Martha was Turnbull's mistress and that his wife set the fire to kill her. Regardless, Martha has never left the house. (In fact, the rathskeller in the cellar has been named for her.) Martha's apparition has been seen staring from the attic window, and even when she doesn't materialize she plays with the light switches, moves objects around the house, opens books, locks desks, and opens the upstairs windows. She also makes strange sounds. One night several years ago, the university police were called to investigate loud, unidentifiable noises in the building, but the officer's K-9—perhaps wisely—refused to go inside.

WASHINGTON COLLEGE

300 Washington Avenue, Chestertown, MD 21620; (410) 778-2800
www.washcoll.edu

Washington College traces its beginnings from the Kent County Free School, which was founded in the 1720s, but the institution of higher learning didn't fully come about until Maryland granted a charter to establish a college in Chestertown in 1782. Although the college had many supporters, it named itself for its main patron, General George Washington. The liberal arts school stands on 114 acres and has an enrollment of about 1,400 undergraduates.

The 150-seat **Tawes Theatre** (also called the Tawes Experimental Theatre) in the Gibson Center for the Arts holds as many as four ghosts: a little girl who skips in the aisles, a student who supposedly died in the playhouse, a custodian who is thought to have hanged himself there, and the so-called "Tuxedo Man" (who's been nicknamed Noel by some students after always nattily attired dramatist Noel Coward). Spectral phenomena in the auditorium have included cold breezes, incoming telephone calls with no one on the other end, and calls being placed to the outside from empty offices. Technical problems during productions are usually blamed on the Tuxedo Man. He seems to particularly dislike musicals.

The historic **Hynson-Ringgold House** has been the official residence of the college's president since 1994. Its most distinctive feature is its grand double staircase—that, and its ghost. Henry and Ilma Pratt Catlin owned the property from 1912 until the college bought it in 1946, but the phantom may date from when Thomas Ringgold, a wealthy local merchant, owned the house in the eighteenth century. (Among other renovations, he installed the distinctive staircase.) Although no one ever saw the spectre during Ringgold's time there, there were already whispers of "ghosts in the attic." The Catlins were the first to acknowledge rumors that the place was haunted. One of their servants, a Jamaican maid, left the house and returned to her home country because a female spirit kept pestering her at night and wouldn't let her sleep. As she lay in bed trying to doze off, the caller from the Next World would show up and brush her fingers on the maid's cheeks. Apparently the apparition also liked to hang out near the left side of the double staircase. Even if the stories are true, visits by that particular spectre may be a thing of the past. There have been no recent sightings—or accounts of unwanted touching in the dark.

There are occasional reports of muffled cries in the building, however, and they're said to come from revenants of escaped slaves who passed through the house on their way to freedom in the North. There's no evidence that the home was ever part of the Underground Railroad, though—despite a persistent, unconfirmed legend that a secret tunnel extends all the way from the customshouse in town through the Hynson-Ringgold House up to the college campus.

MISSISSIPPI

Mississippi University for Women

1100 College Street, Columbus, MS 39701; (662) 329-4750
www.muw.edu

Mississippi University for Women is a four-year university. It was founded in 1884 as the Industrial Institute and College and then in 1920 became the Mississippi State College for Women. The school took its current name in 1974 and went coed in 1982.

Constructed in 1860, **Callaway Hall** is recognizable by its central clock tower. The oldest building on campus, it was originally the Industrial Institute and College's main dormitory. A ghost named Mary haunts the hall. Details about the spirit's former life are unknown, but people outside have spotted her standing at a window on the top floor. Legend says she's trying to find her missing boyfriend. Some first-year girls have said she's appeared in their rooms at night, sitting on the bed and weeping.

University of Mississippi

University Circle, University, MS 38677; (662) 915-7211
www.olemiss.edu

One of the grandest institutions of the Deep South, the University of Mississippi is fondly known by one and all as Ole Miss. Chartered in 1844, the school admitted its first students in 1848 and has been coed since 1882.

Ventress Hall was constructed in 1889 as the university library and is currently home to the school's College of Liberal Arts. Most people who think that the building is haunted merely feel an uneasy presence when they're inside, but window blinds have been known to flatten on their own, and unexplained silhouettes have been seen in a second-story window when the building was supposedly empty.

There have also been phantom encounters around the **Circle,** a small spot of green at the original center of campus. The space was declared a National Historic Landmark in 2008. Eight important buildings can be found around the ring's perimeter, including Ventress Hall. Another, the **Lyceum,** is the only surviving structure of the university's first five buildings. Today, it's the main administration building, but during the Civil War it served as a military hospital, especially for casualties from the Battle of Shiloh. Perhaps that's why the ghosts of several Confederate soldiers have been seen or heard there.

The spirit of Eula Deaton, a deceased faculty member, has returned to the eponymous **Deaton Hall.** In 1985, an electrical failure caused the death of two students in the residential hall's elevator. At least that's the official story; legend has it that Eula's ghost is malevolent and somehow caused the accident.

And finally, **St. Anthony Hall** houses the Fraternity of Delta Psi, a national collegiate literary society. The chapter at Ole Miss was established in 1855. It's said that one of its members died in a car crash in the mid-1900s and has returned to his old quarters, known as the Sigma room. Strange noises emanate from the walls and echo about the room, and the television seems to have a mind of its own. People have heard disembodied footsteps throughout the building, and at least one person has claimed that he saw the ghost materialize in the library at about one o'clock in the morning.

NORTH CAROLINA

Appalachian State University

287 Rivers Street, Boone, NC 28608; (828) 262-2000 www.appstate.edu

Appalachian State University was founded as a teachers college by brothers B. B. and D. D. Dougherty in 1899. The public coeducational university offers both baccalaureate and graduate degrees.

East Residence Hall is the most haunted site on campus. The coed dormitory houses two apparitions: a little girl in a white dress who materializes in the students' rooms and a young boy who shows up in the third-floor women's restroom. No one knows who they are—or were. Residents walking down the corridors of East Hall at night often hear someone walking behind them, but when they turn, no one's there. Other times they have the distinct sensation of an invisible someone—or some*thing*—passing by them. Lights switch off in the halls, and there are disembodied whispers and other strange sounds throughout the building.

CHOWAN UNIVERSITY

1 University Place, Murfreesboro, NC 27855; (252) 398-6500
www.chowan.edu

Dr. Godwin Cotton Moore founded Chowan University as Chowan Baptist Female Institute in 1848. The school was renamed Chowan College in 1910 and became Chowan University in 2006.

The **McDowell Columns** building, which houses the school's administrative offices, was constructed in 1851. A spectral Lady in Brown, also called the Brown Lady, has been appearing on the third floor of the building (or the fourth, depending upon which account you read) since the turn of the twentieth century, perhaps even longer. When her apparition materializes, she's dressed all in brown—hence her sobriquet. More often she makes herself known by turning on lights and slamming or knocking on doors. People also hear the rustling of her gown. According to legend, which dates from the late 1870s or early 1880s, the spectre is Eolene Davidson, the captivating daughter of a well-to-do North Carolina planter. The blue-eyed brunette was promised to New York lawyer James Lorrene, but her parents insisted she finish her studies at the institute before getting married. She acceded to their wishes and returned for her sophomore year, but she fell ill that October and died on Halloween.

Three other buildings on campus have resident spirits as well. The sounds of a piano being played by phantom fingers can be heard from inside the empty **Music Hall.** Residents of **Mixon Hall** run into the spectre of a male student who committed suicide in the building, and **Belk Hall** has two apparitions, both female. One of them died while she was on the staircase, but the other girl killed herself in her room. The latter phantom will suddenly manifest in her old dorm room, laughing or screaming. It's said her arrival is so traumatic that it can drive the current occupants insane.

Lees-McRae College

191 Main Street West, Banner Elk, NC 28604; (828) 898-5241
www.lmc.edu

Lees-McRae College started out as a high school for girls in 1899. The academy merged with a boy's school, becoming Lees-McRae College, a two-year institution, in 1931. It began offering bachelor's degree programs in 1900.

Tate Residence Hall was Grace Hospital before it became a men's dorm for sophomore, junior, and senior students. The "Men of Tate," as they like to call themselves, are haunted by the ghost of a little girl who died at the old hospital. She'll switch the lights off and on, move small objects, and bounce a ball down the hallways. She also wanders out of the dorm and appears in the **James H. Carson Library.**

Louisburg College

501 North Main Street, Louisburg, NC 27549; (919) 496-2521
www.louisburg.edu

Louisburg College, first chartered as Franklin Male Academy in 1787, is a private two-year institution affiliated with the Methodist Church. One of Louisburg College's oldest ghost stories concerns the spectre of a little boy who roams the campus. His name is lost to time, and it's no use trying to take a look at him to figure out his identity. He doesn't have a face.

Old Main, the administration hall, was constructed in 1857, back when the school was called the Female Academy. Like the facilities at many colleges and universities in the South, Old Main was temporarily used as a field hospital during the Civil War. The spirits of men who died there now haunt its third floor.

Merritt Hall, which houses 150 residents on its four floors, has a reputation for being haunted. Chairs get rearranged, lights are switched off, water faucets in the bathrooms turn on, and electrical appliances have a mind of their own.

Queens University of Charlotte

1900 Selwyn Avenue, Charlotte, NC 28274; (704) 337-2200
www.queens.edu

Queens University of Charlotte was founded in 1857 as Charlotte Female University. After a merger with another academy, a move of campus locations, and the expansion of programs, the school received its current name in 2002. The university offers both baccalaureate and master's degrees.

Albright Hall is a coed residence building completed in 1964. The dorm is said to be haunted by the spirit of a young woman who killed herself in her room after her parents discovered she was in a relationship with another female student. People hear rappings or knocks inside the suicide's former room, and the door flies open on its own.

Another dormitory, **Wallace Hall,** was constructed in 1962 and is formally known as West Residence Hall. It also has a haunted room, but there's no urban legend that gives any kind of explanation for the activity, which includes odd knocking sounds and spectral cold spots. Students standing in the hall sometimes hear objects moving around inside the room—even when they know for a fact it's empty.

Folks walking through the courtyards on campus have heard disembodied screaming. Now and then the ghost of a lynched body is seen hanging from a tree. The phenomena on the quads are thought to be revenants from the War between the States.

SALEM COLLEGE

601 South Church Street, Winston-Salem, NC 27101 (336) 721-2600; www.salem.edu

Salem College traces its history from the Little Girls' School, which was founded by the Moravians in 1772. It is the oldest women's institution of higher education in the southern United States.

Mary Reynolds Babcock Hall opened in 1955. An oil portrait of Babcock is prominently displayed, and it's said her eyes follow people as they walk by the painting.

A student committed suicide on the third floor of **Dale H. Gramley Residence Hall,** which opened in 1965, and now it's haunted. Residents and visitors to the third story hear the girl getting ready to take her life. There are also sounds of rapping on the walls, furniture being moved, and marbles rolling across the floor. The dormitory houses first-year students on its three floors and in its residential basement.

The third floor of **Gramley Library** is haunted as well. Electronics go haywire, and there are odd sounds throughout the building. People have also seen dim apparitions. There's a rumor that sometime in the library's past, several students were accidentally electrocuted there.

The identity of the spirit in the **Robert E. Elberson Fine Arts Center** is unknown. It roams the halls and is heard playing a variety of musical instruments.

University of North Carolina at Chapel Hill

Chapel Hill, NC 27599; (919) 962-2211; www.unc.edu

The University of North Carolina at Chapel Hill, also nicknamed UNC, UNC–Chapel Hill, and Chapel Hill, was established by state charter in 1793 and began classes two years later. The coed, public institution has about 29,000 students in its undergraduate and graduate programs.

The Carolina Inn sits on campus and is operated by the university. For seventeen years, one of the school's professors, Dr. William Jacocks, lived in a room on the second floor. His ghost now likes to lock current hotel guests out of his former room.

The **Horace Williams House** is named for a former dean of the philosophy department who willed the property to the university in 1940. His phantom moves objects around the building, including switching the fireplace tools from one side of the hearth to the other. He also rocks in a rocking chair and flushes the toilets.

The school's most famous haunting isn't on the 729-acre campus, but it is part of UNC's folklore because it involves one of its former students. Back in 1833, eighteen-year-old under-graduate Peter Dromgoogle fell in love with Fanny, a local girl. A rival for Fanny's hand challenged Peter to a duel by pistols on nearby Piney Prospect. Peter was shot in the chest and died while lying on top of a large, flat rock, which became stained with his blood. Dueling was illegal, so the other suitor and the two seconds assisting the duelers buried Dromgoogle on the spot and swore one another to secrecy. The three men spread the story that Peter had run off and joined the army or, according to some sources, left for Europe.

Distraught over her lover's departure without so much as a good-bye, Fanny returned to Piney Prospect every day, weeping at the stone. Soon she began to see Peter's phantom walking toward her from out of the forest, only to fade away in front of her eyes. Some say Fanny went mad; others claim she died of a broken heart. Regardless of the cause, poor Fanny soon passed away. Peter's murderer confessed to his crime on his deathbed, sixty years later. Today, hikers on the hill's wooded trails see Peter's apparition from time to time, and the rock is still stained red.

Is there any truth to the story? The university's geology department has studied the rock. The red streaks are copper veins running through the stone, not blood. Researchers also found no evidence of buried human remains anywhere near or under the boulder. As for the rest of the tale, the stone mansion that now sits on the site, Gimghoul Castle, is private property, and the owners don't wish to be disturbed by ghost hunters.

Warren Wilson College

701 Warren Wilson Road, Swannanoa, NC 28778; (828) 298-3325
www.warren-wilson.edu

Warren Wilson College dates from 1893. Much of the current campus was once the Asheville Farm School, which merged with the Dorland-Bell School for Girls in 1942. A junior college division was added later that year. Warren Wilson College began to offer classes leading to four-year degrees in 1967.

Sunderland, a coed residence hall, opened in 1929. In the three-story brick building's early years, the basement was used as a slaughterhouse, primarily of cattle. Students who live in Sunderland sometimes smell the strong odor of raw meat coming from the basement. A very few students have reported seeing phantom cows as well.

Dorland, also a coed dormitory, was constructed in 1956. On the evening of May 15, 1959, Patricia Dennis walked downstairs from her room on the second floor and attacked a former roommate, Rose Watterson, with a hatchet. She struck the victim's face numerous times and nearly killed her. Ever since, students have experienced sudden dips in temperature in Dorland and doors that won't stay closed. Some residents feel a general sense of uneasiness in the halls. Many believe that the ongoing otherworldly occurrences somehow relate to the horrific near-fatal assault.

An oil portrait of a generous donor to the college, Helen Kittredge, hangs in the lobby of the 321-seat **Kittredge Theatre.** She's thought to be the spirit who smashes small objects and blinks lights on and off. Her ghostly footsteps echo all over the building—including up on the roof! The cast and crew can tell when Kittredge doesn't approve of a production: The ethereal activity noticeably increases during rehearsals and the run of the show.

No one is sure what causes the strange happenings in **Jensen Lecture Hall.** The building has an odd shape—some say it would look like an owl from overhead. Inside there are flickering lights and an elevator that operates itself at night. On at least one occasion, a custodian's vacuum cleaner has turned itself on and off.

There are also general reports of ghostly doings at **Bannerman Computer Lab,** the **old well on Suicide Ridge, College Chapel,** and a **former teacher's house next to the sanctuary.**

WESTERN CAROLINA UNIVERSITY

1 University Way, Cullowhee, NC 28723; (828) 227-7211 www.wcu.edu

Western Carolina University grew out of a high school called Cullowhee Academy, which was founded in 1889. It became a state institution to train teachers in 1905, then a junior college, and in 1929 a four-year college. The school attained university status and took its current name in 1967.

The paranormal activity in **Moore Building,** home to the health sciences and nursing departments, has slacked off in recent years, but there are still reports from time to time. Visitors hear the sound of brisk footsteps as well as a woman sobbing or screaming. The noises are especially strong on the third floor, where a spurned admirer killed a female education major in the 1920s. The murderer, who was mentally deficient, eventually had his hospitalization sentence commuted to home detention. His victim's hauntings didn't slow down until the man died many years later.

The spectre of a college-age woman still hangs out in the coed **Harrill Residence Hall.** Many years ago the unidentified girl was staying overnight in her boyfriend's dorm room on the fifth floor. Unfortunately she died of an asthma attack as she lay by his side. Now she makes the elevator descend to the first floor or go to the upper floors on its own.

OKLAHOMA

Oklahoma State University

315 Student Union, Stillwater, OK 74078; (405) 744-5000 www.okstate.edu

Oklahoma State University was established on Christmas Day 1890 as Oklahoma Territorial Agricultural and Mechanical College, or Oklahoma A&M. It became a university in 1957. The current name only became official in 1980. The university, often referred to as Oklahoma State, has several branch campuses with its main campus in Stillwater.

The **Seretean Center for the Performing Arts,** with its six-hundred-seat theater, eight-hundred-seat concert hall, and other facilities, stands on the site of the former Williams Hall. It may be haunted by Joseph Pierre Foucart, who designed Williams Hall and was the first architect to open a practice in the Oklahoma Territory. Although Foucart died in Muskogee, it's said that he was actually buried in a hidden courtyard at Williams Hall.

The six-story Georgian-style **Edmon Low Library** was built in 1953. The centrally located facility holds between two and three million books and one ghost. The invisible spirit—mentioned on links from the university website—has been nicknamed Fred by custodians who have been tapped on the shoulder or have heard the spook call out their names.

Cordell Hall, constructed in 1939, was originally a dormitory but has now been converted into classrooms, labs, and offices. Cordello, its spectre, likes to follow students in the corridors or touch them lightly on the shoulder from behind, but he is never seen. The phantom flicks the lights on and off and sometimes produces odd sounds in the ceiling overhead.

SOUTH CAROLINA

ANDERSON UNIVERSITY

316 Boulevard, Anderson, SC 29621; (864) 231-2000 www.andersonuniversity.edu

Anderson University, a private four-year school, opened in 1912 as the Anderson College for Women. The school switched to a junior college in 1930, the same year it became coeducational. Anderson College went back to offering four-year programs in 1991 and became Anderson University in 2006.

One of the main landmarks on campus is the **Sullivan Building,** constructed in 1916 and today the headquarters for the Campus Ministries and Christian Life organizations. Dr. John E. White and his family lived there when he was the university's president from 1916 to 1927. Many people believe that his daughter Anna is back on the premises. The circumstances of her death are uncertain, as are the dates when the paranormal activity first began. In fact, her spectre has never materialized. Nevertheless she's thought to be the one who slams doors and moves objects on the tables when people are out of the room. Folks have also heard her playing an invisible piano.

BOB JONES UNIVERSITY

1700 Wade Hampton Boulevard, Greenville, SC 29614 (864) 242-5100; www.bju.edu

Evangelist Bob Jones Sr. established Bob Jones University as a private, non-denominational Protestant institution of higher learning in Florida in 1927. The school moved to Cleveland, Tennessee, six years later, and then to its current campus in Greenville in 1947. Three buildings at the university are said to be haunted.

Mack Library, constructed in 1947 and expanded in 1980, holds more than 325,000 books. Its ghost is the apparition of an elderly man who sits quietly reading in the main hall of the library.

Rodeheaver Auditorium, also built in 1947, was one of the first buildings to be completed on the Greenville campus. Designed by Bob Jones Jr., the yellowish-brick building can seat 2,600 in its performance hall. Students and staff have reported hearing ethereal organ music coming from inside the auditorium when it was empty and locked up tight.

Dr. Jones Jr. founded the **Museum and Gallery** in 1951. The art gallery opened with about thirty paintings but now has more than four hundred religious works on exhibition, including oils by such masters as Botticelli, Rubens, Tintoretto, and van Dyck. The spectre of an unidentified young girl wearing a long dress is sometimes seen wandering through the gallery.

University of South Carolina

Columbia, SC 29208; (803) 777-7000; www.sc.edu

The University of South Carolina, a public coeducational school, was founded as South Carolina College in 1801 and began classes four years later. The school was rechristened the University of South Carolina in 1865 and is the state's flagship university.

The university has several libraries on campus. The **South Caroliniana Library,** built in 1840, is located on the Horseshoe quadrangle. In addition to its 75,000 books and microfilms, the collection contains important historical and genealogical records. Staff members have spotted the spectre of J. Rion McKissick, a former university president, crossing the upstairs balcony. Perhaps the haunting is a matter of proximity: McKissick, who died in 1944, is buried in front of the building.

WOFFORD COLLEGE

429 North Church Street, Spartanburg, SC 29303; (864) 597-4000
www.wofford.edu

Wofford College was founded in 1854. The entire Wofford College Historic District is considered an arboretum, and it was placed on the National Register of Historic Places in 1974.

The oldest structure on campus is Main Building. A complete, much-needed refurbishment and renovation of the entire structure ended in 2006. This included the restoration of its **Leonard Auditorium,** which is used as a chapel and for performances. Disconcerted audience members have spotted a ghostly pair of disembodied eyes that sometimes hovers high in the air along the auditorium's east wall. No one knows whose unearthly orbs they might be.

TENNESSEE

AUSTIN PEAY STATE UNIVERSITY

601 College Street, Clarksville, TN 37044; (931) 221-7011
www.apsu.edu

Austin Peay State University opened in 1927 as a teachers training school. It became a four-year institution in 1939, and the school changed its name to Austin Peay State College in 1943. University status was conferred in 1966.

The Trahern Theatre is located in the **Trahern Building,** home to the Department of Theatre & Dance. The whole structure is haunted by a ghost nicknamed Margaret whose real identity is unknown. A few think she's Margaret Trahern, after whom the place is named, but most people think it's someone else—probably a former drama student. The apparition is most often seen on the third floor, and she likes to call out people's names. She also slams doors, flicks light switches on and off, and makes elevators operate without being called. These days Margaret is blamed for just about anything unusual that happens in the theater, including all sorts of strange noises.

The Printing Services office is located in the basement of the **Felix G. Woodward Library.** People working there have reported odd sounds since the 1990s, including a spectral voice calling "hello." Paranormal investigator and author Lorraine Warren, who claimed to be a medium and clairvoyant, visited the rear basement during a lecture appearance at Austin Peay. She received the mental image of rows of hospital cots. As it turned out, that part of the cellar had been converted into a crude hospital during the War between the States.

Students and faculty have seen the apparition of a man walking around campus that they swear is former Governor Austin Peay, namesake of the university. Peay was the first governor of Tennessee after the Civil War to win three consecutive terms in office. He died midway into his third term in 1927, the year the university was founded, at the age of fifty-one.

The school's strangest ghostly activity takes place inside the gymnasium at the Memorial Health Building, which is fondly called the **Red Barn.** The building is haunted by a mule. That's right: a mule. The animal belonged to a group of veterans studying at the university after World War II to help them tend a garden. When their faithful friend died, they received permission to bury the mule in a large empty meadow on campus. Later, the Red Barn was built on the field, and some say the beloved mule now lies directly beneath center court. People have heard its hoofbeats echoing throughout the gymnasium on nights when everything is still.

BELMONT UNIVERSITY

1900 Belmont Boulevard, Nashville, TN 37212; (615) 460-6000
www.belmont.edu

Belmont University sits on about seventy-five acres that were once part of the Belle Monte estate owned by Adelicia Hayes Franklin Acklen Cheatham, a Nashville socialite. She built the Belmont Mansion between 1849 and 1853. In 1889, two Philadelphia sisters bought the house to open a seminary for women. After several permutations, the school became Belmont University in 1991.

Adelicia's ghostly figure has returned to her old home to welcome visitors. Late at night, people have spotted her walking the halls or staring out the windows. She wears an elaborate dress that would have been fashionable in the 1880s. Although seeing her spectre can be startling, she is quite tranquil and will never interact—much less interfere—with the living.

CUMBERLAND UNIVERSITY

1 Cumberland Drive, Lebanon, TN 37087; (615) 444-2562; www.cumberland.edu

Cumberland University received its state charter in 1842. Its original building was burned by the Union army during the Civil War, but classes started up as soon as hostilities ended. The school moved to its current campus in 1892. After the Depression, the university operated as a junior college until four-year classes resumed in 1982.

Two of the university's hauntings take place in and around **Memorial Hall.** Supposedly in the mid-1980s, a science professor teaching a night class experienced chest pains while walking down the stairs as he left the building. Later, back at home, he had a fatal heart attack. His ghost has been seen all over campus but especially on the staircase where his symptoms first appeared. The second ghost story dates from at least the 1940s or 1950s. Supposedly a male student was waiting for class to start in either Room 301 or 302. He leaned back against a windowpane, which broke under his weight, and fell three floors to his death. People say his spirit now walks the halls on the third floor, and even if they don't see him, they feel spooked there at night. (For the record, the university has no record of anyone tumbling out of a window at Memorial Hall.)

EAST TENNESSEE STATE UNIVERSITY

807 University Parkway, Johnson City, TN 37604; (423) 439-1000 www.etsu.edu

East Tennessee State Normal School was founded in 1911 and underwent several name and curricula changes before becoming East Tennessee State University in 1963. So many ghosts haunt the institution that it's considered to be one of the most ghost-ridden universities in the South.

Founding-president Sidney Gordon Gilbreath served until 1925. His glowing ghost, tinged red, has been spotted staring out the attic window of **Gilbreath Hall,** one of the oldest buildings on campus. His silhouette has also been seen by those still inside the building at night. "Uncle Sid," as he's been nicknamed, was a strict disciplinarian, so some say he's come back to keep everyone in line.

Because the school library used to be in Gilbreath Hall, some think it's the ghost of the librarian, not the former president, who fiddles with lights and shuts windows in the building. One of the head librarians retired after twenty years, but she often came back to help out as a volunteer. Unfortunately, one day she suffered a heart attack while in the library and died. But that didn't stop her from returning from the Beyond. Her spectre only materialized a few times, but people frequently felt her presence and sensed they were being watched. Also, if anyone got up for a few minutes and left a book or periodical lying out, it had a funny way of reshelving itself. There are claims that the **Charles C. Sherrod Library** is haunted by a former librarian as well.

Christine Burleson spent many years teaching English and Shakespeare at ETSU. By the time she retired in 1967, her health had declined and she was wheelchair bound. In November 1967 she committed suicide by shooting herself in the head. Her spirit has returned to **Burleson Hall,** home of the English department. Starting around 1988 people began to hear her restless moans. Now, people attribute almost any unusual occurrence in the building to her. The strangest paranormal phenomenon involves an oil portrait of her father that hangs on the second floor. Burleson's eyes seem to follow people as they walk by, and some say it's actually Christine's spirit, not her father's, looking out from the painting.

Lucille Clement Hall opened in 1967 and was fully renovated in 2010. The dorm is haunted by the "Marble Boy." Legend says the young lad died in the building's elevator years ago. Residents all over the dorm hear what sounds like marbles being dropped on the floor overhead, one at a time. If anyone yells at the youngster, he "loses his marbles." (In other words, he drops them all at once.) No one has ever seen the tyke, but he opens water taps, and he turns television sets on and off and changes channels. Though not malicious, he's also been known to throw objects across the room.

Mathes Hall houses the music department. There is no concrete information about the entity that causes the spooky activity there. Inexplicable cold spots pop up, and people have heard disembodied footsteps and muffled voices following them in the corridors.

Some say that a female student leapt to her death from a window on the third floor—the top story—of **Yoakley Hall.** Not long after the young woman took her life, passersby began to spy her apparition leaning out of that same window or jumping. Students who lived in the building would experience unwarranted sadness, even depression. Word got out, and Yoakley soon became one of the least desirable dorms on campus. Eventually the university turned it into an office building.

There are a few more rumors about hauntings on campus, but they don't come with many details. The **Sigma Chi fraternity house** allegedly harbors an impish spirit who likes to move objects from one spot to another. The frat boys also hear the disembodied sound of snapping fingers. The ghost of Congressman B. Carroll Reece is said to roam his eponymous two-story **Reece Memorial Museum,** and the phantom of Ada Hornsby Earnest, a former home economics professor, haunts—what else?—the **Ada Earnest House.**

Sewanee: The University of the South

735 University Avenue, Sewanee, TN 37383; (931) 598-1000
www.sewanee.edu

Sewanee: The University of the South was established in 1857 but didn't open until 1868. The school is officially named The University of the South, but everyone knows it as Sewanee. The 13,000-acre campus is referred to as "The Domain" or "The Mountain."

Like almost every college, Sewanee has a smattering of ghost tales, such as the spectral soldier seen in the stairwells of **Walsh-Ellet Hall.** Also, one particular room on the third floor of **Tuckaway Hall,** a dorm dating from 1929, is cursed. Three students who lived there committed suicide, and their tortured souls have returned from the Other Side to terrorize those who now reside in the building.

The only ghost story that's really stood the test of time at Sewanee, though, is the tale of the headless spectre known as "The Phantom Gownsman." Because of the spirit's recognizable robe, he's believed to have been a student who belonged to the Order of the Gownsman, an honor society unique to Sewanee. According to one legend, the ghost has been appearing on campus since the 1880s. In another, the unidentified young man was decapitated in a car accident while driving on a winding road on Mounteagle Mountain.

The cranially challenged ghost has been seen in buildings all over campus, especially St. Luke's Hall. The Phantom Gownsman's head has turned up as well—but always separate from the rest of the apparition's body. The head has a habit of materializing at exam time, floating in the air. One student even claimed he heard the head bouncing down a staircase, counting the steps aloud as it went!

TENNESSEE WESLEYAN COLLEGE

204 East College Street, Athens, TN 37303; (423) 745-7504
www.twcnet.edu

Founded as the Athens Female College in 1857, Tennessee Wesleyan College is a small liberal arts school affiliated with the United Methodist Church. It offers baccalaureate and master's degrees as well as teacher certification.

In 1780 a British officer was wounded during the Revolutionary War at the Battle of King's Mountain. He was nursed back to health by Nocatula, the daughter of Cherokee chief Attakulla-Kulla. The young couple fell in love and married. The former officer was accepted into the tribe and renamed Conestoga, which meant "the oak."

But the story did not have a happy ending—at least not in this world. One of Nocatula's rejected suitors killed Conestoga with a knife. The Indian princess, unwilling to go through life without her husband, stabbed herself and died. The chief buried them on land that is now on the Tennessee Wesleyan College campus. To signify their undying love, he placed an acorn in Conestoga's hand and a hackberry seed on his daughter's palm. The seeds sprouted, and two large trees soon grew up side by side. In the 1940s, the hackberry tree became diseased. As if in sympathy, the mighty oak also died and, reluctantly, the university cut down both trees. A historical marker was erected on the site to commemorate the tale.

Today, students walking by the grassy area where the trees once stood sometimes hear the soft murmuring of strange, disembodied voices. Other times, people catch a fleeting glimpse of two dark shadows, Conestoga and Nocatula, as they glide over the hallowed patch of earth—together again in the Afterlife.

University of Memphis

3641 Central Avenue, Memphis, TN 38111; (901) 678-2040
www.memphis.edu

The University of Memphis opened in 1912 as the West Tennessee State Normal School. After the school underwent almost a century of growth and change, its name took its current form in 1994.

The Brister Library, named for two-term president John W. Brister, was built in 1928. When the modern Ned R. McWherter Library opened in 1994, the building was transformed into **Brister Hall.** Even before then, people heard a young woman's screams in the old library. Legend has it they belong to a student who was raped and murdered in the tower. Her killer was never found. Campus security has never been able to find a source for the bloodcurdling sounds. The girl's filmy apparition still occasionally appears, always late at night, but if it's approached the spirit will instantly evaporate.

University of Tennessee at Chattanooga

615 McCallie Avenue, Chattanooga, TN 37403; (423) 425-4111
www.utc.edu

The University of Tennessee at Chattanooga, also known as UTC or simply Chattanooga, was established in 1886 as Chattanooga University. It took its new name in 1969 when it became one of the three primary campuses of the University of Tennessee system.

Hooper Hall, built in 1917, is in the university's central courtyard. Rumors have circulated for years about ghostly happenings inside the building. Custodians have seen muddy footprints end in the middle of a hallway. Some have heard the inexplicable sound of raspy breathing on the first floor, and visitors can make out what sounds like heavy footsteps and furniture being rearranged overhead on the second floor, especially when standing where the two wings of the building meet. Cold spots three or four feet in diameter manifest themselves, particularly in the upper stairwells, and rust-colored beads of water have appeared on the walls. There are also slamming doors and footsteps pacing from one end of the vacant corridor to the other, and the elevator sometimes decides on its own to head to the top floor. Many think the spirit of John Hocking, the superintendent of grounds and buildings who gassed himself to death in the physics lab in January 1924, is causing the paranormal activity in Hooper Hall. The fifty-year-old man had never gotten over the death of his wife and child some twenty years earlier.

Patten Chapel, situated next to Hooper Hall, was dedicated in 1919 when the school was known as the University of Chattanooga. Reportedly, an unknown Woman in White haunts the chapel. She's been seen at all hours, day and night. People detect cold spots, and the sounds of disembodied footsteps and doors swinging shut sometimes echo in the hall. Organ music has also been heard coming from inside the empty building late at night.

Brock Hall is one of the academic buildings, holding classroom space for the history, geography, anthropology, sociology, and language departments. No apparitions have been seen, but students and staff have reported hearing disembodied voices and other odd noises. Perhaps the sounds are holdovers from a troubled past: A jail and an execution yard were once located where Brock Hall now stands.

There have been generalized claims that **Development House, Metro** building, and the **Lambda Chi Alpha fraternity house** are haunted as well.

University of Tennessee, Knoxville

1331 Circle Park Drive, Knoxville, TN 37916; (865) 974-1000
www.utk.edu

The University of Tennessee, Knoxville was founded in 1794 as Blount College and then rechartered in 1807 as East Tennessee College. It became East Tennessee University in 1840 and the University of Tennessee in 1879. In 1968 a University of Tennessee system was formed with Knoxville as its flagship campus.

Several ghosts wander the grounds. Part of the Battle of Fort Sanders, fought during the Civil War, took place on the property. The phantoms of Union soldiers killed in the clash have been spied all over campus, and the sounds of troops marching and artillery fire can be heard on still nights. The most active area seems to be the oldest section of campus, which is situated on a gentle rise referred to as "**the Hill.**" There have been similar reports of soldiers appearing at an apartment house near the corner of Fifteenth Street and Lake Avenue.

Supposedly a spectral wolf stalks the Hill, howling. Some say it's the elusive Wampus Cat, a supernatural feline creature that's been part of Appalachian folklore as long as anyone can remember.

Opened in 1931, the **James D. Hoskins Library** served as the university's principal library until 1987 when the Hodges Library opened. The Hoskins Library still holds the special collections, map services, and archives. The building's Collegiate Gothic exterior and interior—with vaulted ceilings, pointed arches, and gargoyles out front—make it look haunted. And it is! The library had two ghosts before the new library opened, and both seem to have stayed. Neither ever materializes, however. The first spirit is believed to be male and a former director of the library. The other, thought to be a female, has been nicknamed "Evening Primrose." She strolls through the library, closing doors, sometimes knocking books off of shelves, and riding the elevator. When she's around there's also often a scent in the air of food being cooked, especially corn bread.

The visitants of **Reese Hall** have a reason to be angry. According to historical maps, the building is on land that contains both a Native-American cemetery and a pioneers' graveyard. No one remembers any human remains being relocated when Reese Hall was put up, so chances are good that lots of bodies are still lying under the basement and the parking lot. Details about spectral activity in the building aren't plentiful, other than the fact that students *do* encounter ghosts from time to time—and the spirits don't look happy. (The students probably aren't too thrilled to see them, either.)

Tyson Hall serves as the headquarters for the Office of Development and Alumni Affairs. The original structure was a modest two-story, Queen Anne–style frame house built by James M. Meek in 1895, but he went bankrupt the same year. Bettie Tyson, wife of UT's military commandant Lawrence D. Tyson, bought the house at auction. Lawrence and Bettie's spirits still amble through their old abode. It's said the former residence is also haunted by the Tysons' dog, Benita, who's buried behind the house. Visitors will hear the canine's bark or see the spectral pooch scampering about. Some claim the dog has returned because the university failed to keep its promise to maintain Benita's grave.

UTK has a couple of other buildings with a "reputation," but there are few specifics. **McClung Museum of Natural History and Culture** was supposedly built on Native-American burial grounds, and some of their spirits now meander through the building's exhibit space. **Hess Hall** is haunted by a female student who committed suicide there.

The University of Tennessee, Knoxville may have said good-bye to its best-known phantom. From the time it opened in 1925 until it closed in 2008, **Strong Hall,** a women's dormitory, was haunted by the ghost of Sophronia Strong, whose house previously stood on the property. The apparition would break up squabbles, lock kids out of bathrooms and their own rooms, and appear as a reflection in mirrors. She almost always showed up on her birthday, February 17. Only twenty thousand square feet of Strong Hall will be incorporated into the new science building that will replace it. It's too soon to tell whether the ghost will return. That's Sophie's choice.

TEXAS

BAYLOR UNIVERSITY

1311 South Fifth Street, Waco, TX 76706; (254) 710-1011
www.baylor.edu

Baylor University, chartered in 1845 by the Republic of Texas, is a private Baptist university. The campus location that's most often said to be haunted is the **Armstrong Browning Library.** The building, which opened in 1951, is named for its special collection of Robert and Elizabeth Barrett Browning materials. Rumor has it that, in the evening hours, a spirit thought to be Elizabeth Browning peers out a window on the top floor. Her delicate apparition, holding a lit candle, has also been seen on the staircase. People hear disembodied footsteps, and there are several cold spots in the library. It's unlikely, though, that the phantom is Browning. Neither she nor her husband ever visited America, and she died and was buried in Florence, Italy. A much more probable suspect would be Preacher Johnson, a construction worker who died in an elevator accident in the building. (In fact, one of the spectral cold spots happens to be very close to the lift.)

For many years an unidentified male ghost haunted Brooks Hall, especially the locked fifth floor—which was closed off in 1987 when the structure was refurbished. The spectre was most often described as wearing a top hat and a cloak. Occasionally he held a candle or played the violin. A still-popular legend says that one time the wraith smashed an upper-story window and glared down at passersby, but the next day the glass pane was unbroken. Whether any of this ever happened is moot: The building was torn down in 2006. **Brooks Residential College** now stands on the spot, and there's already been at least one published claim of apparitions of former students searching its halls looking for their old dorm rooms—which, of course, no longer exist.

Other haunted spots on campus? There have been a few reports of a female spirit in **Marrs McLean Gymnasium.** It's said to be Mrs. Marrs McLean, the building's principal donor, searching for the swimming pool that was removed during renovations. The screeching of phantom cars has been heard in the **Fifth Street Parking Garage,** and students have been followed or assaulted by spectral stalkers on **Bear Trail,** which circles the campus. There are also vague stories of some sort of entity inside **Carroll Library.**

Our Lady of the Lake University

411 Southwest Twenty-Fourth Street, San Antonio, TX 78207
(210) 434-6711; www.ollusa.edu

Our Lady of the Lake University was founded in 1895. Its **Sueltenfuss Library** is named for Sister Elizabeth Sueltenfuss, the fourth president of the university. Construction on the building started in 1998, and it opened two years later. It's said that the ghost of a former custodian has been seen down in the basement. The old library in St. Marin's Hall was also haunted. Its spectre was a nun who had been one of its librarians, and the spectre would turn on the lights and knock books off the shelves at night.

Providence Hall, a coed residence hall housing eighty-two students in single rooms, is named for the university's founding and sponsoring religious order. The dorm is visited by the apparition of a spectral nun.

Texas A&M University

College Station, TX 77843; (979) 845-3211; www.tamu.edu

Texas A&M University, also known as A&M, was founded in 1876 as the Agricultural and Mechanical College of Texas—the first institution of higher learning in the state. Students, alumni, and sports teams are referred to as the Texas Aggies or simply Aggies.

The **Animal Industries Building** was constructed between 1929 and 1931, and originally it housed the animal science department. A meat laboratory was located in the basement directly beneath the building's largest lecture hall. The building is haunted by the ghost of Roy Simms, who used to be the laboratory foreman. On November 14, 1959, Simms was alone slicing a slab of bacon when his knife slipped and cut his femoral artery. He dragged himself into the freight elevator, hoping to make it upstairs to get help, but he bled to death in the lift.

Simms's spirit has since returned. No one has ever seen him, but he's made himself known in other ways. His footsteps and screams are heard in the halls at night, punctuated by the sound of doors opening and slamming. The elevator arrives on various floors, but no one is ever in the car. At first Simms created havoc in the meat lab at night, opening containers, tampering with equipment, and moving around furniture. According to legend, Henry Turner, the custodian at the time, decided that Simms was causing the mess because the ghost couldn't get any rest. Turner got in the habit of leaving the elevator in the basement all night with the door wide open. That way, Simms would have a place to sleep. Apparently, it worked . . . for a while. But these days, Simms is up to all his old tricks, though not in the meat lab, which is now a men's restroom and emergency fire escape. But upstairs, well, that's a different story.

The Romanesque-style building known as **Francis Hall** opened in 1918 to house the School of Veterinary Medicine. Odd things take place there very early in the morning, usually between 4:30 and 6:00 a.m. The cleaning staff—the only ones in the building at that time—see their mops swirl in the buckets by themselves. Carts move on their own. Janitors hear loud coughing and other unusual noises in the stairwells and hallways, including the sound of stall doors squeaking and banging shut in the second-floor bathrooms. They've also spotted a human-shape shadow moving in the corridor. So far there's been no explanation for the hauntings.

Texas State University

601 University Drive, San Marcos, TX 78666; (512) 245-2111
www.txstate.edu

Texas State University, or Texas State, was founded in 1899 as Texas State Normal School. It became a university in 1969. The institution underwent several name changes before taking its current form in 2013.

Butler Hall can accommodate 283 students—and, apparently, at least one ghost. Rumor has it that at night residents hear the disconcerting sound of taps on the windows and rapping at the doors as well as odd, unidentifiable noises throughout the building. Some students also report the sensation of being watched by invisible eyes.

University of Texas at Austin

1 Inner Campus Drive, Austin, TX 78712; (512) 475-7348
www.utexas.edu

University of Texas at Austin, also called simply University of Texas, UT, or UT Austin, was founded in 1883. It's the flagship school of the University of Texas system.

There are strange goings-on in the **Scottish Rite Dormitory,** constructed in 1922 to house the daughters and granddaughters of freemasons. Lights flicker, the fire alarm sets itself off, the heater sometimes won't shut off, and the lift moves from floor to floor without being called. People have heard coughing inside vacant rooms, and unidentifiable sounds come from inside an empty storage room. In the students' rooms, personal belongings move from one place to another on their own. On one occasion the photograph of a former dorm administrator (who didn't like to have her picture taken) fell off the wall, even though all the others around it stayed in place. Rumor has it that the ghost responsible for all the paranormal activity is a former resident who committed suicide by throwing herself down one of the elevator shafts when she found out her boyfriend had died in WWII.

Another ghost on campus that everyone seems to have heard of is Dalies Erhardt Frantz, a renowned pianist and a professor at the university from the 1940s through the 1960s. He died in 1965. His presence is still felt in **Jessen Auditorium,** a three-hundred-seat chamber hall located inside Homer Rainey Hall. At the time of the building's construction in 1942, it was the primary music facility on campus.

Then there's the twenty-eight-story Main Building, commonly referred to as the **Tower.** The landmark entered the news on August 1, 1966, when deranged gunman Charles Whitman, a UT engineering student and former US Marine, went up to its observation deck and began a shooting spree that killed fourteen people (three in the tower and another eleven by sniper fire) and injured many more. Police and citizens eventually made their way to the top of the building and shot Whitman to death.

The assassin's spectre is blamed for lights that turn themselves on and off after hours, and his apparition is occasionally seen in the tower, sometimes wearing workman's clothing, other times materializing as a dark shadow. A few folks think the phantom is a former construction worker, not Whitman. There are other spirits up there as well. Since the tower opened in 1937 at least nine students have committed suicide by jumping from its observation deck. Some of their ghosts have been spied walking around the tower.

University of Texas at Brownsville

1 West University Boulevard, Brownsville, TX 78520; (956) 882-8200
www.utb.edu

From 1991 to 2011, following the merger of the University of Texas at Brownsville (a former branch campus of Pan American University) and Texas Southmost College (a junior college), the combined school was known as the University of Texas and Texas Southmost College. The school subsequently evolved into the University of Texas at Brownsville.

The campus stands on the site of the former Fort Brown, which would explain the phantom soldiers that people have seen going through drills and maneuvers at night. Folks were puzzled when a spectral nurse in a white uniform walked through locked doors and sat behind office desks in **Gorgas Hall**—that is, until they discovered the building was once the fort's hospital.

Paranormal activity also took place in the Arnulfo L. Oliveira Memorial Library, which opened in 1966. Books were seen moving on cabinet shelves, and the Hunter Room door opened on its own. Visitors to the library often felt unseen eyes watching them. Ghost investigators were given access in 2001, and they claimed to have captured an image of a male apparition in one of the hallways. They promptly decided it was Arnulfo Oliveira himself. Most of the library's materials were moved to the new University Boulevard Library, now called the University Library, between 2009 and 2010. Only the special collections and archives are still kept at the old library. The Oliveira Memorial Library building was renamed the **Oliveira Student Center** in 2013. It's too soon to tell whether Oliveira or any other spirits will stay.

UNIVERSITY OF TEXAS AT SAN ANTONIO

HemisFair Park Campus, Institute of Texan Cultures, 801 East Cesar Chavez Boulevard, San Antonio, TX 78233; (210) 458-2300 www.texancultures.com

The University of Texas at San Antonio was founded in 1969 as part of the University of Texas System. The school has three campuses: the original Main Campus northwest of center city, the Downtown Campus, and the HemisFair Park Campus, which is also located in the inner city.

For all intents and purposes, the entire HemisFair Park Campus is just one building, the **Institute of Texan Cultures.** The 182,000-square-foot museum is housed inside the former Texas pavilion from the 1968 World's Fair, which was known as HemisFair '68. The structure was turned over to UTSA when the exposition closed. Today, about a third of the institute's space is used to tell the multicultural history of Texas through interactive displays. As for its ghosts, there are footsteps heard in the halls, books that move around on the library shelves, and the inexplicable scent of pipe smoke wafting through the exhibit area.

University of the Incarnate Word

4301 Broadway Street, San Antonio, TX 78209; (210) 829-6000
www.uiw.edu

The University of the Incarnate Word, a private Catholic institution of higher education, was founded in 1881 by the Sisters of Charity of the Incarnate Word, a religious order. There are at least two haunted buildings on the 154-acre campus.

The **Administration Building** was built in 1922. The ghost of a five-year-old boy chasing a bouncing ball has been spotted on the third floor, and cold spots have been reported throughout the building. The top floor was once used to quarantine tuberculosis sufferers, some of whom died on the premises, but it's unknown whether the hauntings are in any way related to the victims.

Dubuis Hall was built in 1928 and is named for Bishop Claude Marie Dubuis, the founder of the Sisters of the Incarnate Word. The three-story dormitory is coed and houses first-year students. No apparitions have been seen, but residents have said they often feel they're being watched at night. They suspect that the spirit is a former nun.

Wayland Baptist University

1900 West Seventh Street, Plainview, TX 79072; (806) 291-1000
www.wbu.edu

Wayland Baptist University is a private coeducational school affiliated with the Southern Baptist Convention. It was founded in 1906. The school opened as Wayland Literary and Technical Institute and became Wayland Baptist College in 1910. It was made a full university in 1981.

In addition to its main campus, the university has thirteen satellite campuses. **Gates Hall,** on the Plainview campus, was the original administration building constructed between 1909 and 1910. Today the building is haunted by at least one ghost, the unseen spectre of a young woman who was a music major at the university. Her voice can be heard singing into the wee hours on the third floor. Details about the haunting are imprecise. Some say she's accompanied by a piano, others by a flute, but there seems to be no discussion about who's playing the instruments. Most versions of the tale claim the unseen vocalist is singing the aria she used for her senior exams. When the recital didn't go well, she killed herself by jumping off the third floor or the roof. The ghost has been around since at least the 1940s. According to Michael Norman's *Haunted Homeland*, when the class of 1941 met for its fiftieth reunion, former students recalled the time the phantom chased them out of the building when they tried to sneak a cow into the president's office.

In addition to the singer, folks have heard footsteps and doors slamming. A black shadow has passed people in a hallway, and students standing outside the building have seen a strange figure in the upper windows. Some think this last spectre may be Dr. I. E. Gates, the university's first president and the building's namesake.

VIRGINIA

The College of William and Mary

102 Richmond Road, Williamsburg, VA 23185; (757) 221-4000
www.wm.edu

King William III and Queen Mary II of England signed a charter in 1693 that resulted in The College of William and Mary being founded. William & Mary is the second-oldest college in America after Harvard.

College Building, now known as the **Wren Building,** was built between 1695 and 1700. The building was used as a field hospital by colonial and French forces during the Revolutionary War and by the Confederate army during the Civil War. Disembodied footsteps have been heard since the American Revolution, and some people think they come from a French soldier who died in the temporary infirmary. Others claim they belong to the building's namesake, architect Sir Christopher Wren. A more recent ghost—though still more than a century old—is a full-form male apparition that walks the halls upstairs garbed in a Confederate uniform.

The Brafferton Building, the second-oldest structure on campus, is located southeast of Wren. Part of the royal charter for William & Mary's called for the school to teach Native Americans to speak English and to convert them to Christianity. The Brafferton Building was first used for that purpose. Native-American boys were forcibly removed from their families and housed in the building, where they also attended classes. Conditions and discipline were severe. A few of the boys died from the meager food and bad sanitation. These days, the moans and mournful cries of at least two of the youngsters reverberate down the vacant halls at night, and on moonlit evenings their souls are sometimes seen wandering outdoors.

The **President's House** is the official residence of the president of William & Mary, and all but one of them have stayed there. The apparition of the college's first president, the Reverend James Blair, is among the building's spectral occupants. A phantom believed to have been a French soldier has been spied walking down the staircase between the third and second floors. An unknown spirit hugs visitors and occupants, though the spectre is usually felt rather than seen. Also, people on the ground level have heard footsteps and generalized thumping on the floors overhead. At some point during renovations, human bones were discovered sealed behind a wall. It's uncertain whether those remains have anything to do with the hauntings.

Phi Beta Kappa Hall, the college's performing arts center, was named for the first Greek-letter society. The apparition who's seen there most often is a female former student named Lucinda. She's seen on the stage, in the rooms beneath it, and in the balcony of the auditorium. According to legend, Lucinda died in a car accident while in rehearsal for a production of Thornton Wilder's *Our Town*, and her ghostly attire is always some piece of wardrobe from the show. She tinkers with lights, has been known to fix broken organ pipes, and was once heard asking a male music student who was winding up his practice to keep going. Other students and staff have reported entering the playhouse early in the morning (or staying late) and seeing and hearing a female apparition performing on one of the musical instruments. No one knows if that ghost is Lucinda or some other spirit. Another ghost in Phi Beta

Kappa Hall is a Revolutionary War soldier who died from a gunshot wound. He materializes in a tiny third-floor room in the back of the building.

The college's newest ghost shows up in what was the school's first freestanding library, now called **Tucker Hall.** Supposedly a female student killed herself in the building in 1980. According to legend, her phantom now wanders its corridors. A variation of the tale says her suicide took place in one of the bathrooms, and students staring into the restroom's mirrors occasionally see the girl's reflection as she passes behind them.

Randolph-Macon College

204 Henry Street, Ashland, VA 23005; (804) 752-7200; www.rmc.edu

Randolph-Macon College was founded by the Virginia Methodist Church in 1830, making it the oldest Methodist-run institution of higher learning in America. The coed, liberal arts school has approximately 1,300 students and offers four-year degrees in more than thirty-five programs.

Several buildings at the college have had a reputation for being haunted, but only a few have specific stories attached to them. The best-known tales concern **Washington and Franklin Hall,** constructed in 1872. The building is listed on the National Register of Historic Places. An elderly man in a late nineteenth-century tuxedo has been observed staring out of windows, and two men in turn-of-the-twentieth-century attire have been spotted in the halls. Sometimes instead of encountering a humanlike figure, people see a gray cloud or mist. Other phenomena in the building include creaking floors, lights that go on and off unexpectedly, and papers that blow off tables when there is no breeze.

Mary Branch Hall was completed in 1906. Windows and doors open and close by themselves, and there are unidentifiable noises. Curtains and shelves fall without being touched, and objects move themselves. The third floor and the basement are especially troubled. Some think the events—almost all of which happen after dark—are caused by the unsettled spirit of a girl who allegedly hanged herself from a pipe in a bathroom.

Sigma Alpha Epsilon fraternity house was built on the foundations of a military hospital that burned down during the War between the States. Like other places of a certain age, there has always been the odd noise now and then, but the building is also haunted by the ghost of a Civil War soldier. (Some versions of the legend say there is more than one spectral soldier.) The strange thing is, the phantom is only ever seen from the waist up as he moves around the building. Perhaps the hospital stood lower, and the soldier is still walking on the old, long-gone floorboards.

One other spot at Randolph-Macon requires a Ghost Alert. A young man who died on the stretch of railway that runs along the edge of campus has apparently never left the tracks. As part of a hazing ritual, he was put into a box that was then placed on the **railroad tracks.** No, he wasn't struck by a locomotive—nothing that ghastly. Instead, the stress or fear was probably too much for him, and he died of a heart attack. Now he walks the rails, warning others to stay off the tracks.

Sweet Briar College

134 Chapel Road, Sweet Briar, VA 24595; (434) 381-6100
www.sbc.edu

Sweet Briar College owes its existence to Indiana "Miss Indie" Fletcher Williams, who, upon her death in 1900, left a million dollars and her eight-thousand-plus-acre Sweet Briar plantation to establish a woman's college. Today the school sits on 3,250 of the original acres.

Twenty-one of the thirty buildings on campus are on the National Register of Historic Places as part of the Sweet Briar College Historic District. One of the structures is the former main residence on the estate, **Sweet Briar House,** and it's now the official home of the president of the college. As a small child, Miss Indie's daughter, Daisy, and her friends used to love to spin and dance in front of the tall pier mirrors in the parlors. According to witnesses, Daisy, who died at age sixteen, is still there today. They have seen her spirit in the form of a swirling white cloud "dancing" in front of the mirrors.

Not long after the college was founded, someone pried a metal stake from the family cemetery fence and smashed Daisy's marble marker. (It's believed the culprit may have been a relative or someone else who was angry about being left out of Miss Indie's will.) The girl's tombstone was rebuilt, and as part of a new monument, there's a statue at the top of a high vertical column. The sculpture has been nicknamed the **"Screaming Statue"** because it makes a high-pitched whistling sound. Legend says that it's Daisy signaling her presence, but the "scream" is most likely caused by wind blowing through a hole in the statue's hand.

Anne Marshall Whitley was doing research in the college library when she found an abandoned cardboard carton full of old photographs in the rare books room. While drying them out, she discovered a note saying they had been salvaged from the cellar of Sweet Briar House in 1953.

She became excited, hoping there was a photograph of Miss Indie. (None was known to exist.) Two of the photos showed the same unidentified woman at different ages, but Whitley recognized her as being the same person who had previously been identified in a photo as a teenage Daisy Williams. When Whitley removed the photo of "Daisy" from its frame and checked the back, the picture was inscribed PARIS, FRANCE. Daisy had never been to Paris, but Indie had been there when she was sixteen. Whitley called out in excitement to the wife of the college president, whom she thought was standing behind her. She had found not one but *three* photographs of the school's founder! Whitley heard a laugh over her shoulder, but when she turned there was no one there. Perhaps it was Miss Indie acknowledging the discovery. (Although Indiana Fletcher Williams's ghost has never been seen on campus, its dark figure is said to have appeared near the dining room and the upstairs fireplaces in her former mansion at Mount San Angelo, a separate 450-acre estate that Miss Indie left to the college.)

Sweet Briar College didn't have a gymnasium until 1931. The building's name, Daisy Williams Gymnasium, wasn't selected until three days before it was set to open. On the very day the announcement was made, a housekeeper named Mrs. Martindale stumbled across a sixteen-inch-diameter bronze medallion bearing a bust of Daisy Williams in a storage area under the staircase in Gray Residence Hall. Mrs. Martindale had been the director of the residence halls for twenty-five years but, even though she thought knew every square inch of them, she had never seen the medal before. The president of the college quickly had it polished and mounted just inside the front entrance of the gym. Was the medallion's sudden, unexpected appearance coincidental?

Had Miss Indie led the housekeeper to it, or had a grateful mother somehow sent it from the Beyond?

The college doesn't shy away from its numerous ghost legends; in fact, it embraces them. Several more haunted locations are pinpointed and explained under the "Layers" drop-down menu found on the map at www.sbc.edu/map. Also, the Sweet Briar College Public Relations Office maintains a link at http://ghosts.sbc.edu where students, alumnae, and faculty are invited to share their own experiences.

Sweet Briar College was the basis for the episode entitled "Ghostly Girls' School" on the Syfy channel series *School Spirits*.

University of Virginia

1215 Lee Street, Charlottesville, VA 22908; (434) 924-0211
www.virginia.edu

The University of Virginia was founded in 1819. It was conceived, designed, and partially financed by President Thomas Jefferson, who remained involved with the university up until his death in 1826. Presidents Madison and Monroe were also major figures in the institution's early years.

The campus's Federal-style mansion **Montebello** was constructed in 1830 and now serves as housing for distinguished faculty. According to some reports, lights inexplicably appear in the windows at night, and mysterious sounds, including full conversations, come from the building when it's empty.

As part of Jefferson's original design for the campus, ten pavilions were set along a green terraced space known as "the Lawn." Students have given Pavilion VI on the East

Lawn a nickname: the **Romance Pavilion.** Supposedly the daughter of one of the university professors fell in love with a student, but her parents didn't approve. The young couple broke up, but the girl never got over it. She died of a broken heart, and her spirit has taken up residence in the building. Many believe that the legend is what gave Pavilion VI its sobriquet. (Actually, it got the name because Romance languages were taught in the building for more than fifty years.)

The most haunted spot on campus is **Alderman Library,** with its two ghosts. The first spirit is Dr. Bennett Wood Green, a Confederate surgeon whose papers were donated to the university after his death in 1913. His phantom returned to guard the documents in the Rotunda, which was the university's library until 1938. When everything was moved from the Rotunda to the Alderman Library, Green went right along with it. People sense him watching them and hear his footsteps—especially if they happen to be in the building after midnight. Occasionally they catch a peek of the elderly, grayish spectre walking through the stacks and dusting books.

The other apparition is holed up in the library's **Garnett Room,** which houses a special collection donated by the heirs of Muscoe Russell Hunter Garnett. The otherworldly shade is a physician, a family friend who admired the books whenever he visited the Garnett home. After the doctor passed on, some say his ghost returned to his friend's estate to protect the tomes. The tale may or may not be true, but the plantation was abandoned after the Civil War, and remarkably the volumes sat undisturbed in the empty mansion for many years. The phantom physician now seems to be keeping a watchful eye on the books in the Alderman Library.

University of Virginia's College at Wise

1 College Avenue, Wise, VA 24293; (276) 328-0100
www.wise.virginia.edu

The University of Virginia, located in Charlottesville, has one branch campus in Wise. Founded in 1954, the Wise campus is considered a separate college. The four-year liberal arts institution has about two thousand students.

McCrary Hall opened in 1970 as the college's first new dormitory. The wing housing females is haunted by a spirit that many believe to be Emma McCrary, one of the school's first faculty members and the building's namesake. Others think the spectral presence is Lois Lawry, a former housemother who lived in the hall and often sat in the lobby to chaperone students—just to make sure the young ladies and gentlemen behaved themselves. Perhaps she's still in the building keeping an eye on things.

Zehmer Hall, one of the classroom buildings, was constructed above an old cemetery. (Didn't they know that was asking for trouble?) The graves were relocated, but that didn't stop a local crone who said she was a witch from placing a curse on whatever structure would be erected there. When strange things started to occur in Zehmer, the Black Mountain Paranormal Society asked to look into the disturbances. Investigators witnessed shaking doors and recorded an EVP—Electronic Voice Phenomenon—on tape: the voice of a small boy crying out, "Mommy!"

The **John Cook Wyllie Library** is home to a phantom woman wearing a long, white dress. She darts between rows of bookshelves, but when people have followed her into the stacks, she's never there.

The newest haunting take places in the **Gilliam Center for the Arts,** which was dedicated in 2012. When a pine coffin was needed for a theatrical production, students had to go no farther than Crockett Hall, which had held a morgue back when much of the campus property was the county poor farm. The kids were thrilled—and a bit creeped out—to find an old wooden casket in the basement. After the play's run was over, the "prop" remained at the theater instead of being returned to Crockett—which apparently made someone from the Beyond very unhappy. The dim apparition of a man in coveralls and a flannel shirt has begun to appear throughout the playhouse, and the coffin sometimes moves around by itself.

Virginia Military Institute

309 Letcher Avenue, Lexington, VA 24450; (540) 464-7230
www.vmi.edu

Virginia Military Institute is the oldest state-supported military college in the United States, one of six such schools in the country. Cadets pursue a baccalaureate degree, and entry into the military after graduation is optional. Founded as an all-male institution in 1839, VMI became the last American military college to admit women in 1997.

When the college first opened, cadets lived in the former Virginia State Arsenal building, which was falling apart. In 1851 students were able to move into the partially completed **Barracks,** which later became the college's trademark structure. The third floor of the edifice is said to be haunted by a phantom known as the Yellow Peril. Though not destructive, the wraith is terrifying to behold, with a bleeding wound on its repulsive yellow face.

A bronze statue of General Thomas Jonathan "Stone-wall" Jackson stands on the Cadet Battery directly in front of the Barracks. Allegedly Jackson's spirit is so upset when a cadet is ceremoniously drummed out of the corps that the statue turns its head away.

The other two hauntings on campus are connected to the Battle of New Market on May 15, 1864, which resulted in the death of ten VMI cadets. The bronze sculpture *Virginia Mourning Her Dead,* located directly in front of Nichols Engineering Hall, honors those cadets. Remains of six of the ten cadets commemorated by the sculpture are buried in a copper box inside the pedestal. (The other four cadets are not interred on campus.) Inexplicably, what appear to be tears have occasionally been seen running down the face of the statue, and people standing nearby have heard odd moaning sounds coming from the monument.

Inside Jackson Memorial Hall, an 18-by-23-foot **mural** by 1880 VMI graduate Benjamin West Clinedinst portrays the charge of the Corps of Cadets at New Market. Supposedly the painting comes to life at night. Rifles fire, cannons blast, and the soldiers move across the canvas.

WASHINGTON, DC

GALLAUDET UNIVERSITY

800 Florida Avenue NE, Washington, DC 20002; (202) 651-5000
www.gallaudet.edu

Gallaudet University, chartered by the federal government, was the first post-secondary school in the world for the deaf and hard of hearing. (Until 1865, the institution worked with the blind as well.) The university had its start in 1856 when former US Postmaster General Amos Kendall donated two acres of his own land for the endeavor. In 1864 the school began to offer college degrees. It became Gallaudet College in 1954 and Gallaudet University in 1986.

Dr. Edward Miner Gallaudet was the school's first superintendent. His twenty-room Victorian Gothic residence, now the main university building, is considered **House One.** Built in 1869, the mansion is on the National Historic Trust. Although Gallaudet's ghost has never been seen there, his presence is certainly sensed. He opens and shuts doors, his disembodied footsteps are heard, and he's responsible for clattering noises, especially on the second floor.

Georgetown University

37th and O Streets NW, Washington, DC 20057; (202) 687-0100
www.georgetown.edu

Georgetown University, the oldest Jesuit and Catholic university in the United States, was founded in 1789. Classes began two years later. Established as a college, Georgetown received its university charter from the US Congress in 1815.

Healy Hall is the flagship building as you enter the university's main gates. Built between 1877 and 1879, this National Historic Landmark was designed by Smithmeyer and Peltz, the architects of the Library of Congress. Today the building houses primarily academic and administrative offices.

It also has a ghost. The phantom is thought to be a former Jesuit priest who, sometime around the turn of the twentieth century, slipped and plunged to his death from Healy Hall's tower while setting the clock's massive hands. The spirit doesn't interact with students or staff, but it protects anyone who enters the tower, which is now normally locked. (The tower has been closed off, in part, because stealing the arms of the clock hands was a popular prank at Georgetown.)

The exterior of Healy Hall is seen in the film version of the 1971 novel *The Exorcist*. Parts of the 1990 movie sequel, *The Exorcist III*, were shot in one of Healy's hallways and on the main floor of the building. William Peter Blatty, the book's author, attended the university and set his story in Georgetown.

WEST VIRGINIA

GLENVILLE STATE COLLEGE

200 High Street, Glenville, WV 26351; (304) 462-7361 www.glenville.edu

Glenville State College was founded in 1872 as a branch of the West Virginia Normal School, with a focus on training teachers. The Lighthouse on the Hill, as the school has been nicknamed, became Glenville State College in 1943.

There have been hundreds of witnesses of ghostly activity at the school. Some of the otherworldly outbursts have been attributed to the spirit of Sarah Louisa Linn, usually called "Sis Linn," an alumna who opened her home as a residence to female students. In February 1919 she was discovered bludgeoned to death in the house. Her killer or killers were never found, and it's said Linn's ghost returned to the building to look for them.

By then the students had been relocated. In 1924 the college purchased Linn's vacant house, tore it down, and built Verona Maple Hall, a four-story girl's dorm, on the spot.

Apparently Linn's ghost moved in along with the new residents. When Maple was demolished in the 1960s or 1970s, Sis Linn transferred to nearby **Clark Hall.**

Her ghost is never seen, but she certainly makes herself known. According to a 2013 press release from the college, one time when Assistant Professor of Early Education Connie Stout was alone in the building grading papers, she heard metal desks and chairs being dragged across the floors all around her—upstairs, downstairs, and next door. As Stout went to investigate, Sis Linn unexpectedly came to mind, but the moment she did, the noise stopped. Associate Professor of Education Kevin Cane heard the sound of chains being dragged on the floor, followed by the slam of what seemed to be the door of a prison cell. Campus service worker Ellen Minney tells how one night she and her coworkers finished up in Clark Hall, turned out the lights, and locked the doors behind them as they left the building. They hadn't gotten more than a few steps before they looked back and noticed that every light in the building had switched itself on again. Minney's daughter, GSC graduate Sonya Hartshorn, was standing in an empty classroom in Clark when the window blinds began to sway and ripple, and then they opened and closed on their own.

Director of Residence Life Jerry Burkhammer and a security officer remembered meeting some students playing with a Ouija board one Halloween outside Louis Bennett Hall, which at the time was a dormitory. The kids told the dean that the spirit of Sis Linn had come through and told them she would be in Clark Hall at the stroke of midnight. They decided to stroll over to Clark out of curiosity. As they neared the building, a light came on in a second-floor window, revealing what appeared to be a woman hanging from a noose. They ran into the building to investigate, but when they got upstairs, the room was dark and empty.

A bell hung in the clock tower over **The Harry B. Heflin Administration Building** for 105 years, beginning in 1901. Before the bell was removed, it supposedly always tolled thirteen times at the witching hour on Halloween—with no explanation. People still experience hauntings throughout the building, especially in the basement. Lights flick on and off unexpectedly. Keys left in a doorknob jingle on their own, and disembodied voices whisper, "What are you doing here?"

Bennett Hall has ghost stories as well. For five years in a row, back when the building was a men's dormitory, a Lady in White would appear at the foot of the bed in Room 225 on the first night that new freshmen arrived. She'd talk to the student before disappearing into the aether. The residence hall has since been turned into offices. Staff members continue to report various weird phenomena, including the sound of someone running on the fourth floor.

First year-students are required to live on campus. Most stay at Pickens Hall. The six-story building has three sections. In **Scott Wing,** some students have heard furniture being moved or marbles rolling across the floor overhead. The spectre of a little girl carrying a doll wanders through **Wagner Wing.** So far, Williams Wing seems to be ghost-free.

West Virginia University

Morgantown, WV 26506; (304) 293-0111; www.wvu.edu

West Virginia University, or WVU, was established in 1867 as the Agricultural College of West Virginia, but it took its current name just a few months later, on December 4, 1868.

Almost thirty thousand students matriculate in its fourteen colleges, with degree programs being offered at all levels.

Woodburn Hall is probably the most recognizable building on campus. The brick Second Empire structure is crowned by a massive cupola and clock tower. It's said that at some point students managed to lead a cow up into the tower as a prank, only to discover that it was impossible to get the animal to walk back down. They had to kill and butcher it on the spot to remove it. Today the sound of mournful mooing can be heard drifting down from the high dome.

Elizabeth Moore Hall, a three-story Georgian Revival mansion, was built in 1928 to act as a women's gymnasium and dormitory. It was named for a former principal of Woodburn Female Seminary, whose grounds became part of the university campus. Moore's apparition hangs out near the basement pool in her namesake building.

The **Mountainlair Student Union** is one of the central hubs on campus, containing lounges, a game area, restaurants, a convenience store, lockers, a copy center, ATMs, and a ghost. The ethereal little girl, always wearing a pretty yellow dress, is most often seen by the custodial staff in the dead of the night. It's believed she was buried in a cemetery that was once located on the site of Steward Hall.

Last but not least, the **Downtown Campus Library** dates from 1931. Supposedly a maintenance worker fell down its elevator shaft, and his ghost is now spotted entering and leaving the lift on various floors. If anyone goes up to the apparition, it instantly vanishes. Other spectres have been seen roaming between the library shelves. The sound of writing can be heard coming from unoccupied desks, and many of those brave enough to venture into the off-limits storage area on the tenth floor have felt an unspecified presence.

Part Three

MYSTERIES OF THE MIDWEST

As the pioneers moved westward, their beliefs in "things that go bump in the night" moved right along with them. Perhaps the telling of ghost stories is just another one of those good old traditional family values for which the country's central states are known.

And they have lots of tales to tell. The "flyover states," as some have called the great expanse between New York and California, stretch some 2,500 miles or more. Plenty of spirits have decided to call the colleges and universities in our nation's Heartland home. It's time to meet some of the Banshees of the Breadbasket.

ILLINOIS

Bradley University

1501 West Bradley Avenue, Peoria, IL 61625; (309) 676-7611
www.bradley.edu

Established in 1897, Bradley University is a private institution of higher leaning with about 5,700 students.

The **Hartmann Center for the Performing Arts** is home of the Department of Theatre Arts. The building, originally a gymnasium, holds two performance spaces: Bradley Jacobs Theatre, with a thrust stage and seating three hundred people, and the black box Laboratory Theatre, seating seventy-five. It also has several ghosts.

The first is believed to be an athletics coach who allegedly committed suicide in the former gym. His apparition is always hazy, but people can usually smell the strong scent of his cigar smoke whenever he shows up. Also dating from the building's pre-theater days is a young boy who drowned in the swimming pool that was located directly below what is now the orchestra pit. His sobbing can be heard as well as his scratching against the floorboards as he tries to get out of "the water." The ghost of an opera singer, given the sobriquet the Lady in White, wanders around backstage leaving footprints of her high-heel shoes behind. She's been known to comfort performers before they went onstage with gentle strokes of reassurance, and she turns off lights when she thinks it's time for everyone to go home. A fourth presence is the Man in Brown, a regular patron who always wore a brown suit when he attended shows. He invariably sat in the back of the house and became notorious for shushing people if they talked or waking them if they fell asleep during performances. His ghost now does the same thing. Like the phantom coach, the Man in Brown is accompanied by the odor of a lit cigar.

Harper/Wyckoff Residence Hall also has a spirit running around. The complex consists of two separate dormitories joined by a common lobby, game room, and study area. Neither hall accommodates students on its top floor. Harper/Wyckoff's bothersome spectre is never seen, but it likes to push buttons on the elevators and make unusual sounds throughout both buildings.

EASTERN ILLINOIS UNIVERSITY

600 Lincoln Avenue, Charleston, IL 61920; (217) 581-5000 www.eiu.edu

Eastern Illinois University was founded in 1895 as a two-year state normal school to train teachers. The institution, with more than 11,500 undergraduate and graduate students, has operated under its current name since 1957.

The university's main haunting occurs in **Pemberton Hall.** The ghost of the residence hall is Mary, a former third-floor resident assistant who, legend has it, was chopped to death by a crazed janitor bearing an ax back in the 1920s. The killer escaped and was never found.

Supposedly Mary was playing a piano on the fourth floor when she was assaulted. It's unknown whether the custodian was specifically seeking her out or whether Mary was a victim of opportunity, but the cleaner chased the terrified woman down the hallway, down the staircase, all the way to her room. As Mary desperately struggled to open the door, the custodian lifted his weapon and struck. Mary's roommate was inside but, not knowing what was causing the commotion in the corridor, was too frightened to open the door. She found Mary dead, lying in a pool of blood, the next morning.

Mary's spectre still makes her RA rounds, turning off unnecessary lights and either lowering the volume of or shutting off TVs, radios, and music players. She closes windows, makes sure that doors are safely locked, helps keep rooms neat, and generally watches out for the girls. Although she usually remains invisible, a few coeds have seen Mary's apparition as it wandered in and out of their rooms.

Millikin University

1184 West Main Street, Decatur, IL 62522; (217) 424-6211 www.millikin.edu

Millikin University is a private four-year university founded in 1901 by Decatur businessman James Millikin. The school, affiliated with the Presbyterian Church, has approximately 2,300 undergraduate students.

The ghost that haunts **Albert Taylor Theater,** which is located inside Schilling Hall, is the "Rail Girl," a youngster who sometimes materializes along a railing in the upper part of the auditorium. Schilling was the first building on campus, so it's uncertain what era the little girl comes from. Most times the spirit doesn't manifest, but people still hear her making strange noises, walking around the building, or crying. She also likes to snitch small objects and return them to other places. There's been a long-standing tradition of leaving three pieces of candy for her backstage before any performance. If she doesn't get them, she takes her revenge by tinkering with the light and sound equipment, damaging props, or even causing injuries.

The college's first building dedicated solely for use as a gymnasium was constructed in 1911, replacing an athletics room that was in the basement of Schilling Hall. That gym, in turn, was eventually replaced by the Griswold Physical Education Center, and the **top floor of the old gym** was converted for use by the theater department as rehearsal space, a dance studio, and storage facility. Visitors, especially late at night, hear the sounds of bygone sports-related activities, including basketballs dribbling, a person running laps, regular footsteps, cheering, referee whistles, laughter, and wild applause.

Ashton Hall is the college's oldest women's dormitory. Originally known simply as Women's Hall, the five-story building opened in 1907, but it has been completely transformed by later additions. Its ghost is Bernice Richardson, who committed suicide in her room on February 1, 1927, by drinking carbolic acid—an incredibly painful way to die. Her ghost appears only from the waist up. The apparition moves slowly from one end of the third floor to the other, going from room to room by passing through the walls. She also moves objects, makes belongings disappear and reappear, raps on the walls, and messes with the lights and doors.

Blackburn Hall is a coed dorm for first-year students, housed by gender by floor, accommodating ninety-nine students. The apparition of an unknown woman has been seen prowling the premises.

The origin of the **Gorin Hall** ghost story is well known, even though the spectre's name seems to have been forgotten. The male phantom is a former employee who died when he fell down an empty elevator shaft. He seems to stay in the basement—where he landed.

Alumni House on West Main Street was the Mueller family home before the university acquired it. For several years, the building was the Zeta Tau Alpha fraternity house. During that period it was haunted by the ghost of one of the Mueller's maids, who had apparently lived upstairs. The otherworldly servant had a set routine. Frat boys would hear her open the front door, close it, walk across the foyer, climb the stairs, and head toward her former room. Sometimes the unseen spectre would brush against them as she went by. The guys called her Louise and nicknamed the lobby "Louise's Lounge."

The spectral sister of **Delta Delta Delta** sorority is a pale spirit, translucent almost to the point of transparency and dressed in eighteenth-century pioneer garb. She visits rooms and produces cold spots but is considered to be harmless. It's thought that the phantom may have been interred in the John Miller family cemetery that was once located on the property. The graveyard's name last appeared on local maps in 1843, but the burial sites were rediscovered when the house was built in 1913.

North Central College

30 North Brainard Street, Naperville, IL 60540; (630) 637-5100
www.northcentralcollege.edu

Founded in Plainfield, Illinois, as Plainfield College in 1861, North Central College is a private liberal arts institution of higher learning. The school moved to downtown Naperville in 1870. Approximately three thousand undergraduates and graduates study on its sixty-five-acre campus.

Many ghosts have been spotted inside **Pfeiffer Hall,** the college's major performance space. They include a drama professor who committed suicide there and a former custodian, Charlie, who haunts the balcony and west stairwell. Perhaps its best-known spirit is an elderly woman wearing a fashionable white dress who died in Row G Seat 42 while watching her grandnephew in one of the college's productions. Technicians believe invisible spirits sometimes watch them in the light booth, and unidentified spectres appear in photographs taken in the booth and the balcony.

University of Illinois at Chicago

2035 West Taylor Street, Chicago, IL 60612; (312) 996-4350
www.uic.edu

The University of Illinois at Chicago was established in 1982. It has approximately 28,000 students and is located in Chicago's Near West Side.

The **Jane Addams Hull-House Museum** stands on the eastern edge of the UIC campus and is owned by the university. The house was built as a private residence by real estate developer Charles Jerome Hull in 1856. His cousin and heir, Helen Culver, allowed activist Jane Addams to open the first American settlement house there.

Rumors started circulating in 1913 that Addams had taken in a baby that had been cast off by his parents. Legend has it that when a pregnant mother, a devout Catholic, put a picture of the Holy Virgin on the wall of her home, her atheist husband tore it down, screaming, "I would rather have the devil himself in this house!" When the infant was born, he resembled a demon, complete with scaly skin that was ice-cold to the touch, talons for feet, claws for hands, and a tail. Addams accepted the child, but when he couldn't be held still long enough to be baptized, he was supposedly locked in the attic. Ever since, passersby have been able to see the Devil Baby—or occasionally just his eyes—peering out the window on the top floor.

The terrifying tot isn't the only apparition at Hull House. Charles Hull's wife died in an upstairs bedroom facing Halsted Street, and people encountered her spirit even before Addams took over the property. (Addams reportedly saw it, too.) People have spotted the apparition of the Woman in White in the bedroom and in the main staircase. A glowing mist has appeared in photographs and has shown up on video as the hazy spectre heads toward the attic. Inexplicably, the wraiths of four monklike figures have also been photographed on the staircase between the first and second floors. Window shutters open and shut on their own, lights go on and off, fire alarms go off without cause, and motion detectors pick up movement in the building at night, even when it's vacant.

WESTERN ILLINOIS UNIVERSITY

1 University Circle, Macomb, IL 61455; (309) 298-1414; www.wiu.edu

Founded in 1899 as Western Illinois Normal School, Western Illinois University has two campuses: the main branch in Macomb and the Quad Cities campus in Moline. The hauntings all occur in Macomb.

Simpkins Hall is the home of the English and journalism departments. It's said that several ghosts are also headquartered there. The stories seem to date from around the 1970s. The apparition of an adult male is "Harold," a former custodian; others suggest the phantom may be a former graduate assistant. Whoever he is, the spectre often hangs out in Room 343. He'll open and shut doors, jangle keys, and click away at keyboards. The spectre of a woman is heard sobbing in a first-floor restroom. Also on the ground floor, folks have seen the spirit of a young or 'tween-age girl who likes to follow people as they walk down the hall. A few have spotted a little boy as well. The children may date from between 1939 and 1967, when the building was used as the teachers training school.

The sound of disembodied footsteps resonates in **Seal Hall,** especially on the stairs. Doors open and shut, too. The activity may be caused by the unsettled revenant of Steven Hyde, a nineteen-year-old freshman who was gunned down by fellow freshman Clyde R. Johnson in 1972. The shooting took place on the staircase between the third and second floors as Hyde attempted to flee the building. Johnson pled self-defense and was acquitted of voluntary manslaughter.

Washington Hall, a fourteen-story coed dormitory, is available to upper-level students. A former female resident apparently likes to keep in touch. The phone in her old room rings, but no one is ever on the line. The girl allegedly killed herself in the room after a huge argument with her boyfriend.

INDIANA

EARLHAM COLLEGE

801 National Road West, Richmond, IN 47374; (765) 983-1373
www.earlham.edu

The Quakers founded Earlham in 1847 as a residential high school for teenagers, but it morphed into Earlham College just twelve years later. About twelve hundred undergraduates study on its eight-hundred-acre campus.

In addition to its regular residence halls, the school owns several modest houses that were formerly private homes. **Wilbur House** has belonged to Earlham College since 1986 and can room nine students. Supposedly at some time in the past before the house was acquired by the school, a group of elderly women, all of whom had lung cancer, rented it. One by one they died on the property, and many of their spirits are still in the house. So, too, is the apparition of an unknown little girl, who also allegedly died there. Passersby have seen the youngster's spectre drifting by one of the windows.

Franklin College

101 Branigin Boulevard, Franklin, IN 46131; (800) 852-0232
www.franklincollege.edu

Franklin College is a private liberal arts institution, founded in 1834. More than a thousand students work toward their degrees on the 187-acre campus.

Old Main was hit by fire in the 1980s. Much of its interior was damaged, and according to rumor a student died in the attic. (Supposedly people heard screams coming from the top floor during the conflagration.) The landmark building has been restored to its former glory, but the inexplicable scent of burning flesh sometimes lingers in the air.

Indiana State University

200 North Seventh Street, Terre Haute, IN 47809; (812) 237-6311
www.indstate.edu

Indiana State University was founded in 1865. Frequently named "Best in the Midwest" by the *Princeton Review*, the school has more than twelve thousand undergraduate and graduate students on its 234-acre campus.

Two of ISU's dormitories are haunted. **Burford Hall,** which is coed by floor, houses first-year students. Residents hear low disembodied whispering and unusual, unidentifiable noises. Personal belongings have a way of shifting around in the rooms without being touched. Some of the activity may be caused by a student named Barb who died in her room after drinking too much. People hear her apparition crying or vomiting, or see her weaving down the halls.

Cromwell Hall is located in the southwest corner of a four-tower complex. The spooky goings-on in Cromwell date from the suicide of a male student who leapt from the window of Room 1221. Some people have seen a glowing white cross in its window. Actually, the entire twelfth floor of the building is haunted. Students hear the young man's restless footsteps pacing up and down the hall, and other odd sounds are attributed to his phantom as well.

INDIANA UNIVERSITY

107 South Indiana Avenue, Bloomington, IN 47405; (812) 855-4848
www.indiana.edu

Indiana University was established in 1820. It consists of two core campuses, one in Bloomington—considered to be the flagship campus—and another in Purdue. There are also six smaller campuses scattered throughout the state as well as three extension centers. The hauntings are on the main campus.

Read Hall, also called Read Residence Center, consists of four separate wings (Beck, Clark, Curry, and Landes) laid out in an X-shape and connected by a central hub. During an argument, a medical student stabbed his girlfriend—also a student at the university—hitting her in the throat with a scalpel. She died within minutes. Somehow the young man managed to drag her bloody body down to a tunnel running off the basement and hide the corpse without anyone seeing him. When the police talked to him, however, he confessed almost immediately. The girl's ghost, sporting a black mane of hair and wearing a yellow nightgown, has returned to haunt the building, especially her killer's third-floor room. Another female banshee also frightens occupants of Read Hall. Years back, a sixth-floor RA, remembered as Paula, threw herself down the stairs and died. On December 12, the anniversary of the woman's suicide, students in the hall hear her bloodcurdling scream echoing down the stairwell.

The Lilly Library holds many sets of rare books, including special collections once owned by Elisabeth W. Ball, Robert S. Ellison, Joseph Benjamin Oakleaf, and library founder J. K. Lilly Jr. Folks have credited odd happenings in the building to the various benefactors, figuring that their ghosts have descended on the hall to make sure the current curators are taking care of their treasures.

The **Indiana Memorial Union** is one of the largest student unions in the country at 500,000 square feet. Several ghosts roam its premises, all former students who supposedly killed themselves by jumping from the building's upper levels. The phantom of an unknown canine has also been spotted.

Rumor has it that the **Career Development Center** was once the campus health services building, and before the 1970s one of its doctors performed illegal abortions for female students who had nowhere else to turn. A woman's disembodied shrieks bounce down the halls, and people encounter indistinct apparitions thought to be the spirits of the lost babies.

SAINT MARY-OF-THE-WOODS COLLEGE

3301 Saint Marys Road, West Terre Haute, IN 47885; (812) 535-5151 www.smwc.edu

Founded in 1840, Saint Mary-of-the-Woods College is the oldest Catholic women's college in the United States. Also known as SMWC or "The Woods," the college is a four-year liberal arts institution. The school's graduate degree programs are coeducational.

The best-known ghost story on campus is about a faceless nun who used to turn up in the now-razed Foley Hall. The sister was doing a self-portrait and had painted everything but her face when she unexpectedly died—which is why her ghost had no facial features when it appeared. (An alternate version of the tale suggested the spirit wasn't really faceless, but it always manifested between the viewer and a bright light. As a result, the apparition's face was obscured.) Her befuddled spectre often would show up in Foley Hall and ask people who she was or why she was there. She would also mumble that something had gone wrong with the masses done for her after her death. And here's another oddity: Sometimes when the spectre materialized, it would be seen by only one individual in a whole roomful of people. Around 1980 a special mass was held during which the spirit was asked to leave Foley Hall. It complied, for the most part, but students still reported seeing the mysterious sister from time to time. Unfortunately, fire destroyed the hall in 1989, and it had to be torn down. For now, the whereabouts of the phantom nun are unknown.

Foley Hall stood next to the **Conservatory of Music,** which was constructed in 1913. The building holds the historic 750-seat Cecilian Auditorium. The place is thought to be haunted by one or more spirits. A spectral nun manifests inside the theater, and another (if, indeed, it is a separate phantom) can be heard walking on the marble staircases. Security guards have also noticed piano music coming from the vacant practice rooms on the second floor.

Ghosts in the form of shadows seem to like making their presence known in the **tunnels** that run beneath and connect many of the buildings on campus. Besides providing access for maintenance workers, electrical wires and heating pipes line the shafts. The tunnels are lit but are still creepy. Some are large enough that they can be walked through even while standing erect; others are little more than crawl spaces.

Guerin Hall, which dates from 1913, holds administrative offices and classrooms. In the past, the four-story Renaissance Revival building was a dormitory. Some say that a student hanged herself in Room 334. Although most people discount the story, it's as good an explanation as any for the ghostly activity that sometimes occurs there, including objects that move, strange noises, and dark figures.

The Italian Renaissance–style **Le Fer Hall** contains a ballroom, a formal parlor, and three floors of student lodging. A human-shaped silhouette sometimes appears on one of the corridor walls, most often between midnight and four in the morning, and slowly makes its way from one end of the hall to the other.

The revenant of a nun who killed herself in **O'Shaughnessy Dining Hall** has returned to the building. No apparition is seen, but bloodstains appear on the spot where she committed suicide.

University of Notre Dame

Notre Dame, IN 46556; (574) 631-5000; www.nd.edu

The University of Notre Dame du Lac, more commonly known as the University of Notre Dame or simply Notre Dame, was founded by Father Edward Sorin in 1842. The school awards post-secondary degrees on all levels.

The university is famous for its iconic football team, which is known as the Fighting Irish. Even non–sports fans have heard the quip "win one for The Gipper." Back in 1920 George Gipp was one of the team's star players. He came back to his dorm after curfew one night and found himself locked out. He went to the back door of **Washington Hall,** the music and theater building, knowing it often remained unlocked at night. Unfortunately the hall was shut up tight as well. Gipp curled up and fell asleep on the stairs. Within days he had developed pneumonia. From his hospital bed he made his coach, Knute Rockne, promise that whenever things looked tough on the field he should exhort the boys to, well, "win just one for The Gipper"—a scene immortalized in the 1940 Ronald Reagan film *Knute Rockne, All American*. (Reagan played Gipp and many years later used the phrase as a political slogan.) Gipp died of strep throat—it was before the discovery of penicillin—at the age of twenty-five on December 14, 1920.

George Gipp's ghost lives on, and it's often seen in the predawn morning sitting on the steps of Washington Hall. He goes inside as well: His spectre has appeared on the stage in the 564-seat auditorium as well as in the green room where actors relax and meet with friends. (Gipp also has been credited with making tombstones near the front entrance to the university dance in the dead of night.)

There are also hauntings in Washington Hall not caused by Gipp. Things fly off the walls, poltergeist-style, and female custodians have complained of being poked hard by invisible fingers, so strong that they left marks. The ghost of Jim Minerva, a former graduate professor, plays his trumpet after everyone's gone from the theater. People have also heard harpsichord music. Finally, the phantom of Brother Canute Lardner, who spent fifty-five years at the university, pops in now and then, but he never hangs around for very long. He's very recognizable: elderly, balding, and speaking with an Irish accent.

Notre Dame sits on land that was once occupied by the Potawatomi Native Americans. A brave who lived on the property more than a century ago materializes on campus as a spirit on horseback. The rider and his steed gallop up and down the front staircase of **Columbus Hall.** Some people have seen a whole group of mounted tribesman on the steps.

IOWA

BUENA VISTA UNIVERSITY

610 West Fourth Street, Storm Lake, IA 50588; (800) 383-9600
www.bvu.edu

Buena Vista University, a private four-year school affiliated with the Presbyterian Church, was founded as Buena Vista College in 1891. The name was changed to its current form in 1985 when the school began to offer graduate degrees.

There's been a long-standing rumor that three-story **Swope Hall** is haunted by the ghost of Mary Swope, a student who committed suicide by jumping out of a window of the dorm around 1985. A group of male students got together on a lark in the fall of 1997, changed the story around, and spread a new tale: The dorm stands on land that was once the Swope family farm. Mary was actually the Swope's daughter, and she went crazy from drinking water from the lead-lined pipes. After her parents locked her in the attic, Mary leapt to her death from the window trying to get out. The brokenhearted family moved to Pennsylvania and donated their property to the college. The young men added a key element to the legend that persists today. The garret in the Swope's farmhouse was situated at approximately the same spot that Room 305 in Swope Hall is located today. The room number has stuck and is now part of the mythology.

Pierce Hall is part of a two-building residence hall complex with White Hall. The second floor of Pierce is where the odd stuff takes place. People hear banging on the walls, footsteps in the vacant corridors, and barely audible mumbling. The elevators move when they want, and electrical devices run themselves. Not only that, a nonspeaking spirit also manifests in the rooms, standing by the bed.

Edson Hall was dedicated in the 1920s as the school's new gymnasium and later became a dorm. The building was remodeled in 1997 for use by the music department. Strange activity in the hall includes the sound of disembodied footsteps, lights that turn themselves on, and pianos that play themselves. People return to rooms to discover that objects have moved on their own while they were gone, and an apparition of an unknown person is seen in the second-floor sound studio. Hauntings are supposedly related to an unknown "someone" who died in the building while it was a dormitory.

There have also been generalized reports of paranormal phenomena in **Lage Communication Center.**

COE COLLEGE

1220 First Avenue NE, Cedar Rapids, IA 52402; (319) 399-8000
www.coe.edu

Coe College, founded in 1851, is a four-year liberal arts school affiliated with the Presbyterian Church. Coe offers more than forty majors and BAs, bachelor's degrees in music and nursing, and a Master of Arts in teaching.

An old legend on campus concerns an eighteen-year-old student named Helen Esther Roberts who died of pneumonia and cardiac arrest brought on by the Spanish influenza in the fall of 1918. She pledged to the Delta Delta Delta sorority and lived in **Voorhees Hall.** When Helen got ill, she was moved to an infirmary on the third floor of the building, where she died.

For some reason, Helen's spirit took up residence inside a grandfather clock that her family had given the college. At night Helen's apparition would leave the clock in the lobby, go to the parlor, and play the piano. Often she'd go upstairs to the west wing where she had resided and visit the rooms. She'd slam doors and pull at blankets or bedspreads, and sometimes she would materialize, dressed all in white, at the foot of someone's bed. Supposedly, she never failed to show up on the anniversary of her death, October 19, so students would stay up at night and huddle around the clock hoping to see her apparition.

The visitations ended for the most part after the clock was moved to Stuart Hall and placed outside the president's office, but supposedly Helen occasionally still turns up in Voorhees and elsewhere around the campus.

Iowa State University

100 Enrollment Services Center, Ames, IA 50011; (515) 294-4111
www.iastate.edu

Iowa State University was founded in 1858. The school's full name is the Iowa State University of Science and Technology, and it's among the most haunted universities in the nation.

Its student union, **Memorial Union,** was completed in 1928, but the original five-story structure has been greatly expanded with eleven separate additions. The building contains **Gold Star Hall,** a war memorial, where the names of Iowa State graduates who died in service to the country are carved into the walls. Inexplicable low moans come from inside the chamber. Elsewhere in the building, people hear disembodied footsteps and doors slamming shut. The spectral activity is thought to be caused by the spirit of Hortense Elizabeth Wind, the only female among all the names engraved in the memorial hall when it first opened. She died of the flu in the Great Pandemic of 1918–1919.

Frederica Van Trice Shattuck was a professor of public speaking at Iowa State from 1907 to 1956. She also founded the student acting troupe, the Iowa State Players, in 1914 and produced and directed many of their shows during the next twenty years. The campus theater was named for her in 1960, and her spectre moved in after her death nine years later. People reported encounters with Shattuck's apparition in the auditorium and backstage until the theater was torn down in 1979. Her ghost now occupies a newer playhouse on campus called the **Fisher Theater,** which opened in the Iowa State Center in 1973. Her presence there was reported in the student newspaper in 1978 after her old wheelchair rolled into the middle of the Fisher stage all by itself.

The Iowa State Center's main hall is the **C. Y. Stephens Auditorium,** named for the benefactor who financed the building's construction. The patron's ghost is seen sitting in the third row of the balcony during rehearsals. His footsteps are also heard, and cold winds are felt in the walkways beneath the auditorium.

The Farm House, constructed between 1860 and 1865, is now a museum. It also has a couple of ghosts: two sisters whose family lived in the house for about fifty years. They switch lights on and off, open windows, lock doors, shake furniture, open curtains, and play with plates and cutlery.

The **Nuclear Engineering Laboratory** is home to the wraith of Joseph Keichel, who died in 1946 after working on the Ames Project, which helped produce uranium for the Manhattan Project. Students who have problems with their lab trials only half-jokingly point to Keichel. They claim his angry spirit is messing with their work because he blames his death on exposure to radiation.

Then there are the residence halls. Four-story, coed **Barton Hall** is thought to be haunted by its namesake: founder of the American Red Cross Clara Barton. Needless to say, she's a helpful presence.

Birch-Welch-Roberts Hall is a complex made of up three connected male dormitories. There's no suspect in mind for the phantom who causes problems with the lights, moves objects, and carries out all of the other annoying paranormal phenomena.

Freeman Hall, a four-story residence hall on the east side of campus, opened in 1916 as East Hall. It was renamed for Alice Freeman Palmer, who at the age of twenty-six became the president of Wellesley College—the first female head of a nationally known institution of higher learning.

Supposedly her ghost likes to open doors and lingers in the parlor of her eponymous dorm.

Friley Hall is one of the largest residence halls in the country. The building is plagued by strange noises and unexplainable drafts. There's a legend that security guards once chased a large, mysterious stranger (later nicknamed "Mr. Big") through the corridors about one in the morning. The spectral intruder was dressed in a cape and top hat and eventually eluded his pursuers. No one knows whether the same phantom causes the ongoing oddities in the hall.

Coed **Linden Hall,** built in 1957, can house up to 321 students on its five floors. Its apparition is an unnamed football player who shows up in full uniform on the nights before Cyclone home games.

Finally, Iowa State University has had a **cemetery** on its property since 1876. The two-acre swath is located in the northwest corner of campus. Through the years there have been many reports of misty apparitions wandering among the headstones, but none of the visitants has ever been distinct enough to be identified as being one of the more than seven hundred people buried there.

LUTHER COLLEGE

700 College Drive, Decorah, IA 52101; (563) 387-2000
www.luther.edu

Luther College, a private four-year liberal arts institution, was founded in 1861. The school is affiliated with the Evangelical Lutheran Church in America.

Larsen Hall, which opened in 1907, is named for the college's first president, Laur Larsen. It's the oldest residence hall on campus, and it can accommodate 142 students. Disembodied footsteps of a woman wearing high heels are heard clicking down the corridors, most often in the health services offices. The third floor of Larsen Hall has a ghost of its own: Gertrude. She's a pesky presence who sets off fire alarms, goes through students' drawers, and switches their clothing with vintage apparel. The funny thing is that Gertrude was never a student at the college, much less a resident of Larsen Hall. She was a Decorah High School graduate who had wanted to go to Luther College, but at the time the institution admitted only men. The college became coed in 1936, but Gertrude didn't live to see it. She was struck and killed by a car in 1918 as she rode her bicycle down West Broadway Street.

Palmer College of Chiropractic

1000 North Brady Street, Davenport, IA 52803; (563) 884-5000
www.palmer.edu

Palmer College of Chiropractic was established in 1897 by Daniel David Palmer, more often referred to as D. D. Palmer. The college is generally accepted to be the first chiropractic school in the world. The institute also has campuses in San Jose, California, and Port Orange, Florida.

The Alpha Grand Chapter of **Pi Kappa Chi** fraternity is located on the Davenport campus. Its frat house is said to be haunted by the ghost of a hefty man, always dressed in a winter coat with an upturned collar. The spirit will walk in the front door, go up the stairs, and enter the front bedroom. Before the building belonged to Pi Kappa Chi, it was a private residence. It's believed the phantom was a homeless man the former owner took pity on and brought in from the cold in 1922. The stranger died in the upstairs bedroom that the apparition now seeks.

SIMPSON COLLEGE

701 North C Street, Indianola, IA 50125; (515) 961-6251
www.simpson.edu

Founded by members of the Iowa United Methodist Church in 1860, Simpson College sits on seventy-five acres found about twelve miles south of Des Moines. Simpson is a coed liberal arts institution offering more than eighty programs to its fifteen hundred or so full-time students.

Several spirits hang out at **College Hall,** which opened in 1870. The most common ghost story associated with the building says that on May 6, 1935, twenty-two-year-old Mildred Hedges was descending the staircase from the third floor while loaded down with books. She tripped and tumbled over the railing, falling thirty-five feet to her death. It's said that if you stand on the college seal set into the patio in front of the building on any Friday the thirteenth at midnight, Mildred's face will appear at a window on the third floor. The tale received credibility when prominent ghost hunters Ed and Lorraine Warren visited Simpson College in 1979. They investigated Old Chapel, as it was then known, and proclaimed that Mildred's spirit "remains in the building because she is not ready to die."

Hauntings have been reported inside College Hall as well, including bizarre noises, peculiar lights, and people being tapped on the shoulder by invisible hands. The activity may not all be coming from Mildred, however. Some sources, including Dennis William Hauck's seminal *Haunted Places: The National Directory*, suggest that the paranormal phenomena could be caused by any number of people who supposedly died in the hall, including at least one other person who fell in the stairwell. There was also a female student who hanged herself from the ceiling in 1924, a woman who hanged herself from a chandelier, and a male student who killed himself in the tower.

UNIVERSITY OF IOWA

Iowa City, IA 52242; (319) 335-3500; www.uiowa.edu

The University of Iowa, also known as UI or simply Iowa, is the oldest university in the state. Technically named the State University of Iowa, the school was founded in 1847. Approximately thirty-one thousand men and women study on its nineteen-hundred-acre campus.

Currier Hall, built in 1912, is the oldest dormitory on campus. For many years it housed women only, but today it is coed. Its most regular hauntings come from three former female students who shared the same room. Legend has it that all three committed suicide when they realized they were hopelessly pining for the same guy. It's said that when roommates in the dorm fight now, the ghostly trio shows up to mediate. Also, a male ghost is seen in the E-300s section of the building. He's an older man, thought to be a worried father looking for his long-gone daughter, who was once a resident there.

Slater Hall is a modern, multistory coed residence hall that can accommodate 499 students. Its ghost is a former male resident who, overcome by the pressures of college, jumped to his death from the ninth floor. His spectre, always with a sad look on his face, plods down the halls. Some people hear only his footsteps or his anguished screams. A recent addition to his saga says he carries a hatchet.

The dormitory has another urban legend associated with it: Back in the 1800s a serial killer named "the Penguin" was apprehended and hanged nearby. His ghost now prowls Slater looking for victims. When he was alive, he went after babies. Now he seeks older fare: college kids. In another version of the myth, the murderer is an obese, cannibalistic female RA who stalks the first floor, looking for first-year students to eat. There's even a variation that suggests the resident assistant is the reincarnation of the nineteenth-century predator.

UNIVERSITY OF NORTHERN IOWA

1227 West Twenty-Seventh Street, Cedar Falls, IA 50614 (319) 273-2311; www.uni.edu

The University of Northern Iowa was founded in 1876 as the Iowa State Normal School. The institution took its current name in 1967. The school has about twelve thousand undergraduates and an additional two thousand graduate students in ninety different majors.

Lawther Hall, a women's dorm, was constructed in 1933 and expanded in 1948. Paranormal activity started in the hall in the 1970s. At first there was no apparition, but residents would hear footsteps in the empty attic, and personal belongings sometimes went missing. They would also encounter unexpected cold spots. Then one night a man dressed in a pin-striped suit walked unannounced into the building. He swiftly climbed the stairs, got out a set of keys, and unlocked the attic. No sooner had he gotten on the other side of the door than campus security arrived. The guards thoroughly checked the garret, but the man was gone. He was a ghost! The legend arose that the building was once an army hospital, and the ethereal outsider was actually a soldier named Augie who died there. The upper loft where he disappeared was even given a sobriquet: "Augie's Attic."

The **Strayer-Wood Theatre** opened in 1978. The building's resident ghost haunted an earlier theater on campus as well, but when the Department of Theatre moved to Strayer-Wood, Zelda (as the phantom's been named) came right along with it. Her spectre has never materialized. Instead, she makes do with producing weird noises, screaming, playing a piano, shouting at audience members, and fiddling with sound and light equipment.

KANSAS

Kansas State University

Manhattan, KS 66506; (785) 532-6011; www.k-state.edu

There seems to be only one haunted university in Kansas, but its ghost stories are real doozies! Kansas State University was founded as Kansas State Agricultural College in 1863, making it the oldest public university in the state. The school obtained full university status in 1959.

The **Purple Masque Theater** is nestled underneath the seating of the East Stadium in Kansas State's Memorial Stadium. Its good-natured ghost has been named Nick, and it's believed he was a football player for the school's Wildcats. In fact, legend persists that he was fatally injured during play in the stadium, even though there's no record of such a death. Nick has never been seen, but his loud footsteps have been heard throughout the theater, and his voice has been captured on audiotape (known in the paranormal world as EVP, or Electronic Voice Phenomena). He rearranges chairs in the theater and items in the dressing rooms, plays music at night, spills paint, sets off fire extinguishers, and carries around objects, thereby making them appear to float.

A second ghost has been seen in the theater. The unidentified man is always dressed in a Confederate uniform and sitting in a spectral chair, often on the stage.

The spectre at **Pi Kappa Phi** was already there when the fraternity moved into the house. In the early twentieth century, the building was occupied by Theta Xi fraternity. During one of their initiation ceremonies, a pledge named Duncan was accidentally struck on the head and died from the concussion. Phi Gamma Delta moved into the frat house in 1933, and they found some of the Theta Xi paddles hanging on a library wall. Underneath one of them was a deep reddish stain on the wall—the color of dried blood. No matter how hard they tried to remove the spot or how often they painted over it, the mark showed up again. Finally they paneled over the wall, and in 1965 they threw out the paddles. Bad move! That's when the hauntings began. The awakened spirit slams doors, flicks lights—all the usual hijinks. He even leaves the house. His lifeless-eyed apparition has been spotted all over campus. Reports have lessened but not ended since Pi Kappa Phi moved in and refurbished the library.

The **Delta Sigma Phi** fraternity house has two phantoms from the time the building was St. Mary's Hospital. One of them, a nurse, may have crossed over to the Beyond because she was last seen in the 1960s. The other spectre, George, was an aged patient at the hospital, and he's still around. On the day he was to be moved to a new facility, he rolled off his bed and became jammed against the wall. He suffocated before he was found the next day. George is never seen, but he throws things and rearranges the furniture, and occasionally he's heard shuffling around on the third floor where his room used to be. His most memorable stunt happened in 1973 when an ice storm cut electricity throughout much of the town. George was a *Star Trek* fan, and one night during the blackout the television came on just long enough for a rerun of the show to air.

Kappa Sigma fraternity's ghost was a sophomore who hanged himself in a file room. His phantom appears as a white mist on the stairs, the second floor, and the roof.

MICHIGAN

CENTRAL MICHIGAN UNIVERSITY

1200 South Franklin Street, Mount Pleasant, MI 48859 (989) 774-4000; www.cmich.edu

Central Michigan University was founded in 1892. There are more than twenty thousand students on its campus in Mount Pleasant.

The distinctive brick **Warriner Hall,** with its five-story central tower, was built in 1928. According to the June 2, 1937, edition of the student newspaper *Central State Life*, the hauntings in the building stem from an accident that occurred on May 29 of that year. (Other sources claim it happened on June 1.) The details of the tragedy vary, but everyone agrees that nineteen-year-old cafeteria worker Theresa Elizabeth Schumacher died from some sort of head injury. The simplest version of the tale says she stuck her head into the elevator shaft to see if a car was coming and was struck as it descended. Many people think she was decapitated.

Regardless of how her death took place, it was years before people started to hear her disembodied footsteps on Warriner Hall's center staircase. There is also the sound of objects being dropped on the floor—even though nothing is ever found out of place—and loud knocking, especially in Rooms 503 and 504. Other phenomena include lights that go haywire and the elevator door opening and shutting without being called. People on the street will see lights on the "sixth floor," which is merely a few feet of empty space between the fifth floor and the roof. Sometimes Schumacher will manifest throughout the building as a flashing blue light. When her ghost does appear in a recognizable form, it's most often seen on the top floor of the tower, near the radio station, or in the building's Plachta Auditorium. Other spectral activity has occurred in the theater as well: The custodian's vacuum cleaner turns itself on and off, and the fire curtain has a tendency to fall for no reason.

The **Myron A. Cobb Residence Hall** opened in 1970 as a women's dormitory but became coed three years later. In 2009 a first-year female student in Room 406 woke to see an apparition leaning over her laundry basket. Moments later the spectre was sitting in a nearby chair. Strange things still happen: The room's doorknob rattles, and the bathroom sink seems to "whistle." The shower also turns itself on and off.

Charles C. Barnes Hall opened its doors in 1939. Allegedly at some point a female student hanged herself in the study after her boyfriend broke up with her. She now haunts the building, especially the second floor. Her favorite tricks seem to be moving around personal objects and causing interference on TVs. Students placate her by placing tchotchkes that they think will amuse her around the room.

The **R. D. Calkins Hall** ghost, who has never been seen, began making prank telephone calls from the building in 2004. The police received a distress call from someone in a room on the first floor, but when they investigated they discovered that no one was living there. Similar calls have occurred several times over the years. When students *do* live in the room, they're the ones receiving the spooky calls.

The **Mae K. Woldt Hall** opened as a residence hall in 1964. A young lady living there came out of a shower to see the words HELP ME written in the steamed-up mirror. Frightened by the message, the student soon quit the university. The phantom is thought to be a female student who committed suicide in her dorm room there.

A staff member at **Carlin Alumni House** once entered the empty building to hear the disembodied voices of a man and woman chatting. The moment the security switch was disarmed, the noises stopped—as if the ghosts quit talking as soon as they realized they could be heard. A toilet has flushed itself, a male spectre's laugh has been heard, and a white cloud has been seen floating around the rear of the building. It's unknown whether the spirits are alumni. Also, the place has a dirt basement, and there are rumors that bodies are buried there.

In the 1930s, a junior music student named Emily died in **Powers Hall** while practicing piano. Reportedly she was buried at her parents' request under an array of hedges forming the shape of a piano in the building's foyer—what's sometimes called the Piano Garden. Today, the sound of Emily's ethereal playing occasionally emanates from that area of the lobby, although some versions of the tale say the music actually comes from the practice room where the young woman died, even when it's empty.

Unidentifiable noises have been heard from the **Ronald W. Finch Fieldhouse.** The sounds may be ghostly echoes from a rifle range that was once located on the level beneath the building's main floor.

In the 1930s, one of the school's football players died during practice. **Alumni Field,** the site of the tragedy, is located between the Health Professions building and Finch Fieldhouse. Today, people standing on the grassy expanse feel distinct cold spots, which are thought to signify the presence of his ghost.

One of the university's most famous revenants is Carolyn, a first-year female student who died in 1951 of unknown causes. At first her apparition, always dressed in a white nightgown, appeared in her old dorm, Bernard Hall. The building was razed in 1996, but the spirit has now shown up elsewhere on campus, including the **pathway alongside Park Library Pond.** According to a few people, Carolyn has also moved into the new **graduate residence hall** located where Bernard Hall once stood.

Finally, the large **CMU Seal** is one of the most recognizable landmarks on campus. According to legend, two students from the school fell in love, but the young man's parents disapproved because of the girl's lower social standing. That winter the pair decided to elope. Their meeting place would be the Seal. Unfortunately, on the night in question the boy was delayed due to car trouble, and his girlfriend froze to death while waiting for him. He died soon after of the proverbial broken heart. Legend has it that if a loving couple goes to the Seal at midnight, the spirits of the long-deceased pair will materialize to show them their support.

Eastern Michigan University

900 Oakwood Street, Ypsilanti, MI 48197; (734) 487-1849
www.emich.edu

Eastern Michigan University, established in 1849 as Michigan State Normal School, was the first normal school to be founded outside of the original thirteen colonies. A four-year curriculum was introduced in 1899. The institution was transformed into Eastern Michigan College in 1956 and achieved university status three years after that.

Starkweather Hall, built in 1896 with a ten-thousand-dollar grant from Mary Ann Starkweather, is the oldest building on campus. The donor had stipulated that the edifice be used for religious purposes, but over the years it has served many functions. Today it houses the graduate studies office. There are rumors that Mary Ann isn't happy about the repurposing of her namesake building, so her unsettled ghost now roams the halls. Reported hauntings include a custodian was who touched by invisible hands in the basement and a female student who claimed the light in the basement ladies' restroom kept turning itself off.

Pease Auditorium, a fifteen-hundred-seat grand concert hall, was constructed in 1914. Originally named for John D. Pierce, Michigan's first superintendent of instruction, the hall was rechristened in 1915 to honor Frederic H. Pease, Head of the Conservatory and a music professor from 1858 to 1909. Pease himself is said to haunt his eponymous auditorium. He'll show up in the corridors, the dressing rooms, and onstage, as well as on the catwalks overhead. The sightings didn't begin in earnest until a fictional story about Pease's apparition was printed in the university newspaper, the *Eastern Echo*, in 1980.

According to another legend, the building also houses the spectre of a homicidal music student. Supposedly in the early 1900s, two students—a female soprano and a male trumpet player—fell in love. They would meet every day at

Pease Auditorium and go for lunch. One day the boy was surprised when he entered the theater and found his girlfriend talking to a young man he didn't recognize. She casually introduced them, but over the ensuing weeks the trumpeter become jealous as the girl seemed to get friendlier with the interloper. Things came to a tragic end when the boyfriend snuck into the hall's balcony and caught the girl singing privately for the other guy—something she previously had done only for him. He crept down to the first row of the balcony, sat down on a chair, pulled out a gun, and shot the couple onstage. He then turned the gun on himself and took his own life. To this day, students hear disembodied footsteps on the stairs heading up to the balcony and see one of the front-row seats drop by itself, as if someone were sitting in it.

Back in the late 1960s, a former EMU student named John Norman Collins went on a murderous rampage in the Ypsilanti area and became known as the "Co-ed Killer." By the time he was caught, seven young women were dead. It's said that the ghost of one of his victims is seen near the intersection of Geddes and Laforge Roads, close to where a farmhouse once stood that was used for one of his killings. Purportedly, you can also see a long-gone silo, which is also haunted by the female spirit. Sometimes, as you drive through the crossroads, the trunk of your car pops open.

While studying at Eastern Michigan University, Collins lived at 619 Emmet Street, and it may have been the site of some of his slaughters. Today the building at that location is the university's **Alpha Xi Delta sorority house.** Strange voices are heard in its rooms, and doors swing shut by themselves.

MICHIGAN STATE UNIVERSITY

138 Service Road, East Lansing, MI 48823; (517) 355-1855
www.msu.edu

The mighty Michigan State University began in 1855 as the Agricultural College of the State of Michigan. It officially changed its name to Michigan State University in 1964.

Mary Mayo Hall is thought to be the university's most haunted building. Built in 1931 and the school's oldest residence hall, the dormitory was originally called Sylvan Lodge because it was located in a small park. The building was renamed for Mary Anne Mayo, who was on the governing committee of the Michigan Agricultural College and an advocate for women's studies. Stories began to circulate almost immediately after Mayo Hall opened that the place harbored an apparition. The female figure—never positively identified but thought to be Mayo—strolls through the corridors, flips lights on and off, messes with electrical appliances, and is responsible for strange noises and the piano playing itself at night. Folks have felt cold gusts of wind and invisible fingers touching them. Furniture rearranges itself. The paranormal phenomena seem to be particularly active in the West Lounge, a basement hallway, and the corridor linking the two wings of the building. An oil portrait of Mayo hangs on the first floor, and her eyes seem to follow people as they move around the room. The ghost may indeed be Mayo, but the fact that she died in 1903, twenty-eight years before the dorm was constructed, dispels the rumors that she committed suicide in the attic or was murdered in the basement.

There's the matter of the Red Room in the attic on the fourth floor. Supposedly another woman hanged herself there. Also, it's said that satanic rituals were held in the garret in the building's early years, and animal sacrifices took place in the 1950s and 1960s. People passing by the building see inexplicable lights and shadows through the fourth-story windows, which is odd because the chamber has been shut up tight for decades and is strictly off-limits.

Mason Hall opened as a men's dorm in 1938. An elderly man allegedly got locked inside the "oak room" in the basement in 1975, suffocated, and died. His spectre is now spotted there. He's also thought to be responsible for banging noises in the early morning, erratic lights, toilets that flush themselves, and an uneasy presence in the laundry room.

Yakeley-Gilchrist Hall was constructed in 1948. The hall's ghost story began in the summer of 1995 when a panicked female student called security around midnight to report someone banging on her door. When the police arrived, they could hear the pounding and see the door shaking, but no one was standing there. The incident lasted only a few minutes, but the tale has been repeated so often that there are now frequent claims about turning doorknobs and thumping at the doors.

Williams Hall, dating from 1937 and named for the wife of MSU's first president, is actually the second Williams Hall on the same site. The first building was destroyed by fire. Eerie sounds escape empty rooms, and electrical devices such as appliances and the TV in the lobby flip themselves on and off. Also, dark, unidentifiable figures have been caught dancing in a room that used to be the cafeteria.

Three residential halls are located in the East Neighborhood on the northeast side of campus, and two of them are haunted. **Holmes Hall,** the university's largest dormitory, opened in 1965. The most reported ghostly phenomena take place on the sixth floor in the West building (or wing), where an unknown male spectre enters the elevator. The doors close behind him and then immediately reopen, revealing the car to be empty. In the wee hours of the morning around 3:00 a .m., two male apparitions occasionally show up and enter the lift. The elevator is often unpredictable, and sometimes an unexplainable wind is heard rushing through the shaft. Elsewhere in the dormitory, lights, appliances, doors, and windows have a way of working themselves.

There's a similar elevator story at the other haunted East Neighborhood dorm, **Hubbard Hall.** The spectre of a mystery man enters the elevator on the top floor of the South wing and takes the lift down to the ninth floor. When the doors open, no one is in the car, and a breeze blows out of the compartment. The entire top floor is a hotbed of spirit activity. Windows open and close on their own, lights and electrical appliances turn on and off, and doors slam shut. Students hear the sound of running footsteps and laughter in the deserted hallway.

The **Wharton Center for the Performing Arts** is in the River Trail Neighborhood. A young man known only as Bill haunts the theater, and it's thought that he was beaten to death in the 1980s. He doesn't materialize often. One of the few times he did show up—in a dressing room in 1989—he was wearing a white button-down shirt and black chinos. Most often he remains invisible, but his spirit opens and closes doors, flips light switches, and makes strange noises throughout the playhouse.

Each year for a few days at the end of October, the MSU Auditorium is turned into a haunted-house attraction as a fund-raiser for student organizations and initiatives. The **Fairchild Theatre,** found on the east side of the building, has an actual ghost year-round. The spirit is a little boy whose apparition is usually seen walking through the rows of seats. He also wanders the hallways, and sometimes his face looks out of the third-floor windows. Visitors to the building have reported hearing the sound of his laughter as well as whispering, footsteps, and a bouncing ball. Often the noises come from the empty wings of the stage.

Late at night at the **W. J. Beal Botanic Garden,** people have seen dark ghostly figures strolling across the grounds and have occasionally heard screams.

The nearby Collegiate Gothic–style **Beaumont Tower,** completed in 1928, is one of the most recognizable structures on campus. If what students claim is true, the bells in the tower sometimes peal on their own. A male student who died in World War II has appeared in the tower. It's believed he's looking for the girl he left behind when he went off to war. On foggy mornings, the ghosts of romantic couples wearing attire from the late nineteenth and early twentieth centuries are spotted outside the tower, strolling through the mist holding hands. Spectres of other former students roam the immediate area as well. They used to attend classes at College Hall, which once stood on the spot. (That building, which collapsed in 1918, was the first building on campus and the first in the United States dedicated to "the teaching of scientific agriculture.")

In the early morning and evenings, the apparitions of deceased students also wander the **now-vacant site of Saints' Rest,** the second building constructed at the Agricultural College. Completed in 1856, it was the school's only dormitory until 1870. The building never had a name; after it burned down in 1876, it acquired the nostalgic sobriquet "Saints' Rest" from a 1650 Puritan devotional written by Richard Baxter entitled *The Saint's Everlasting Rest.*

At least one intern has had his arm tugged by an invisible hand as he rushed down the stairs of the **Central Services** building. He then heard the disembodied voice of a female youngster calling out his name.

At the **Physical Plant**, technically the Infrastructure Planning and Facilities building, it's said that sometime in the past a man killed seventeen puppies in Room 25 in the basement. Ever since, on chilly nights and at noon on Saturdays in July, people can hear the sound of children crying in the cellar.

NORTHERN MICHIGAN UNIVERSITY

1401 Presque Isle Avenue, Marquette, MI 49855; (906) 227-1000
www.nmu.edu

Northern Michigan University was founded in 1899 as the Northern State Normal School to train teachers. After several name changes throughout the years, the institution became a university in 1963.

The 515-seat **Forest Roberts Theatre** opened in 1963 as The Little Theatre as part of a three-building complex for the College of Arts and Sciences. The playhouse was renamed in 1969 for a former head of the English department. The facility is haunted by the ghost of Perry Fezatt, who was a custodian at the university for thirty years. The short, stout man was popular with students and staff alike. He died of a heart attack while working in the theater's elevator.

The lift has been "spirited" ever since. Sometimes when it's called, it goes in the opposite direction, and occasionally people riding in the elevator feel it move, but when the doors open they discover they're on the same floor where they started. Fezatt's presence isn't confined to the elevator;

his essence is felt throughout the theater, and the sound of his whistling is unmistakable.

University of Michigan

500 South State Street, Ann Arbor, MI 48109; (734) 764-1817
www.umich.edu

The University of Michigan was founded in Detroit as the University of Michigania in 1817. The school moved to Ann Arbor in 1837, and the first classes were held four years later. It's the state's largest university, with satellite campuses in Flint and Dearborn.

Despite the institution's having almost six hundred major structures on its three-thousand-plus acres, only one of its buildings seems to be haunted, and it's not even on campus. The story just came to light recently because it was featured on television in "Sorority House Terror," the first episode of *School Spirits* on the Syfy channel, which premiered on June 20, 2012. Otherwise, the tale seems to be undocumented.

The name used for the sorority on TV, Gamma Alpha Gamma, was a pseudonym. It's believed the story refers to **Phi Rho Alpha,** but none of the footage was shot in their sorority house. According to the TV show, three new sisters who moved into the house in 2009 experienced strange things, such as disembodied footsteps on the stairs, maggots in their food, an infestation of bats, and other phenomena—including the appearance of a ghost. One of the girls recognized the phantom from a photo in an old book as Joseph Walser, a UM graduate who lived in the house with his family in the 1890s.

MINNESOTA

COLLEGE OF SAINT BENEDICT

37 South College Avenue, St. Joseph, MN 56374; (320) 363-5011
www.csbsju.edu

SAINT JOHN'S UNIVERSITY

2850 Abbey Plaza, Collegeville, MN 56321; (320) 363-2011
www.csbsju.edu

The College of Saint Benedict for women and Saint John's University for men are liberal arts schools whose students attend classes at both institutions. The campuses are located about three and a half miles apart. Although they're operated separately, they have a single academic program and share a 3,200-acre campus. They consider themselves equal partners and are usually paired under a single name: the College of Saint Benedict and Saint John's University. Their combined enrollment is approximately four thousand students.

Saint John's University was established first, in 1857. The massive, redbrick, twin-towered **Great Hall** served as the school's church until the current **Abbey Church** opened in 1961. During the Great Hall's construction a young monk fell to his death from a scaffold. Unhappy with the abbot's explanation for the accident, the monk's mother made a scene at the building's dedication. On her way home, her carriage overturned into a lake and she drowned. The woman's unhappy, unseen spirit came back to haunt the sanctuary. Worshippers could sense her troubled soul in the room, and she often left a trail of wet footprints in the center aisle. Her ghost may still be there, but she traveled, at least briefly, to the Abbey Church as well. Shortly after the new house of worship was consecrated, a crack appeared in the newly laid floor of the central aisle. Many believe the angry mother produced the fissure.

Anselm Bartolome, one of the brothers at Saint John's University, died by drowning in **Sagatagan Lake,** which borders the campus. His apparition materializes on the lakeshore as well as in some of the university buildings. Like the disgruntled mother, he, too, leaves watery footprints as evidence that he was there. Even though Brother Bartolome is no longer flesh and bones, he still has to be careful: The banks of the lake are haunted by a bear that, somewhere along the line, acquired the name Murro. Police shot the animal after it mauled a student who had hit it with an oar. The animal's spectre now roams the waterside looking for victims.

Saint Francis House, commonly called Frank House, was opened at Saint John's University in 1904. The three-story brick hall was built as a residence for the nuns who prepared the meals. The building was converted into student housing in 1964. Then, Saint John's Seminary took it over in 1993. There's an urban legend that sometime in the past a student killed himself in one of the rooms, and his playful wraith bothers residents to this day.

The Benedictine Sisters founded the nearby College of Saint Benedict in 1913. It's the only Benedictine college for women in the United States. Its campus is haunted by a phantom nun who is buried in the **convent cemetery.** Fortunately she only appears to students who are walking by the graveyard and, even then, only if they are undergoing some sort of emotional distress. Rumor has it that, some years ago, one of the dormitories was haunted for several days by a student who became sick and died in her room. Shrieks and moans soon began to emanate from the vacant chamber, causing the sisters to seal off the room until the paranormal activity ceased.

Concordia College

901 Eighth Street South, Moorhead, MN 56562; (218) 299-4000
www.cord.edu

Concordia College is a private liberal arts institution of higher learning that was founded on Halloween 1891 by a group of Norwegian pastors and lay settlers. The school, which is located on 113 acres, has around 28,000 students and is affiliated with the Evangelical Lutheran Church in America.

Hoyum Hall, constructed in 1965, is now a coed residence hall. The dorm's ghost is an unknown spirit who haunts the fifth floor. It appears at the foot of girls' beds while they're sleeping and cries out their names. The spectre also turns on radios and TVs when no one's in the room, floods the bathrooms with hot water, and screws around with students' schoolwork.

Fjelstad Hall, built in 1938 and fully refurbished in 1984, is an English Tudor–style dormitory. It's home to Dolly, the apparition of a student who, overwrought with the pressures of college life, hanged herself on the third floor in the mid-twentieth century. She sets alarms, locks kids out of their rooms, and switches around roommates' belongings, especially clothing.

The **Frances Frazier Comstock Theatre** is a 434-seat playhouse with a proscenium/thrust stage. The building also contains a media center, language lab, the Cyrus M. Running Art Gallery, and a ghost. The spook's name is Al Gersbach. Hauntings date from around 1980, when the program for an upcoming show came back from the printer with Gersbach's name in it. The problem was, no one had ever heard of him. He wasn't a student, and he certainly had nothing to do with the production. The printer returned the list of names that had been submitted to him and there, handwritten in pencil at the bottom, was Al Gersbach's name. Ever since, any time a producer or director is foolish enough to leave the mysterious name off the playbill, the show is beset with technical difficulties.

It's uncertain how the young woman died who is now the spectre on the fourth floor of **Old Main,** but according to legend she became romantically obsessed with one of her professors. He rebuffed her approaches, but she still continued to leave love letters on his desk. She told him that if she couldn't have him, she would die. Apparently she did.

MINNESOTA STATE UNIVERSITY, MANKATO

Mankato, MN 56001; (607) 389-1866; www.mnsu.edu

The Mankato Normal School was founded in 1868. It became a state teachers college, then a state college, and finally, in 1972, Mankato State University. The institution took its current name in 1998. The university offers undergraduate, master's, and doctoral degrees to approximately sixteen thousand students.

There have been rumors since at least the 1960s that the Crawford-McElroy Complex of dormitories is haunted. At the **Crawford Residence Community,** the spectre of a male student supposedly locks himself in his old room and rings some sort of buzzer to open the door. Also, rolls and rolls of toilet paper go missing from the building's storeroom, presumably stolen by another spirit.

The ghost story most associated with the university is a light-fingered phantom that steals women's undergarments from the four buildings that make up the **McElroy Residence Center.** (Some sources say the phenomenon is confined to the third floors.) It should be noted, however, that in 2006, Robb Murray, a reporter for *The Free Press* in Mankato, did an exhaustive inquiry into the legend of the panty-snatching spectre. He contacted current and former residents of the dorm, the director of residential life, former hall directors, a maintenance man, and other employees whose jobs regularly took them into McElroy. None of them had ever run into a ghost, much less seen one run off with anyone's underwear.

Some think that Room 113 in the **Memorial Library** is visited by several entities from the Beyond. The room used to be a tech lab, and one of the spectres that appears is a female student looking for her missing project. It gets very cold when she enters the room, and she doesn't always open the door when she comes and goes; sometimes she passes right through it. An amiable male phantom nicknamed Doug offers to help students with their lab work. He's believed to be a former university student from the 1990s who disappeared on the Pine Ridge Reservation in South Dakota in 2001. Many students think they're being watched by invisible spirits known as the Shadow People when they're in the room late at night. And, as so often happens when ghosts are around, lights have a tendency to work themselves.

The original Old Main was one of the first buildings on campus. A 1922 fire destroyed it, but a new building opened in its place two years later. That structure, located on the old lower campus, is now a senior citizens' home. It's said that the apparition of a female college student wanders its halls. The young woman allegedly committed suicide by jumping down one of the three-story elevator shafts. The lift is now covered over, but residents of the retirement home claim that you can hear its car moving up and down behind the wall.

SAINT MARY'S UNIVERSITY OF MINNESOTA

700 Terrace Heights, Winona, MN 55987; (800) 635-5987
www.smumn.edu

Saint Mary's University of Minnesota, a private institution of higher learning, was established in 1912 by Bishop Patrick Richard Heffron. It's operated by the Winona Diocese.

Heffron Hall, named for the university's founder, was built as a men's dormitory in 1920. Today the building's third floor is haunted by the malevolent apparition of Father Laurence Michael Lesches. On August 27, 1915, Father Lesches shot Bishop Heffron while the latter was reading in his library. Lesches fired twice: One bullet penetrated Heffron's lung and the other grazed his skull. But the priest survived. In fact, he lived another twelve years, dying in 1927 at the age of sixty-seven. Details about the incident vary depending upon their source, but all of them agree that Heffron had correctly assumed Lesches was mentally unstable and had prevented him from getting a parish of his own. Lesches was sent to the State Hospital for the Dangerously Insane in St. Peter, Minnesota. He was eighty-four when he died there in 1943.

Lesches's evil, vengeful spirit returned to campus shortly after his death. People regularly hear his footsteps and the tapping of a cane on the third floor of Heffron Hall. (Lesches used a gold-handled walking stick.) Residents feel extreme cold spots, and inexplicable winds occasionally whip down the corridor. Students trying to get to the third floor have sometimes found themselves being pushed back by an unseen force.

One night a student became terrified in the bathroom when blood-colored liquid started flowing from the faucets and running down the side of a urinal. He fled the room but was chased by an invisible spirit—he could hear the footsteps following him. He managed to escape, but the next day he was found dead in his bed, his mouth agape and the sign of a cross burned into his chest.

In 1945 the ghost knocked on the door of resident Mike O'Malley, and when the seminarian answered it, the cloaked and hooded figure of Father Lesches attacked him. O'Malley fought back, breaking his hand when he punched the very solid spectre. Over the years, several students have been similarly assaulted. Some say that the letters A, C, and M are often later found scribbled near the door.

One more bit of folklore: On May 15, 1931, the charred body of Father Edward Lynch, another Lesches foe, was found on his bed. His bible was also burned, but nothing else in the room was damaged. Supposedly the bible was opened to 1 Thessalonians 4:16, an apocalyptic verse that Lesches had used years earlier to intimidate Lynch. The death was ruled an accidental electrocution, but urban legend suggests that Lesches, who was miles away in a mental institution at the time, had somehow projected his murderous spirit to the hall and killed Lynch.

St. Cloud State University

740 Fourth Avenue South, St. Cloud, MN 56301; (320) 308-0121 www.stcloudstate.edu

St. Cloud State University was founded in 1869. With more than sixteen thousand students in its undergraduate and graduate programs, it's Minnesota's second-largest university.

Lawrence Hall is the oldest building on campus, having been constructed in 1904. For years people have seen the ghost of a bald man standing in doorways. Flickering lights and stereos that turn themselves on also plague the building. Legend has it that the ghostly activity may be connected to the murder of two professors in their offices by one of the cleaning staff around 1950.

Opened in 1913, **Riverview Hall** is the oldest classroom building on campus and is on the National Register of Historic Places. The spirit of an unknown woman walks the corridors and sometimes enters the restroom without ever coming out. She's been seen and heard by faculty, students, and staff, but most often people simply hear the distinct footsteps of her high-heel shoes. The apparition also opens doors, plays with the lights, and moves furniture from one room to another. Riverview Hall is also haunted by the spectre of a child bouncing a ball. The youngster dates from the days when the building housed an elementary school.

Shoemaker Hall, one of ten residence halls on campus, overlooks the Mississippi River and can house five hundred students. Around the turn of the twentieth century, a female resident had an affair with one of the custodians. When she became pregnant she hanged herself in the meat locker located in the kitchen in the basement of the building. Her ghost is blamed for TVs and lights turning themselves on and off, personal belongings moving on their own, and clocks going haywire. Every so often her spirit is seen floating above students' beds. Another version of the legend—or perhaps a separate tale altogether—says it was a kitchen worker, not a student, who hanged herself in the meat locker. The cook's paranormal phenomena are confined to the basement, however, and includes her unlocking the door to the area.

Finally, **James W. Miller Learning Resources Center** was built on top of an unmarked cemetery, a long-standing rumor that was apparently corroborated in recent times when human bones were unearthed. Many hauntings have occurred inside the library, but the most common is the appearance of a ghost dressed in a nineteenth-century soldier's uniform. The phantom fighter paces the hallways.

St. Olaf College

1520 St. Olaf Avenue, Northfield, MN 55057; (507) 786-2222
www.stolaf.edu

A delegation of clergy and farmers of Norwegian descent led by Pastor Brent Julius Muus founded St. Olaf College in 1874. The college is affiliated with the Evangelical Lutheran Church in America.

The school has been haunted almost since its inception. The first issue of the student newspaper, the *Manitou Messenger*, reported in 1887 that "two ghosts were seen parading the upper floor at Ladies Hall Friday night." Ladies Hall was the college's first building and was the school's only women's dormitory for more than three decades, starting in 1875. The building was torn down in the summer of 1926.

Mellby Hall is a coed dormitory with several ghosts. One of them is a Woman in White with long black hair. She manifests on the staircase between the second and third floors, although some residents merely feel her pass by when they're on the stairs. People outside the building have seen the apparition in two of the windows on the third floor. The spirit is believed to be the building's namesake, Agnes Mellby, a former preceptress and the first woman to graduate from a Norwegian Lutheran college in the United States. There are sporadic accounts of one or two other ghosts wearing Victorian clothing in the building. Along with Agnes, they walk the stairs, the fourth floor, and the lobby. Another Mellby Hall spectre is an older man who wears a hat and a black trench coat.

Hilleboe Hall was the site of a suicide. The young woman, alone in one of the upper-story rooms, leapt to her death from her window. She left behind notes scrawled on the walls saying a disembodied woman's voice drove her to kill herself. The students in the next room told police they had heard screaming in the room right before the girl jumped. One summer a resident life associate heard a youngster singing along with the sound of the piano in the downstairs lounge. The woman checked the room, but no one was there. When she went back upstairs she found a child's handprints on the outside of several windows on the third floor. Also, the faucets had been turned on in all the third-story bathrooms.

A female resident of **Thorson Hall** once reported being awakened by the sound of a screaming child. She caught sight of the youngster, who continued to yell for several minutes before the phantom turned around and vanished on the spot. The student checked the door; it was locked. Her roommate slept through the whole thing! In fact, no one else in the building saw or heard anything out of the ordinary that night. Residents *do* see the ghost of a little boy in a red baseball cap, however. He was first reported by two female residents who were outside and spotted him standing in the window of their room. At one point, several women who lived in the hall got together and politely called on the lad to leave. For a time he complied, but there are still stories about him turning up. It's thought that he "lives" on the first floor. The apparitions of two young men also materialize together in various rooms, sometimes quietly playing cards on the floor. There has been other odd paranormal activity in the building, too. One student's CD player would start or stop playing if certain songs were on any of the discs. Apparently the ethereal entities didn't like Led Zeppelin's "D'yer Mak'er," but they didn't mind classical music.

Kelsey Theater is one of two playhouses located in the campus Theater Building. The performance space is named for Elizabeth Walsingham Kelsey, who was a guiding light in the theater department for more than thirty years. Hauntings in the building began in the mid-1990s. A male student was working in a sound booth late one night, syncing up some prerecorded violin and piano music. As he was leaving, he heard the sound of a piano, yet he knew he had turned off all his electronics. When he looked into the studio, the apparition of a woman wearing a lavender dress was seated at the piano, playing the same song that was on the tape. Needless to say, the technician skedaddled. As he rushed through the lobby, his eyes were drawn to a portrait of Kelsey hanging on the wall—a picture he had walked by countless times before. It was the woman he had just seen at the piano! Since that time, many students have caught sight of Kelsey's spectre. Some claim to have heard her voice as well.

Rolvaag Memorial Library was visited on at least one occasion by the ghost of former English professor and librarian Charlotte Jacobson. A student walked by a woman pushing a cartload full of books on one of the landings. When the girl reached the study area, she saw a portrait of Jacobson hanging on the wall. It was the woman she had just passed! The student rushed back to the cart, but no one was anywhere near it. She later found out that the long-deceased faculty member used to volunteer at the library after she retired, and her duties often included reshelving books.

University of Minnesota

Minneapolis, MN 55455; (612) 625-5000; www.umn.edu

The University of Minnesota was founded in 1851 and has more than 69,000 students in its five-campus system. Its main branch, known as the University of Minnesota, Twin Cities, has facilities in both Minneapolis and St. Paul.

The **Walter Library** was constructed in 1923 and opened the following year. It now houses the Digital Technology Center, the Learning Resources Center, the Digital Media Center, the Minnesota Supercomputing Institute, and the College of Science and Engineering library. The inexplicable and unidentifiable sound of howling is heard throughout the building. It's impossible to tell whether the noises are animal or human in origin.

Built as the chemistry laboratory in 1890, **Nicholson Hall** was also once the student union. A "one-off" haunting was reported in 1996, but it's still being cited as evidence of poltergeist activity in the building. A campus security guard was on the receiving end of a phone book that was tossed across the room by invisible hands. For the rest of the night, he could hear only static on his two-way radio. Today the building is home to the College of Liberal Arts and several other departments. Time will tell if the spunky spirit ever returns.

These ghost stories are minor compared to the spectral activity on the **Washington Avenue Bridge.** The crossing spans the Mississippi River and connects the east and west sides of the campus. Many people have committed suicide by jumping off the bridge, and some of them have chosen to return from the Beyond. People walking across the bridge encounter cold spots and hear disembodied footsteps, especially at night. Others have been approached by different apparitions who disappear in front of their eyes. One of the spectres seems to have psychiatric problems, and, as it turns out, there is a record of a mental patient who hurled himself off the Washington Avenue Bridge shortly after being released from an institution.

MISSOURI

COTTEY COLLEGE

1000 West Austin Boulevard, Nevada, MO 64772; (417) 667-8181
www.cottey.edu

Virginia Alice Cottey Stockard established Cottey College, a private women's school, in 1884. For most of its existence, the institution offered two-year associate degrees, but in 2011 it began offering baccalaureate degrees in a few select programs as well. Cottey College is owned by the P.E.O. Sisterhood.

Three spirits are said to haunt the campus. On May 15, 1920, twenty-one-year-old senior Vera Neitzert was cooking in her dorm room in Main Hall when her nightclothes caught fire. (Cooking over an open flame was not allowed in the residence halls to prevent just such an occurrence.) Vera was rushed to the nearby Amerman Sanitarium, where she died two days later. According to legend, Vera's ghost soon began to wander both **Main Hall** and Rosemary Hall. (The two buildings were connected.) The latter structure was demolished in 1990, but Vera's spectre is still encountered all over campus. Most often, she finds a piano and plays it when no one is in the room.

Some folks say the phantom is actually Madame Blitz, who was head of Cottey College's music department at the beginning of the twentieth century. She died in 1904 in her house just off campus by drinking carbolic acid. Like Vera, her apparition supposedly roams the entire campus.

The third apparition at Cottey is male and thought to date from around the Civil War, predating the college's existence. He's always dressed in black, and some believe he's an African American. It's unknown why his spirit would want to return to the site.

NORTHWEST MISSOURI STATE UNIVERSITY

800 University Drive, Maryville, MO 64468; (660) 562-1212
www.nwmissouri.edu

Northwest Missouri State University was founded in 1905 as the Fifth District Normal School. The institution's name changed in 1919 to the Northwest Missouri State Teacher's College when it started to offer bachelor's degrees. The word "Teacher's" was dropped in 1949 as the curricula expanded. The school acquired university status in 1972.

Even the university's website mentions Roberta, the school's most famous ghost. On April 28, 1951, a gasoline storage tanker was parked on a railway siding of the Wabash

Railroad tracks directly behind the Women's Residence Hall, the only female dormitory on campus. The car exploded, sending steel beams and debris into the building and setting the structure on fire. Thirty female students were hurt, four of them critically, including one named Roberta Steel. She died a year and a half later of complications from her injuries. The rebuilt dorm was named **Roberta Hall** in her memory.

Roberta's ghost is a playful prankster. For instance, she loves to throw hairbrushes at the girls. She'll turn lights off if they stay up too late, and she'll turn the volume down on loud music. She's quite the musician herself; she often plays the piano in the empty basement. Roberta makes other, unidentifiable noises as well. She's also been known to lock (and unlock) doors and windows, and she seems to have a thing for keys, because they often go missing. When Roberta appears, it's usually in the form of a dark, indistinct shadow, but on at least one occasion, the spectre fully materialized and tried to climb into a bed already occupied by a student. When the resident pushed Roberta out, the phantom began dancing in circles on the floor.

Delta Chi fraternity house harbors the phantom of a little girl, whom the guys have nicknamed Lillian. People hear her disembodied voice in the cellar. Over in **Hudson Hall**, poltergeist-like activity has been reported on the fourth floor, including small objects being thrown around the rooms.

SAINT LOUIS UNIVERSITY

221 North Grand Boulevard, St. Louis, MO 63103; (314) 977-2222
www.slu.edu

Saint Louis University is a private Jesuit institution of higher learning. It was founded in 1818 as the Saint Louis Academy by the Reverend Louis William DuBourg, the Catholic bishop of Louisiana. The school became Saint Louis College two years later, and in 1832 it received university status.

The school purchased land to move to a new location in 1867, but construction on DuBourg Hall, the first building on its current campus, didn't begin until 1886. The grand edifice officially opened on July 31, 1888. It now holds administrative offices, an art gallery, and the Welcome and Information Centers. The building has an unusual haunting. Supposedly people can sometimes catch a whiff of the scent of unwashed socks, and the overpowering odor has been encountered throughout the entire hall. No one knows the reason for the strange phenomenon.

DuBourg Hall is notorious for supposedly being the actual site of the exorcism dramatized in both the novel and horror movie *The Exorcist*. (Based on a real-life exorcism of a young boy in 1949, the book and film set the events in the Georgetown district of Washington, DC.) It's said that the fourth-floor room in which the rite took place is now sealed off and can't be entered. Some versions of the legend say the victim was kept in Verhaegen Hall, not DuBourg. Recent research has shown, however, that the school played no part in the exorcism, and at no time was the child on the Saint Louis University campus. There's an unrelated legend, however, that a few students were once caught trying to perform some kind of ritual using pentagrams and candles in the area between DuBourg and Verhaegen Halls.

Stephens College

1200 East Broadway, Columbia, MO 65215; (800) 876-7207
www.stephens.edu

Stephens College was founded in 1833 as the Columbia Female Academy. It's the second-oldest all-female institution of higher learning in the United States. The school changed its name to Stephens College in 1870 following a major endowment from James Stephens Sr.

Senior Hall was already standing on an eight-acre piece of property when Stephens College acquired it in 1857. Today the ghost of Sarah June Wheeler haunts the building—perhaps along with one or more spectres. Sarah was a student living in Senior Hall at the Columbia Female Baptist Academy, as the school was called at the time of the Civil War. She hid a wounded soldier in the dormitory and nursed him back to health. In the process they fell in love. Their story had a sad ending, however. In one version of the tale, they drowned in a swollen river while trying to elope. In another, the soldier, sometimes identified as Isaac Johnson, was captured and executed. In the latter variation, Sarah committed suicide immediately after her lover's death, either by hanging herself from the tower of the residence hall or by throwing herself down the stairs.

Sarah's ghost returned to Senior Hall, the last place that she found happiness on earth. (Others think she's come back to look for Isaac.) She's usually spotted alone in the tower, although it's been said that Isaac's apparition sometimes joins her. According to campus lore, you can count on seeing Sarah, if at no other time, on Halloween night. A related myth says that a different female ghost is occasionally spotted in the tower. The woman supposedly hanged herself there around 1915.

An entirely different story claims that an unnamed female resident fell in love with a young artist, also during the Civil War era. He murdered her, and to hide the body he dragged it to the tower by the student's long blonde hair. Every Halloween at midnight, her screaming spectre runs down the long-gone staircase that once led from what is now Room 131A to the tower.

The ghosts don't confine themselves to the tower, however. A student might catch a fleeting glimpse of one of them anywhere in the building, usually out of the corner of an eye. Or, the spirit might manifest itself as a cloud of light. Back in 1986 one student told the student newspaper that she had seen two spectral women, both wearing ball gowns, walking together in Senior Hall.

Wales Hall lays claim to its own phantom. Some students think it's Lucy Ann Wales, Columbia Female Academy's first headmistress. Others whisper that it's a student who died in Room 318. The banshee shows up at midnight on Halloween with a chalky white body and a gleaming greenish face. She drifts from room to room, searching the right-hand corner of every dresser drawer before returning to the site of her death, accompanied by the sound of clanking chains. This legend is relatively recent, dating from around 1933.

TRUMAN STATE UNIVERSITY

100 East Normal Avenue, Kirksville, MO 63501; (660) 785-4000
www.truman.edu

Truman State University was founded by Joseph Baldwin in 1867 as the First Missouri Normal School and Commercial College. The name was changed to its present form in 1996 to honor President Harry Truman, who was born in Missouri.

Grim Hall, the smallest dormitory on campus, was originally the nurses' residence quarters for the nearby Grim-Smith Hospital. The university didn't acquire the building until the 1930s. The apparition of a boy has been roaming the corridors since the 1980s, but the building's main ghost is named Charlotte. She was a nursing student at Truman State, and folklore suggests she died when she stayed on campus during a frigid winter break, some say in 1931 (although it's unsure whether the college owned the dormitory at that time). Most versions of the tale say the heat went off in the hall and she froze to death. Others think that she had an epileptic seizure or was diabetic and ran out of insulin. A few suggest she hanged herself from a tree outside the hall. Charlotte slams doors, pushes books off shelves—all the "usual" ghost activity. In fact, she's blamed for just about anything out of the ordinary that happens in the building.

Centennial Hall is the largest residence hall on campus. It's coed and houses approximately six hundred students in suites—two double rooms sharing a living area and common bath. The dorm is supposedly occupied by a spirit known as Joan, although not much else is known about her.

The university also offers housing in three campus-owned apartment complexes, one of which is **Campbell Apartments,** located near the tennis courts. Some students who live there claim they've been visited by the spectral soul of an elderly woman.

At least three phantoms produce poltergeist-like activity in the university's main building, **Baldwin Hall.** This is actually the second Baldwin Hall; the first one burned down in 1924. Enough unnerving phenomena have occurred that the building has been investigated by the Carroll Area Paranormal Team, among others. Two of the spirits are young folks who are possibly former TSU students. They've been nicknamed P. J. and Zoey. The other phantom is Max, a onetime custodian who makes himself known by tapping on water pipes.

UNIVERSITY OF MISSOURI–KANSAS CITY

5100 Rockhill Road, Kansas City, MO 64110; (816) 235-1000 www.umkc.edu

The University of Missouri–Kansas City was founded in 1933 as the University of Kansas City. The main campus, Volker Campus, is on property donated by entrepreneur William Volker. There is also a Hospital Hill campus. In 1963 the university changed its name to its current form upon entry into the University of Missouri system.

Epperson House was constructed between 1919 and 1923. The television show *Unsolved Mysteries* called it one of the five most haunted houses in America. The building's ghost is Harriet Evelyn Barse. An organ student at the Kansas City Conservatory of Music, she was invited by Uriah and Elizabeth Epperson to live with them in their new home even before it was completed. Harriet was ten (some say twenty) years older than Elizabeth, but the couple often referred to her as their adopted daughter. Harriet designed a custom organ for the loft of the house, but in 1922, before it could be installed, she died suddenly of a perforated gall bladder. (There were nasty rumors that she actually died of a botched abortion and that the child may have been Uriah's).

UMKC students have heard phantom organ music in the building even though the instrument was removed years ago. There are other strange, unidentifiable noises as well. Batteries seem to drain quicker than normal in the house, and guards have heard footsteps and seen inexplicable lights in the empty halls at night. In May 1979 an officer was parked outside the house when his car was rear-ended, and he heard the sound of breaking glass. When he got out to investigate, there was no damage to his car, no glass, and no other vehicle—but skid marks in the road showed his car had been shoved forward about eight inches.

Just as puzzling was a phenomenon that took place while two patrolmen were making rounds inside the building. They both saw a man's disembodied arm in a blue coat appear out of thin air, reach out, and turn off a light switch. On another occasion, a shadowy, unknown figure was spied in the corner of the basement but instantly vanished when a flashlight was turned in its direction. Some folks have spotted Uriah Epperson's ghost in the house, and a few have seen him walking with a girl thought to be his daughter—despite the fact that the Eppersons never had children. (One totally unfounded legend says the younger spectre was a daughter-in-law who hanged herself in the attic when she wasn't allowed to see a dockworker she fancied.)

The ghost that most people claim they've encountered in the house is Harriet Barse, her recognizable spirit attired in the sort of evening gown she might have worn at recital. Sometimes she's singing or rocking what appears to be a swaddled baby in her arms.

NEBRASKA

HASTINGS COLLEGE

710 Turner Avenue, Hastings, NE 68901; (402) 463-2402 or (800) 532-7642; www.hastings.edu

Hastings College, a private liberal arts school affiliated with the Presbyterian Church, was founded in 1882. The first building on its current campus, McCormick Hall, was completed two years later. Today the college has forty major buildings sitting on 120 acres.

In 1912, Dr. Hayes M. Fuhr established a music department at Hastings. In the early years classes met in two studios in one of the dormitories. Notable among his early staff was piano instructor Ruth Johnson, who later became his wife. She left the college by the end of the 1930s, but Dr. Fuhr continued at the school, leading the program for forty-nine years. In 1956 the college named its new **Hayes M. Fuhr Hall of Music** in his honor. Ruth Fuhr died in 1968, her husband in 1975.

The apparition of an adult male has been seen roaming Fuhr Hall of Music, although it's most often seen in the form of a glowing light floating through the building. The spectre is also given credit for turning lights on and off. Could the phantom be Dr. Fuhr himself?

Nebraska Wesleyan University

5000 Saint Paul Avenue, Lincoln, NE 68504; (800) 541-3818
www.nebrwesleyan.edu

Nebraska Wesleyan University was established by the United Methodist Church in 1887. The private school offers 106 majors in both undergraduate and graduate degree programs. The story of its most famous ghost, Clara Mills, can be found in several spots on the university website.

Urania Clara Mills taught piano, music theory, and the history of music at NWU for twenty-eight years beginning in 1912. She died on April 12, 1940, most likely of a heart attack, and was discovered slumped over her desk in the **C. C. White Building.** Flash forward to October 3, 1963. Mrs. Coleen Buterbaugh was secretary to the dean, Dr. Sam Dahl. At about nine in the morning, she entered one of the rooms in his first-floor office suite looking for a visiting lecturer. She had taken no more than a few steps when she realized the air in the room was musty despite the fact that the window was open. There was also no ambient noise; the room was completely silent, even though classes were going on next door.

Suddenly she noticed what turned out to be the apparition of a woman standing by a cabinet in an inner office. The stranger was partially turned away reaching into a drawer, so Buterbaugh couldn't see her whole face. The spirit was tall and slender with black hair, and she was wearing a long-sleeved white blouse and a skirt down to her ankles. Almost at the same time, Mrs. Buterbaugh became aware of the presence of a man sitting at a desk to her left. When she turned to look at him, there was no one there.

What happened next was strangest of all. The secretary glanced out the window and realized what she saw outside was oddly different than it should have been. Buildings were missing; streets were gone. It was as if she were seeing what the campus had looked like decades earlier. (In some versions of the tale, the weather was markedly different from when she entered the building as well.) Mrs. Buterbaugh fled from the room in a panic and rushed to Dr. Dahl's personal office. They went back into the haunted room, but everything was back to normal.

The identity of the spectral man remains unknown, but it was decided that the ephemeral female was Clara Mills. Not only did the description match the former music professor, but the room had been her office—the one in which she had died.

As for the change in scenery, what Mrs. Buterbaugh experienced may have been retrocognition and not a haunting at all. Also called postcognition, the phenomenon is a sudden overlap of time in which the past and the present briefly coexist. Typically people from the two periods don't interact; the past is merely observed. Usually the encounter is brief, but there have been reported instances in which several hours elapsed.

Whatever the haunting was, it seemed to open the floodgates. Before long, light switches were working themselves, there were sounds of unexplained footsteps in the hallways, and piano music was coming from the basement.

The paranormal activity came to an abrupt end in the C. C. White Building when it was torn down in June 1973. A few folks have reported experiences in the **Smith-Curtis Administration Building,** which now stands on the site, but according to most people Clara's apparition simply moved to nearby **Old Main.** Her spirit has been seen in the windows, and a shadowy form was spotted in the basement. A piano has also been heard playing in empty rooms. Whenever anyone goes to investigate the music, it stops as soon as the person enters the room. Various legends say that Clara's ghost, unpleasant scents, and the sound of piano music also appear in and around one of the apartments in town where she used to live.

There is a vague legend about another haunting at Nebraska Wesleyan University. The revenant is the spectre of an unnamed male music professor who purportedly taught the organ at NWU. The figure materializes sitting at or near the instrument in the school's music building, and organ music emanates from the hall when it's vacant.

University of Nebraska–Lincoln

1400 R Street, Lincoln, NE 68588; (402) 472-7211; www.unl.edu

The University of Nebraska–Lincoln, commonly called Nebraska, UNL, or NU, was chartered by the state in 1869. It is the oldest university in the state and the largest. It's also the flagship school of the state university system.

At the turn of the twentieth century, Chancellor Benjamin Andrews approached oil magnate John D. Rockefeller Jr. for his assistance in financing a building to house student activities. The result was the **Temple,** constructed between 1906 and 1908. The building is the home of University Theatre. In the 1940s a student fell to his death from the catwalk to the stage while preparing for a performance of *Macbeth*. Ever since, paranormal events occur around the theater, and his spectre appears whenever that particular play is produced. He shows up at other times as well. A spectral human form that may or may not be him has also been spotted in the light booth. In the 1970s he popped up in the student television studio located in the basement.

According to theater lore, the tragedy of *Macbeth* is cursed—some say because of its themes of witchcraft and the supernatural. There seem to be stories of mishaps backstage or actors being injured whenever the show is put on, during both the rehearsals and the actual run. A deeply held superstition among actors says that mayhem or disaster will result if anyone says the play's name out loud while inside a theater. As a result, actors refer to it as "the Scottish Play." Any offender must leave the theater, perform some sort of cleansing rite, and then wait to be invited back inside the building. Rituals might include spinning in a circle, walking around the theater three times, swearing, spitting over one's shoulder, or reciting any line from a Shakespearean play that asks for forgiveness or protection.

One of the UNL's drama professors, Dallas Williams, is a relatively recent ghost in the Temple. He used to watch performances from one particular seat in the auditorium. After he died of a stroke in 1971, actors began to see his shadowy form back in his favorite chair. They recognized him from his distinctive crew cut. His footsteps have been heard, and he's also credited with opening and closing doors. Williams's ghost, the phantom stage crew member who fell, or another spirit entirely might have been responsible for the pounding noises coming from the uppermost rooms of the Temple throughout the 1980s.

Neihardt Hall, originally known as Raymond Hall, was constructed in 1931. Among the dormitory's many ghost stories, one student reported a stereo that turned itself on and off. The building's resident ghost is Sara, who died during a long-ago influenza epidemic. She materializes now and then; she also may be the invisible, unnaturally cold presence that's said to roam the halls.

Pound Hall was a thirteen-story coed dormitory. Work began on the building in 1963, and its first students—all female—moved in six years later. Its ghost, Lucy, haunted one of the rooms on the fifth floor. She lived in the residence hall in the 1960s and was reportedly a "hippie" type. She committed suicide by jumping from her dorm window. Her delicate, misty spectre was occasionally spotted in her old room, and objects would sometimes fly through the air. Pound Hall was put out of service as a residence hall at the end of the 2013–2014 academic year. Plans were announced to raze the building eventually, although no firm date has been set. As a result, Lucy's future is uncertain.

NORTH DAKOTA

NORTH DAKOTA STATE UNIVERSITY

1340 Administration Avenue, Fargo, ND 58102; (701) 231-8011
www.ndsu.edu

North Dakota State University is officially the North Dakota State University of Agriculture and Applied Sciences. It was founded as North Dakota Agricultural College in 1890 with classes beginning the following year. The campus encompasses 258 acres and has more than a hundred buildings.

Arguably the university's most historic buildings are in the southern area of campus. These structures include **Ceres Hall.** The state legislature approved construction of the building in 1909, and the yellow-brick edifice was the first female residence hall on campus. Today the building holds university offices, including admissions, counseling, and military and veterans services.

It also holds a ghost or two, particularly in the basement, on the third floor, and (according to a few sources) on the fourth floor as well. The spirit in the cellar is a disturbing, malevolent presence that's felt but not seen. The third-floor apparition is thought to be a man who hanged himself from a pipe in the building during World War II.

As a macabre side note, the building was supposed to have been named for the college's first female student, Jessie Slaughter, but it was feared people might refer to the dorm as the "Slaughter House." No sense tempting fate.

UNIVERSITY OF NORTH DAKOTA

264 Centennial Drive, Grand Forks, ND 58202; (701) 777-2011
www.und.edu

The University of North Dakota, or UND, was founded in 1883, six years before the territory became a state. The school, which sits on 500 acres and has about 240 buildings, is the oldest and largest in North Dakota. It offers both undergraduate and graduate degree programs.

Tunnels connect five of the campus dormitories with Wilkerson Hall, where the Wilkerson Dining Center is located. The ghost of a girl described as being around 5'5", having short dark hair, and wearing a nightgown has been seen in the **passageway that leads to West Hall,** one of the dorms. It's said that the apparition was a student who froze to death about sixty feet from the residence hall around two o'clock in the morning in December 1962. Supposedly she was heading in the direction of Wilkerson when she slipped on the ice, was knocked unconscious, and died from exposure. The details are unusually specific for an urban legend, so it's too bad none of it is true. Oh, there have been sightings of a ghost all right, but there's no evidence that a death ever occurred in the University of North Dakota tunnels.

OHIO

BOWLING GREEN STATE UNIVERSITY

1600 East Wooster Street, Bowling Green, OH 43403 (419) 372-2531; www.bgsu.edu

Bowling Green State University is a public institution of higher learning on a 1,338-acre campus. Founded in 1910, the institution has approximately eighteen thousand students.

Both the **Joe E. Brown** and **Eva Marie Saint Theatres** are haunted by the apparition of a former drama student known only as Alice. Some say that the theater ghost was playing Desdemona in a university production of *Othello* when a light fixture fell and killed her. Others claim she died in a car accident. In an alternate version of the story, she was on her way to the theater to accept an award; in another, to meet an agent. Regardless of who Alice was and the circumstances of her death, her spirit has returned to her beloved theaters. Many people have seen her apparition. The most notable instance was when she appeared onstage standing on a staircase during a 1986 performance of *Othello*. Alice is quite the diva and really doesn't like being ignored. The stage manager has to invite her to every performance, set a seat aside for her, and leave the ghost light on at night when the theater is closed. If not, Alice's ghost will cause havoc. There'll be problems with the lights and other electrical devices, props will break or go missing, sets will crash, and the auditorium will be filled with inexplicable loud noises.

(For those not familiar with theater lore, the ghost light or ghost lamp is the single bare light bulb on a tall pole that's placed in the middle of the empty stage and left on at night when everyone leaves the theater. Its practical purpose is the safety of those who have to walk through an otherwise dark auditorium. People who believe in the paranormal know that the real reason it exists is to scare away the theater's ghosts, who prefer to come out when all the lights are off.)

Kohl Hall opened in 1939 as the first men's dormitory on campus. Despite the fact that the structure was purpose-built, legend says that its ghost, a little boy named Joey, was killed in a fire in a bakery that used to be located on the first floor. His apparition is never seen, so residents can decide for themselves who their live-in spirit might be. The spectre likes to play tricks such as shutting off alarm clocks, unplugging electronics, opening the refrigerator and leaving the door open, hiding personal belongings, locking doors, and playing with the lights and TVs. The phantom also runs in the halls and knocks on doors, only to dart away before anyone answers.

The **Chi Omega sorority house** is haunted by Amanda, a first-year student and pledge to the sorority who died on a set of train tracks in the area. According to one rumor it was a hazing gone awry on the night of her initiation. (In a different version of the legend, the ghost is a little girl who died in the building that stood on the site before the sorority house was built.) Amanda's brunette apparition is seen in the kitchen and in a room that, fittingly enough, has been nicknamed "Amanda's Room." One closet in the house locks itself. Objects tend to disappear throughout the building and turn up later in the utility room.

Kent State University

800 East Summit Street, Kent, OH 44240; (330) 672-3000 www.kent.edu

Kent State University was established as a teachers training school in 1910. It had university status and was offering graduate degrees by 1935. In addition to its flagship campus in Kent, which has about twenty-nine thousand students, there are eight regional campuses.

Kent State University will be forever associated with the tragic events of May 4, 1970, in which members of the Ohio National Guard fatally shot four students and injured nine others during antiwar demonstrations on campus. The incident and its aftermath are beyond the scope of this book except for the assertion that ghosts of the students who were killed have been encountered on the university grounds, though they are almost never seen together. It's alleged that the students' spirits sometimes hover over the site where they fell. More often, their apparitions appeared in the commons area of the now-demolished Stopher Hall, where their bodies were taken for several hours immediately after the bloodshed. There have also been sporadic claims that the four spectres show up in their former dorm rooms and apartments. For instance, there are reports that one room in Engleman Hall where significant paranormal activity takes place used to be occupied by Allison Krause, one of the two females who died in the incident.

There are also plenty of phantoms on campus not related to the Kent State shootings.

Allyn Hall and **Clark Hall** are connected buildings that were dedicated in 1963. The ghost of a little girl named Sarah wanders around Allyn Hall asking people to play with her. She also likes to tug on blankets and sheets. She's also been known to visit Clark Hall on occasion. No one knows where she came from.

Engleman Hall, dedicated as a women's dorm in 1938, was the third residence hall on campus. According to legend, a female student was raped and murdered in the dorm in the 1940s or 1950s. Her spirit has been spotted in the hallways at night, and her reflection is sometimes seen in mirrors. People have run into a dark, hooded figure on the third floor and heard knocking on their windows. There have been suggestions that the dampness on the boiler room walls is caused by a resident who died by drowning; another tale says the phantom of a male student who hanged himself in the boiler room now drags a chair across its floor.

Koonce Hall is one of three dormitories in the Tri-Towers residence complex. It's the only Kent State building that's named for a former student. Judith E. Koonce must have appreciated the honor, because her apparition has come back to "live" in the dorm. Koonce graduated in 1957, but she died the following year trying to rescue an eleven-year-old girl who was drowning in the Little Miami River near Dayton, Ohio. Koonce's ghost, which never materializes, rewards model residents in her eponymous hall in little ways, such as holding the elevator a tad bit longer for them. On the other hand, she creates mischief for those who are troublemakers. Apparently Judith also likes to open and shut doors and bang on pipes.

Moulton Hall was one of the university's first residence halls. Today it houses the Learning Technologies Center. Passersby have seen a strange blue light floating in the air through the third-story windows.

The Music and Speech Center holds several performance facilities. The **Wright-Curtis Theatre** is haunted by G. Harris Wright, one of the university's first theater directors and also one the theater's namesakes. People can tell when he's in the smoke-free hall from the telltale scent of his cigars. Elsewhere in the building, **Room B-005** has acquired the nickname "Boo-5," which is fitting since it may have a ghost of its own.

Van Campen Hall is one of the smallest dormitories on campus. The most famous urban legend about Van Campen is that the sound of marbles can be heard dropping onto a hard surface overhead. (This is true even for those who live on the top floor.) Students also hear disembodied giggling and see unfamiliar faces next to their own when they look into mirrors. A few people have caught fleeting glimpses of unknown ghosts as the apparitions waft down the hallways.

Kenyon College

106 College Park Street, Gambier, OH 43022; (740) 427-5000
www.kenyon.edu

Kenyon College, a small liberal arts school founded by Bishop Philander Chase in 1824, was the first private college in Ohio. According to its website, Kenyon opened as an all-male institution to train and educate clergy "for frontier America." The college became coed in 1969.

At one time **Bolton Dance Studio** was the Shaffer Pool Building. The conversion took place in 1981, but visitors to the hall still hear the splashing sounds of a phantom swimmer or someone bouncing on a diving board. Wet footprints are seen in the area of the former locker room; sometimes they lead up to a wall that wasn't always there. Lights turn themselves on after people leave for the night, and on occasion passersby see a pale face with wet hair combed back looking out the windows. The spectre was around even before the building was turned into a studio. Lifeguards used to hear disembodied calls for help; folks heard the shouts even when the pool was drained. The apparition is known as the "Greenhouse Ghost" because the building used to have a glass roof. Legend has it that the spirit either drowned in the pool or perhaps died from a diving-board injury, but there's no record of either mishap having occurred.

Caples Hall is home to a male spirit who died from falling down the building's elevator shaft in 1979. The circumstances of his "accident" are cloudy, but it took place right after an argument with his girlfriend, who lived there. The boy went to the dorm to visit and found her with another guy. To keep her unexpected caller out of the room, she pushed her dresser up against the door. After the student's death, his girlfriend repeatedly woke up to find her chest of drawers back against the door. On occasions she'd feel the touch of his cold, dead hands on her face. These days if his ghost appears in the building, it's usually in a girl's room. The spectre is often seen leaning against a piece of furniture, or he'll move a bureau up to the doorway. Although he's not usually dangerous, it's claimed that he once tried to smother a girl with her pillow. Most of the ongoing activity seems to take place on the eighth floor.

The **Hill Theater** is located in the Shaffer Speech Building. Along with other phenomena, curtains open when no one's around and light bulbs become unscrewed. Rumor has it that the building was constructed on or near the site of a fatal drunk-driving accident. The two victims of the crash now supposedly haunt the theater. People have also heard a loud thud from the middle of the stage: an ethereal echo of a stagehand who fell to his death from the catwalk. Security guards have actually run into his ghost!

Lewis Hall is haunted by a freshman who hanged himself in the attic. His bothersome spectre rattles doorknobs, knocks on doors, flushes toilets, and flips lights on and off—not the best way to make friends with his housemates.

Manning Hall's phantom is a female student who died before classes began one year. Perhaps that's why she's constantly moving around furniture in the dorm: She never got to decorate her own room. An urban legend claims that Manning Hall was built on top of a passageway to Hades known as "Hellmouth."

Similarly, there's a popular myth on campus that there's a portal to the Next World in the basement of **Mather Hall**. The **gates on Main Path** and the **twin columns on Middle**

Path may also be entryways to the Beyond—or in the latter case, some say to hell.

Norton Hall is one of five residence halls set aside for first-year students. A former occupant, overcome by his insomnia, killed himself in his room. Even now he's unable to rest in peace. People have seen his apparition throughout the dorm.

Old Kenyon was the college's first permanent structure, built between 1827 and 1829. Used as a residence hall, the building caught fire on February 27, 1949, and nine male students were killed. The dorm was rebuilt the following year, and the hauntings started almost immediately. The most common phenomenon is the sight of one or all of the victims gliding down the corridors. They are visible only from the knees up, however. It's thought that the figures are cut off because the new foundation is approximately ten inches higher than it was on the old building. The ghosts are "walking" on the old floor. In fact, some people claim to have seen the spirits' legs poking through the ceiling overhead. Other spooky activity includes toilets flushing, lights flashing on and off, doors rattling, and sleeping residents being woken by disembodied screams of "Fire!" and "Get me out!"

Old Kenyon is also haunted by the apparition of eighteen-year-old Stuart Lathrop Pierson, who died on October 28, 1905—the night he was to have undergone initiation into Delta Kappa Epsilon fraternity. He was struck and killed by a train either on or near the trestle over the Koskosing River. Debate continues to this day over whether the brothers had merely told Pierson to wait there until they called for him or whether the pledge died as part of a terrifying hazing gone wrong. Regardless, on the anniversary of his death, Pierson's spectre appears in Old Kenyon, where he was living.

He peers out of the bull's-eye windows on the fourth floor, slams doors, opens windows, and walks the halls. Often whoever is living in Pierson's old dorm room vacates it for the day to give the ghost a wide berth.

MIAMI UNIVERSITY

501 East High Street, Oxford, OH 45056; (513) 529-1809
www.muohio.edu

Miami University, founded in 1809, is Ohio's second-oldest liberal arts college and the tenth-oldest public university in the United States.

Several spectres have taken up residence on campus in **Peabody Hall.** The building dates from 1871 and was named for Mrs. Helen Peabody, the first principal of Western Seminary, in 1905. Peabody's ghost wanders the corridors. Supposedly she's returned to keep young men away from her girls. If anyone tries to go up to the spirit, she instantly vanishes. Another frequent haunting is the furious flapping of window shades when there isn't any breeze. Room 210 is thought to have bad vibes: Two student suicides took place in the room, years apart.

Shriver Center opened as a student union in 1957. The entire building—but mostly the top floor—is haunted by a shadowy, faceless figure.

People hear an apparition groaning in **Wilson Hall.** The entity has also been known to toss around furniture. The culprit is thought to be one or more of the souls who died there when the building was a tuberculosis hospital.

The former Fisher Hall, originally Oxford Female College, became a freshmen residence hall for Miami University in 1925. It was named for Judge Elam Fisher, a former trustee, two years later. His wraith has been blamed for a number of things going missing from the building, but he had nothing to do with sophomore student Richard Hamman's disappearance from his room on April 19, 1953. The young man was never found. Some people believe Hamman's ghost joined Fisher's in haunting the building before it was demolished in 1979. Fisher's phantom is said to still materialize on the grounds where the building once stood.

OHIO NORTHERN UNIVERSITY

525 South Main Street, Ada, OH 45810; (419) 772-2000
www.onu.edu

Founded as a normal school by Henry Solomon Lehr in 1871, Ohio Northern University is a private institution of higher learning affiliated with the United Methodist Church. At least five of its buildings have ghosts.

Stambaugh Hall is a coed dormitory. Its apparition is definitely male, which created quite a ruckus back when Stambaugh was a women's dorm—especially since the dark form is usually seen near or in the restrooms heading toward the showers. The spectre always disappears before he gets there.

5 University Place, usually written 5UP and pronounced "Five Up," is a three-story women's residence hall. Before it was a dormitory, it served for a time at a frat house. Two deaths have occurred in the building, and both of the deceased have returned as spirits. The first is a fraternity boy who was accidentally killed during his initiation. The pledges had to run up the staircase as the brothers rolled beer kegs down the steps. A metal cask hit one of the freshmen in the head, killing him. The other ghost in 5UP is a former female student who committed suicide in her room.

As one might expect, the male ghost is always seen zigzagging up the stairs. The female apparition has been spotted in her old quarters.

Not in service since at least 2009, two-story **Clark Hall** was a coed dormitory. Its ghost was a female phantom named Phoebe. She would stroll the halls or stare at residents in their rooms. Plans call for the building's demolition as part of a major revamp of campus housing, so Phoebe's days may be numbered—that is, if she hasn't vanished already.

Presser Hall is the university's main concert hall. Its ghost, a male spectre named Brad, is said to have died on his way to the building for a recital. He hates music in D minor, so he bangs on pipes whenever a piece is played in that key. And—shades of *Phantom of the Opera*—he's been known to make the chandelier sway to the tempo of the composition being played.

Lastly, the **Lehr-Kennedy House** is home to career services and several offices for multicultural activities. Lights work themselves and ethereal music is sometimes heard, but the most frequent haunting is the sound of disembodied footsteps, possibly those of Henry Lehr himself.

OHIO STATE UNIVERSITY

Columbus, OH 43210; (614) 292-6446; www.osu.edu

Ohio State University, commonly called Ohio State or OSU, was founded in 1870 as the Ohio Agricultural and Mechanical College. It took its current name in 1878. The university has several branch campuses and more than 57,000 students on its haunted flagship campus in Columbus.

Bricker Hall was called the Administration Building when it opened in 1924. It's named for John Bricker, a former Ohio governor, US senator, and OSU alumnus and trustee. The building's ghost, however, is Herbert Atkinson, another former trustee, whose ashes are entombed on the second floor behind a plaque on the wall. He makes the lights flicker, and his recognizable ghost appears drinking a cup of punch in the lobby.

A ghost named Christopher haunts **Drackett Tower.** Not much is known about him—even his name is a sobriquet—but he turns electrical devices on and off, and he knocks items off of desks and shelves. He does materialize now and then and has even been known to talk to students.

Canfield Hall echoes with disembodied footsteps, and an unidentified apparition has been spotted in the corridors. People standing in the courtyard have sometimes felt an unexplainable sense of sadness and loss.

Hayes Hall, built in 1893, is the oldest building on campus. Its residents have a guardian angel of sorts: the building's namesake, former president Rutherford B. Hayes, who, as governor of Ohio, had a part in the founding of OSU. From around 1915 to 1920, the building was used as a residence hall. One time a student was locked out after curfew, and a bearded gentleman let the boy in, claiming to be the curator of the building. The young man later recognized him from a photograph as Hayes.

In the 1960s a female art student had a mental breakdown while trapped in an elevator overnight in **Hopkins Hall.** The custodian had turned off the electricity when he left for the night, not only stopping the elevator mid-floor but leaving the building—and the girl—in pitch darkness. The student passed the time by scrawling on the walls of the car. She was rescued the next day and later graduated, but apparently she never got over the trauma. Years later she died in an automobile accident, and today people will enter the lift to discover she had been there, scratching angry messages on the walls.

The area where the **Ohio Union** is located was still sparsely forested when the university opened. Early students saw open flames in the woods, but when they investigated they never found anyone. It came to be believed that they were seeing the campfires of the Native Americans who used to live in the environs. A miniature statue of an Indian woman that was found in the grove was taken back to campus, but it soon vanished. Before long the sound of a flute began emanating from the copse, and a legend grew that it was being played by a ghostly young man who had retrieved the carving, which was a likeness of his lost love. People can still hear the strains of that flute while standing in the second-floor lobby of the Union.

Orton Hall is named for Edwin Orton, the first president of the university and, as it turns out, the building's ghost. But Orton's apparition isn't alone. Students have seen— and there's no explanation for this—the revenant of what appears to a caveman. The Paleolithic spirit doesn't speak; he only grunts.

Though now used as office space, **Oxley Hall** was the first women's residence hall on campus. There are inexplicable footsteps inside the building, and windows open and close by themselves, especially in the attic. Also in the garret, ceiling lights swing despite there being no draft. It's said that a woman's screams can be heard in her former third-floor dorm room on the anniversary of her demise, December 17. Although she was rumored to be a suicide, no one is able to pin down the student's name or how, when, or even if she died. The whole thing may be an urban legend.

Pomerene Hall has been used for many functions since the first part of the building was completed in 1922. In 2012 the second and third floors became the home of the Department of History of Art. A few folks have seen an indistinct apparition in Room 213, but the more common phenomena are the sounds of footsteps and doors slamming. Doors also lock themselves, and people in the Office of Disability Services on the first floor have heard their voice-generating computers "talk" even when they're turned off.

The ghost of Pomerene Hall may be former professor Dr. Clark, who convinced several of his peers to invest in an Alaskan oil deal at the beginning of the twentieth century. When the enterprise went bust, he returned to campus and had to face those who had lost their savings. He later shot himself where Pomerene Hall stands today.

After Clark's widow died in the 1920s, her spirit also returned to campus, dressed in a long pink dress. She most often appeared between late fall and early spring, always at night. Known as the Pink Lady, she usually materialized first as a pinkish mist and then slowly took human form as she floated (or in winter months, seemingly skated) over **Mirror Lake.** (Some suggest that the ice-skater, the Pink Lady, and Mrs. Clark are three different spirits.) Though not seen in recent years, the Lady of the Lake as she's also known, is still an active part of OSU folklore.

The guys at **Phi Gamma Delta** fraternity are pretty mum, at least in public, about any ongoing ghost activity in their house, but Alpha Delta Pi (the sorority that preceded them in the building) was certainly open about it. Things disappeared from locked rooms and turned up elsewhere. Doors opened and chandeliers swayed. There was the sound of unexplained footsteps, and on several occasions a resident felt the weight of an invisible entity sit at the foot of her bed or saw an indentation sink into the bedspread. The ghost of a girl—thought to have lived in the house before it became a sorority—walked the halls, appeared in mirrors, and stared out of windows. A few people thought some of the spectral happenings were caused by a six-year-old boy who died in the house when it was still a private residence. Also, the spirit of a former sorority sister showed up shortly after her fatal car accident in 1994, but she never became a regular visitor.

It's only natural that ghosts wander around **Starling Loving Hall,** built in 1917. Today it houses offices and classrooms, but originally it was the Homeopathic Hospital—and it contained a morgue. Even when the hall's spirits don't manifest, folks can still hear their voices.

Finally, a strange phenomenon occurs when people stand on a flight of stairs built into a curved wall in front of **Wexner Center.** Folks at one end of the wall can whisper and, because of the bend, those at the other end can hear them clearly. If someone speaks while standing in the center of the curve, it will create an echo. But that's just architectural acoustics. Supposedly anyone who stands on the staircase at the midpoint of the wall on Halloween Day will hear the incorporeal voices of deceased OSU faculty and staff members.

Ohio University

1 University Terrace, Athens, OH 45701; (740) 593-1000 www.ohio.edu

Founded in 1804, Ohio University is the ninth-oldest public university in the United States. It is also one of the most haunted universities in the country. Ghost activity has occurred in so many places on campus that it's hard to know where to begin, so let's hit them alphabetically.

Brown House is now the Contemporary History Institute, but it was originally a private two-story residence deeded to the school by Mildred Francis Brown. Legend has it that people see her ghost looking out of the windows. Others hear the sound of children playing in the long-gone swimming pool that was once behind her house.

Residents on the top floor of **Bryan Hall** hear someone moving overhead in the tower, even though it's a locked storage area. There are also odd lights in the building and scratching sounds on the walls and doors.

Bush Hall, constructed in 1954, is one of fourteen residence halls on the East Green. The building's most common haunting is the sound of marbles being dropped on the floor overhead—sometimes dozens or even hundreds at a time. Electrical lights turn themselves on and off, as do faucets in the bathroom. There's also the infernal sound of water dripping when there are no apparent leaks.

The **College Green** marks the nominal center of Ohio University. The Quad is haunted by the headless ghost of a buffalo that was killed by Confederate soldiers during the Civil War. Somehow the animal acquired the name Stroud, and supposedly the last rebel to be captured by Union forces hid a fortune inside the buffalo's head. Rumor also has it that Stroud's head was the one put on display—minus the secret treasure—in the Buffalo Wings and Rings restaurant in town. Of course none of that explains why the decapitated beast's spectre would want to return to roam the Green, but it has. A separate quad known as the **West Green** was allegedly built on sacred Native-American burial grounds. Spectral chanting from the departed tribe can be heard there, as can the babbling of a river that used to flow through the area.

The **Convocation Center,** commonly called the Convo, holds the basketball court as well as student housing around its perimeter. Residents hear furniture being moved above them even when they know no one's on the next floor. One particular closet won't stay locked, and things stored inside it have a way of winding up on the floor. There are at least two purported ghosts roaming the halls. One is a female RA who was killed by her jealous boyfriend (even though she was, in fact, faithful). She is still making her rounds, checking on rooms and locking doors. The other spectre is a student who died of natural causes in her sleep. At least one subsequent person staying in her room has awoken to feel an invisible something pressing her down against the bed. (An alternate story says the spirit was actually trying to hug the startled resident.)

Ghost activity at **Crawford Hall** began soon after one of its residents, Laura Bensek, fell from the window of Room 404 on Easter Sunday 1993 and died. Guess who's blamed for all the strange goings-on in the dormitory? The activity is pretty standard haunted fare: Lights go on and off, and doors slam on their own. Laura was supposedly a Bob Marley fan, and some residents have claimed that they've had trouble playing Marley's music on any of their devices. On at least one occasion, an RA was confronted by the full-form materialization of a spectral college girl, who may or may not have been Bensek, who burst into his first-floor room. The ghost then backed out, apologizing for any inconvenience. The apparition has also been seen in the hallways.

Cutler Hall has an unknown spirit in its bell tower. Its favorite trick is changing the time on the giant clock.

There's a story that members of **Delta Tau Delta** fraternity once removed a headstone from the city's very haunted Simms Cemetery and placed the marker in a place of honor inside the fraternity house. Before long the house fell victim to all sorts of petrifying manifestations, from objects flying across the room to a window shattering. Once the brothers realized their mistake, they hauled the tombstone back to the graveyard, and the spooky activity ceased.

Jefferson Hall, built in 1956, is a four-story, coed dormitory named for President Thomas Jefferson. The building shares a haunting with Bush Hall: the sound of marbles being dropped on the floor upstairs. They can even be heard overhead by people on Jefferson's top floor. Lights go on and off without assistance, toilets flush on their own, and toilet paper unrolls itself. According to an oft-told tale, one night in the fall semester of 1996, several students snuck into an unused attic and saw the apparition of a woman dressed in 1950s clothing seated at a desk—except that they could see through her, and she was actually floating off the floor. The kids freaked! They rushed to get an RA. When they got back, the room was locked *and* empty.

Lin Hall is home to the Kennedy Museum of Art, but for many years it was a mental institution. At the time the university acquired the building, it was known as The Ridges. On December 1, 1978, a patient named Margaret Schilling escaped from her ward. She wasn't found until January 12, but by then she had died of natural causes. Her naked body was discovered in an unused part of the facility that hadn't been searched. She had folded her clothes neatly and placed them in a pile by the window. Her body left behind a permanent stain on the concrete floor. Her soul has returned to walk the hallways of the former asylum, and she may be joined by others who died there as well.

A ghost or ghosts has been reported by students staying in **Perkins Hall.** It turns on electrical appliances, and residents have heard a woman's voice and laughter.

The log cabin used as the **Visitors Center** was once the Athens County courthouse. It then became a private home before being moved onto campus. Doors lock themselves, and folks hear footsteps when they're alone in the building.

At least one room in **Voight Hall** has been visited by the phantom of a woman wearing a dark, long-sleeved, high-collared dress dating from the turn of the twentieth century. The spirit messed up things on the desk and typed on the computer keyboard.

There are two explanations for the spectral basketball team—yes, *team*—that dribbles balls and clatters its way throughout **Washington Hall.** In one story the players are all male, and they lived in the building when it was a men's dorm and the attic was a rec room. In another they're female players, and they were killed on their way back to the university after an away game. Yet a third tale says they were members of a girls' high school basketball team that stayed in Washington Hall while visiting Ohio University. Their bus crashed on the way back to their hometown, and all the girls died. They returned to the dormitory as a group to relive their happy memories on campus. While the hauntings pervade the entire building, they are especially active on the archway that connects Washington and Read Halls.

Wilson Hall was built in 1965, and it's gained a reputation for the number of its ghosts. Furniture will rearrange itself when students are out of the room, sometimes in mere seconds. Smoke or sparks will come from computers, but after students leave their rooms to seek help, they return to find the devices undamaged. In the 1970s an RA named Susan Manch was confronted by an invisible spirit on several occasions, such as the time a glass bottle was thrown against a wall and when her towel bar fell apart without being touched. Her taunter did appear once—in the guise of a bright light. Others have seen dark, shadowy forms in the corridors. Room 428 is thought to be particularly haunted. Among the room's claims to fame is that students discovered what looks like the image of a face in the wood paneling. Legend has it that some of the activity in Wilson Hall may be caused by a former resident who committed suicide in the building, but there are no police records of such a death. Also, for what it's worth, folklore says that the hall is located at the dead center of a giant pentagram formed by five or more cemeteries located in and around Athens—even though no one seems to agree on which graveyards they are.

University of Dayton

300 College Park Avenue, Dayton, OH 45469; (937) 229-1000 or (888) 253-2383; www.udayton.edu

The University of Dayton is a private Roman Catholic school with about eleven thousand undergraduate and graduate students. It traces its origins from the St. Mary's School for Boys, founded in 1850. After going through many changes, the institution took its present form and name in 1920.

Considering the university's humble beginnings as a children's school, it's little wonder that the ghosts of several youngsters have been seen playing near the **Chapel of the Immaculate Conception** in the heart of campus. A spectral priest also wanders by. The building's distinctive blue cupola is reflected in the university's logo. In the 1950s and 1960s, an otherworldly man—tall and wearing a cloak—also roamed the campus. It was believed that he was somehow associated with the disappearance of one of the students.

Liberty Hall has a grotesque apparition: the wraith of an ugly, older man. He has terrible teeth and walks with a distinct limp. Although the building holds offices today, there was once an infirmary there. It's unknown whether the spectre was one of its patients.

The phantom of **Theta Phi Alpha sorority house** is male. Those who have seen the ghost describe him as a rough young man; others think he may have been the protective father of one of the former sisters. The spook likes to rearrange furniture when everyone's away, turn lights on or off, and confiscate personal belongings, only to return them (sometimes days later) to a different location. There are also cold spots in the house, and residents sometimes feel invisible eyes spying on them. Now and then, girls will wake up with their energy totally drained.

WILMINGTON COLLEGE

1870 Quaker Way, Wilmington, OH 45177; (800) 341-9318
www.wilmington.edu

Wilmington College was established by the Quakers in 1870. The private institution has its main campus in Wilmington and two branch campuses in Cincinnati. The school is probably best known for its agricultural program.

College Hall, also known as Old Main, was originally built for Franklin College, which had moved its campus from Albany, Ohio, to Wilmington in 1865. The college went bankrupt, and the building was acquired—only partially completed at the time of the auction—by the founders of Wilmington College.

The building is haunted by two horses. The first is Ole Bill, which belonged to Colonel Azariah Doan, who had represented the Quakers in their acquisition of the property. He laid the remains of his trusty steed to rest inside College Hall between the second and third floors. Its skeleton was found when a new elevator was installed in 1957. The skull was put on exhibition in the hall. The second phantom horse died in College Hall as a result of a student prank gone wrong. A fad swept American colleges and universities in the late nineteenth and early twentieth centuries in which unlikely farm animals—primarily horses and cattle—were smuggled into campus buildings at night so they could be discovered the next day. (Getting the beasts into a bell tower was a particularly popular challenge.) In the case of College Hall, the mischief makers managed to get a horse up to the top floor, but then the animal went wild and eventually had to be put down.

No one has seen either of the horses' apparitions, but people have heard their hooves stomping up and down the hallways. Often the clops are accompanied by neighs, snorts, and whinnies—exactly the sounds you'd expect to hear if the horses were alive. Ole Bill echoes throughout the building, but the noises produced by the unnamed horse occur only on the floor where he died.

Wittenberg University

200 West Ward Street, Springfield, OH 45504; (937) 327-6231 or (800) 677-7558; www.wittenberg.edu

Wittenberg University was founded in 1845 by a group of clerics from the English Evangelical Lutheran Synod Ohio. Their leader, and the university's first president, was the Reverend Ezra Keller.

Myers Hall, built in 1846, is a coed dorm. Its ghost story is very similar to the one at Wilmington College, just thirty miles away. According to legend, in 1863 student tricksters coaxed a horse up to the building's cupola. It was only after they succeeded that they began to worry what would happen if their identities were discovered. They tried to get the horse back down the stairs, but it refused to budge. They panicked and shot the beast. In an alternate version of the tale, Myers Hall was supposedly transformed into an army hospital during the Civil War. A wounded general made a dying wish: to see his cherished horse one last time. The staff complied, but after the patient passed, it was impossible to get the horse downstairs. Eventually, it had to be killed. Regardless of which story you prefer, the haunting is the same: Late at night, the horse's hooves can be heard clomping in Myers Hall, particularly on the staircase as the equine apparition makes its way up the steps. (For the record, Myers Hall was never a field hospital during the War between the States. It was a temporary infirmary during the Spanish flu pandemic, however, and many World War I soldiers were treated there.)

SOUTH DAKOTA

Mount Marty College

1105 West Eighth Street, Yankton, SD 57078; (605) 668-1545
www.mtmc.edu

Mount Marty College is a coeducational Benedictine liberal arts institution founded in 1936. More than eleven hundred students matriculate on its eighty-acre campus.

Its ghosts include a female former student who lived in **Corbey Hall** but one day mysteriously vanished. She's now seen riding the elevator. Sometimes people waiting for the lift can feel her invisible presence when the door opens.

All sorts of spooks visit the rooms in **Whitby Hall.** One is a male figure dressed in gray polyester pants. Another is a white shape that stands in the corners of the rooms, and a couple of uninvited spectral guests show up in students' rooms wearing blue suits and hard hats. Room 200 is especially haunted. In fact, rumor says it was kept unoccupied for several years because there was so much paranormal activity. Among its peculiarities: The inside of its door always seems to be in shadow, even if light is aimed directly at it.

One more ghost, thought to be a former construction worker, roams the entire campus. He'll turn on showers and use water fountains. Usually people see only his dark outline, but they've also heard his disembodied footsteps.

WISCONSIN

MARQUETTE UNIVERSITY

1442 West Wisconsin Avenue, Milwaukee, WI 53233 (414) 288-7250; www.marquette.edu

The Most Rev. Martin J. Henni founded Marquette College in 1881. It's named for the French Jesuit missionary and explorer Rev. Jacques Marquette, a member of the Society of Jesus. The school achieved university status in 1907 and later became the first coed Catholic university in the world.

There are at least seven currently haunted buildings (four of them dormitories) on Marquette's ninety-three-acre campus.

Humphrey Hall used to be the Children's Hospital of Wisconsin. Present-day residents would probably prefer not to know that the first floor once held the morgue. There have been general complaints such as malfunctioning electronics throughout the building, but a few students have reported a strange feeling of unease at a very specific spot just outside the elevator on the sixth floor. Apparently the spectre of a little girl appears in the elevator at night. She'll stare at riders with a contained fury, and sometimes she temporarily traps them by stopping the lift if they're using it at midnight. The ghost of a more sheepish girl likes to hide near the main reception desk and also sneaks around the fifth floor. Students have seen several spectral children, but more often they only hear the youngsters' laughing, crying, singing, and screaming. Supposedly the kids' spirits also have been seen and heard on security cameras near the back entrance to the building, where a playground used to be, but no video footage exists as proof of their visitations.

Cobeen Hall is the only all-female dorm at Marquette. No one knows who the house spirit might be, but it has an annoying habit of removing artwork and posters from the walls. Usually the paranormal activity takes place when the occupant is out of the room, but girls have also woken up in the morning to find some or all of their pictures and prints on the floor. Another irksome phenomenon that occurs day and night is the sound of water dripping, even when there are no leaky faucets.

Starz Tower is another residence hall for students. The building used to be the Milwaukee YMCA, and the dorm's workout area still has the old "Y" swimming pool. It's said a young boy named Petey drowned there, and he's come back to haunt the pool area and the locker room. He's never seen, but he'll unroll toilet paper in the bathroom stalls and open and shut doors. Mostly he whispers to people—even calling them by name—which has gained him the nickname "Whispering Willie."

Carpenter Tower, a coed residence hall, was a hotel in the 1950s. The decorative exterior bricks and art deco lobby are reminders from that era. Although historical records don't seem to back up the story, it's believed that a seven- or eight-year-old boy died there in a fire. He's still seen leaning out of a top-floor window or heard yelling to passersby for help.

Johnston Hall, now home to the J. William & Mary Diederich College of Communications, opened in 1907. Allegedly the hall was built on top of an old Native-American burial ground belonging to the Mascountens. The ghost of an angry tribesman appears in the basement, accompanied by a cold spot and a faint blue light. Legend has it that two Jesuit priests committed suicide by jumping from a fifth-story balcony, and they've returned to haunt that floor. There are disembodied voices and footsteps as well as sudden shifts in temperature. The men also supposedly haunted the elevator, which was replaced in 2011. The old lift would skip floors, open when it wasn't supposed to, rattle, get stuck, or stop completely.

The **Varsity Theatre** is a two-level multipurpose auditorium that can seat almost twelve hundred people. It's said that a projection operator was taking a cigarette break when he fell into a huge ventilation fan just off the balcony. He was sliced to bits. The poor man apparently doesn't blame the theater, because he's become a helpful spirit, locking up doors and turning off lights.

The **Evan P. & Marion Helfaer Theatre** is one of the main playhouses for Marquette University's Theatre Arts program. In addition to the auditorium, the building contains several rehearsal spaces and studios. One of the theater's artistic directors died in Studio 13, and people have been seeing his apparition in the room ever since.

Ripon College

300 Seward Street, Ripon, WI 54971; (920) 748-8115
www.ripon.edu

Ripon College was established as a college preparatory school in 1851. Today the 250-acre campus has twenty-five main buildings. An inordinate number of them seem to be haunted.

Brockway Hall, a dormitory for upper-level men on the south side of the Quad, opened in 1958 as East Hall. (It took its current name in 1971.) At one time Delta Upsilon, now Lambda Delta Alpha, was housed in the building. According to legend, a member of Delta Upsilon named John was killed in a car accident in the early 1960s, and his frat brothers dutifully placed a plaque on the wall to commemorate his passing. Spooky stuff started happening almost immediately. During fraternity meetings things would fall from shelves. At other times there would be the unexplainable sound of footsteps, temperature shifts, and doors that opened and closed on their own. On occasion a resident would be awakened by a knock at his door, only to find no one there when he answered. More disturbing still, students would sense—and occasionally see—a spectral presence in their rooms. All of the hauntings have been attributed to John.

The **Tri-Dorms**—Evans, Shaler, and Wright—are three adjoining residence halls set in a "U" formation. Students on the second floor hear the sound of a basketball being dribbled on the third floor, but if anyone goes upstairs to check it out, the noise stops. Doors open on their own. A few of the paranormal activities happened only once. These include a drinking glass that flew to the middle of an empty room and then crashed to the floor and a clothing iron appearing in the center of a locked room.

The **C. J. Rodman Center for the Arts** opened in 1972. Its theater ghost, Raphael, first made himself known in a local church that the college was temporarily using for its productions after the school's Red Barn Theatre burned down in 1964. The spook never materialized. Instead he contented himself with causing electrical troubles and opening and shutting doors. People would also hear his footsteps, howling, and general banging around in the basement and in the church spire. Raphael then transferred along with students and staff to the Rodman Center, where he's continued his electrical disturbances. He also flicks on lights and locks doors. On at least one occasion, a female student briefly saw his radiant form.

University of Wisconsin–Madison

Madison, WI 53706; (608) 263-2400; www.wisc.edu

The University of Wisconsin–Madison is the flagship campus of the University of Wisconsin system. It was founded in 1848, the same year as the state. It's Wisconsin's oldest public university and, at 933 acres, also its largest.

The **Union Theater,** which opened in 1939, has not one but two ghosts. The first is a construction worker who died while building the playhouse. The other was a timpanist with the visiting Minneapolis Symphony who died during a performance on March 12, 1950. Both have been blamed for fiddling with the lights in the control booth. Many people feel an unseen presence in the auditorium, especially if they're alone in the facility at night.

Two spooks are also said to haunt the **Memorial Library.** One is the spirit of Helen Constance White, a former English professor and novelist who died in 1967. Ghost aficionados point out that White was fond of saying "I hope our paths will cross again" when saying good-bye. Well, they might, because her spectre has been seen roaming the library stacks. There's also an urban legend about a student librarian in the research section hearing a disembodied voice softly whisper, "Sally Brown." As the tale has been passed down through the years, the location of the haunting has changed. The Sally Brown story was first mentioned in an article by library shelver Katie Buller Kintner. In her original version, the voice was heard at the **SLIS Library,** not Memorial.

Two pioneer settlers, Samuel Warren and William Nelson, were buried on the campus grounds in the 1830s, but their graves were lost and forgotten until they were accidentally disturbed in 1909 during the placement of the Abraham Lincoln statue in front of **Bascom Hall.** Now the pair's grinning ghosts are sometimes seen hanging out by the sculpture. Others have heard them quietly chattering away inside the building. The newest ghost tale is that Honest Abe's phantom has also started to wander the area.

Science Hall is home to the university's Department of Geography. Constructed in 1887 and occupied the next year, the building originally housed almost all of the school's science classes, including courses in anatomy. Skeletons and cadavers for dissection were stored in the attic, far away from prying eyes. The anatomy classes relocated in 1956, but human remains were still being found in Science Hall as late as 1974. Although details of paranormal phenomena in the building are sketchy, it's generally believed that the souls of some of the departed haven't really departed. One of their more irritating activities was knocking glassware off laboratory shelves. No ghosts were ever spotted, but students saw beakers move by themselves, fall, and shatter.

UNIVERSITY OF WISCONSIN–RIVER FALLS

410 South Third Street, River Falls, WI 54022; (715) 425-3911
www.uwrf.edu

The University of Wisconsin–River Falls is part of the statewide university system. The school has a 226-acre main campus on the Kinnickinnic River plus two laboratory farms. It was founded in 1874 as a teachers preparatory school and took its current name in 1971.

Of its thirty-two major buildings, only one is said to be haunted: the **Blanche Davis Theatre.** Its spirit is a man of medium height with long hair, slim though not skinny, and always dressed in jeans and a red short-sleeved shirt. He is usually seen walking the stage, minding his own business. He doesn't interact with the living, and if anyone tries to follow him into the wings, he is simply gone.

People have no trouble recognizing him. He is (or was) Sanford Syse, the former assistant professor of speech and theater who designed the complex. Tragically, he died of cancer on November 28, 1973, at the age of forty. Since his life was cut short, Sanford Syse may have returned because he has more to accomplish. Perhaps his love for the Davis Theatre was such a strong connection that it called him back from the Other Side. Or maybe he just wants to be remembered.

University of Wisconsin–Washington County

400 University Drive, West Bend, WI 53095; (262) 335-5200
www.washington.uwc.edu

The University of Wisconsin–Washington County belongs to the statewide university system and held its first classes in 1968. The institution is a two-year campus, but through credit transfer arrangements with other colleges and universities, the school also is able to offer baccalaureate programs.

The only spot on campus known to be haunted is the library, which is located in the southeast corner on the second floor of the main building. The collection contains more than forty-five thousand books, subscriptions to eighty newspapers and periodicals, hundreds of CDs and DVDs, computers with Internet access, and Wi-Fi. At night, when everyone has gone, the lights in the library sometimes turn themselves on. Doors open and slam shut, and books topple from the shelves. So far there's been no inkling as to the identity of the spectral librarian.

Part Four

WRAITHS OF THE WEST

"Go West, young man." So said newspaper editor Horace Greeley.

It stands to reason that academic apparitions haven't been around in the West as long as they have been in the East. It was well into the nineteenth century before pioneers started arriving en masse. That being said, there's still more than a century of ghost stories about hauntings at institutions of higher learning between the Rockies and the Pacific. Here, then, are some of the fresher faces on the phantom scene.

ALASKA

UNIVERSITY OF ALASKA ANCHORAGE

3211 Providence Drive, Anchorage, AK 99508; (907) 786-1800
www.uaa.alaska.edu

The University of Alaska Anchorage started as the Anchorage Community College in 1954 and became a four-year institution in 1976. It is the largest school of higher education in Alaska.

The school's **Wendy Williamson Auditorium** is named for the late musician and UAA professor John Wendell "Wendy" Williamson. The place is filled with architectural oddities. It's also filled with spooks.

Finances became tight after construction began in 1973, so there are now unused elevator shafts, a useless catwalk, unfinished rooms, and doors that lead nowhere. It's also been a temporary hideout for escapees from the nearby Alaska Psychiatric Institute and McLaughlin Youth Center, a detention center for troubled juveniles.

The ghost activity has been ongoing since the late 1970s. Staff members have placed charms around the theater to ward off the spirits, but it doesn't seem to have worked. The most haunted part of the building is the lobby. Unexplainable reflections appear in the windows of the outer doors, and the piano plays itself. Women trying to leave the handicapped restroom sometimes feel the door being held shut from the other side. Females with long brown hair are often shoved from behind as they descend the left staircase in the lobby.

Inside the auditorium, ghostly orbs of light float above people's heads, props fling themselves off tables onstage, eerie shadows appear on the walls, and lights burn out with a pop both onstage and in the house. In the light booth, the crew hears disembodied footsteps, and the temperature will suddenly drop. They'll suddenly and irrationally find themselves overcome by fear or frozen in place.

Backstage, water faucets and showers in the women's dressing rooms will turn themselves on at night. People feel cold spots and lights work themselves. Security staff will hear their names whispered in the vacant halls.

There are multiple spirits in the building, but most of their identities are unknown. Among them, the translucent phantom of a man appears in the lobby, in the auditorium, and standing in the wings. A Woman in White materializes in the auditorium from time to time. The whole audience saw her during a performance of *The Monkey's Paw* in 2001. (It's thought that she's a theater lover who used to frequent the auditorium.) The spectres of children are heard laughing and running near the green room, and their voices have been picked up on employees' walkie-talkies. Their ghosts have been seen floating in the air upstairs. The phantasm of a teenage boy shows up, but not very often. According to a psychic who visited the theater, he was killed in a car accident on 36th Street, but he was drawn to the theater because of all the hustle and bustle. The only ghost who's been recognized and seen in all parts of the building is Wendy Williams. Some even believe that he's the phantom pianist in the foyer.

ARIZONA

UNIVERSITY OF ARIZONA

1401 East University Boulevard, Tucson, AZ 85721; (520) 621-2211
www.arizona.edu

The University of Arizona was chartered in 1885, a full twenty-seven years before Arizona became a state. The institution was Arizona's first university.

Old Main was the first structure on campus, back when the school was called the Territorial University of Arizona College of Mines. Supposedly the building rests on the site of an ancient Native American village. But that's not where its ghost comes from. The spectre is Carlos Maldenado, who helped supervise Old Main's construction and lived in Tucson from 1841 until his murder in 1888. Old Main was converted into an officers' training facility after the attack on Pearl Harbor in 1941. It was during the building's refurbishment that Maldenado's spectre first appeared, frightening the workers. He's been seen by students, staff, and faculty ever since.

Maricopa Hall, a three-story dormitory for women, has been called the "Crown Jewel of Residence Life," and it's known for its large foyer, the crystal chandeliers in the public rooms, and the "sleeping porch." The ghost of an unknown young woman haunts the building. She didn't begin appearing until after a major renovation in 1992. The phantom, always wearing a mantle or cloak, materializes in the basement for short periods. The spectre isn't seen by many people because she usually appears exceptionally early in the morning.

Centennial Hall is the university's performing arts center. Known as simply the Auditorium when it opened in 1936, the building received its new name after a major refurbishment in 1985 for the university's hundredth anniversary. Two phantoms walk its halls. One is an effervescent female who seems to enjoy classical music. The other is a young man in his twenties. He's seen both backstage and on the catwalks overhead. People know he's in the house when they hear his distinctive, raucous laughter.

CALIFORNIA

California State University, Long Beach

1250 Bellflower Boulevard, Long Beach, CA 90840; (562) 985-4111
www.csulb.edu

California State University, Long Beach is the second-largest school in the Cal State University system with more than 36,000 students matriculating on its 323-acre city campus. Students use several shortened forms of their campus's name, especially Cal State Long Beach.

Its most haunted building is the **University Student Union.** No spectre has ever been seen, at least not in human form, but some have identified a strange fog that appears in the USU as a ghost. Other phenomena include elevators that stop where they haven't been called and doors that open and shut themselves.

California State University, Fullerton

800 North State College Boulevard, Fullerton, CA 92831
(657) 278-2011; www.fullerton.edu

Founded in 1957, California State University, Fullerton (commonly called Cal State Fullerton) is the largest of the twenty-three campuses in the Cal State University system and the second-largest university in California. Originally known as Orange County State College, its first classes were held in 1959. The school took its present name in 1972. Several phantoms call it home, and all of the hauntings seem to be the result of horrific murders.

Physics professor Edward Cooperman was shot and killed on the sixth floor of **McCarthy Hall** by a former student, Minh Van Lam, on October 13, 1984. Ever since the teacher's death, the elevators in the building have acted strangely. The lifts will open and close when no one is in them, or they'll arrive when the call button hasn't been pushed. They also tend to get stuck, or at least delayed, on certain floors.

The **Pollak Library** was the site of unspeakable carnage on July 12, 1976. Custodian Edward Charles Allaway strolled into the basement and shot nine staff members with a .22 caliber semiautomatic rifle, killing seven of them. The assailant thought that the coworkers were making pornographic movies with his ex-wife. Found guilty by reason of insanity, Allaway is now in Patton State Hospital. One or more of his murder victims may be linked to the paranormal phenomena at Pollak. A spectral voice has been heard, and the motion-sensor towel dispenser in the women's restroom sometimes goes crazy and shoots out paper until it empties itself. A student assistant at the library said that she followed a girl into that same restroom, only to find no one there when she got inside.

The Gamma Omicron Chapter of Phi Kappa Tau fraternity was established in 1960. Its distinctive house, fondly called **"The Barn,"** is just off campus at the corner of State College and Yorba Linda Boulevards. Many believe that the spirit haunting the house is Wendy Osborn, a fourteen-year-old girl from nearby Placentia who was kidnapped on her way to school, raped, and killed in January 1974. Although paranormal activity has waned in recent years, the spirit plays with lights, turns on spigots, opens cabinet doors, and whispers residents' names. The temperature in rooms will suddenly drop, the girl's touch is felt, and she's been blamed for temporarily paralyzing one of the frat brothers as he lay on the couch. Her brown-haired ghost even has been seen doing the dishes in the kitchen. A member of the fraternity has also reported seeing another phantom: a man in a jacket standing in one of the closets. Could it be the girl's killer, Raymond Barthlett, who was executed in 2006?

CALIFORNIA STATE UNIVERSITY, SACRAMENTO

6000 J Street, Sacramento, CA 95819; (916) 278-6011; www.csus.edu

The California State University, Sacramento (informally known as Sacramento State) was established in 1947 as Sacramento State College. It sits on a 288-acre campus, has about twenty-eight thousand students, and offers degrees at all levels. The school became part of the state university system in 1972.

The Department of Theatre & Dance is located in Shasta Hall. The larger of the two theaters, the **University Theatre,** is a proscenium auditorium. The playhouse is haunted by the spirit of a young man who was killed while the building was being constructed. He fell from the second story and was impaled on exposed steel girders below. His apparition doesn't manifest itself, but students and staff are acutely aware of his phantom presence, particularly on the catwalks, in the tech booth, and near the elevator that runs between the scene shop on the first floor and the costume shop on the second.

CALIFORNIA STATE UNIVERSITY, STANISLAUS–STOCKTON CENTER

612 East Magnolia Street, Stockton, CA 95202; (209) 467-5300
www.csustan.edu/stockton

California State University Stanislaus–Stockton Center, usually referred to as Stockton Center, entered the California State University system in 1997 as a satellite campus for Cal State Stanislaus. The school is located in the former Stockton Development Center, a training hospital for the developmentally challenged that closed in 1976. Before that the grounds had been used as a state mental asylum.

Acacia Court dates from the complex's earliest days. Rumor has it that back when the place served as a mental institution, some of the staff lived on the third floor. One of the nurses became so distraught over the plight of her charges that she hanged herself. Her spirit supposedly still "makes the rounds," and her apparition is occasionally spotted through one of the third-story windows. Doors also slam on their own.

Naval Postgraduate School

1 University Circle, Monterey, CA 93943; (831) 656-3411 www.nps.edu

The Naval Postgraduate School is a fully accredited university operated by the US Navy. NPS is not a "military school." Most of the students are already active-duty officers from all branches of the military, civilians working for the government, or members of foreign militaries. The school offers master's and doctoral degrees.

In 1951 the school moved from Maryland to Monterey, California, and took over the former Hotel Del Monte, which had been financed by railroad magnate Charles Crocker. Now called **Herrmann Hall,** it's the third hotel constructed on the site. The first one was destroyed by fire in 1887, as was its replacement in 1924. The Hotel Del Monte already had a ghost when the government bought the property, and he apparently didn't bother to move out when the fleet came in. He's a Man in Gray, so called because of the color of his clothing and the overall hue of the apparition. His identity is uncertain, but most people assume it's Crocker himself.

OCCIDENTAL COLLEGE

1600 Campus Road, Los Angeles, CA 90041; (323) 259-2500 www.oxy.edu

Occidental College, a private liberal arts school, was founded in 1887 by a coalition of Presbyterian clergy, missionaries, and laic friends. It opened in the Boyle Heights section of the city under the name "The Occidental University of Los Angeles, California." The campus moved to Highland Park in 1898 and to Eagle Rock in 1914.

Two of Occidental's dormitories have ghosts. The first, **Newcomb Hall,** is one of four residence halls that house the majority of first-year students. Legend has it that years ago a female student on the second floor got so homesick she hanged herself in her room. Students who are assigned to it now feel the depressed girl's lingering spirit. They also experience the usual minor oddities that happen in many haunted rooms, but this spook's specialty seems to be playing around with settings on alarm clocks.

The two-story **Erdman Hall** was built in 1927 and renovated in 1979. Reports about the haunted room in Erdman never specify its number. It's described, however, as being located in the center of the second floor on the front side of the building. Two spirits occupy the room: one good, one evil. Perhaps it's more correct to say that the latter spectre is playful—messing with the lights, removing the chain from the door, turning the water faucets on and off, and leaving messages on the wall. The other, thought to be a male, is dark and brooding and lives in one of the closets. He doesn't show himself, but students sense his presence at night, when he stands by the door watching them as they try to fall asleep.

SAN DIEGO STATE UNIVERSITY

5500 Campanile Drive, San Diego, CA 92182; (619) 594-5200
www.sdsu.edu

San Diego State University was founded in 1897 as San Diego Normal School. It became a state college in 1935, part of the California College System in 1960, and a university ten years after that. The school is the largest and oldest post-secondary institution in San Diego County and the third-oldest university in the Cal State system.

Zura Hall was built in 1968 as the first coed dorm at SDSU. In 1974, first-year student Tanya Gardini was sexually assaulted, stabbed, and strangled to death in her room in the southeast corner of the building. The attacker, Ellis Lee Handy Jr., pled guilty to first-degree murder and was convicted. There is at least one ghost, maybe more, in the residence hall, but surprisingly the hauntings don't seem to be connected to the Gardini murder, nor to the female student who allegedly jumped to her death from a Zura balcony. Instead, the apparition is a short man who, according to a few students, sometimes dresses like Charlie Chaplin's Little Tramp. The mystery man likes to plays small pranks, including turning television sets on and off. His voice calls to students in the hallways, especially on the second, fourth, and eighth floors, and people sometimes hear a hard object, possibly a ball or marble, bouncing on the bathroom floors.

SAN FRANCISCO ARTS INSTITUTE

800 Chestnut Street, San Francisco, CA 94133; (415) 771-7020
www.sfai.edu

The San Francisco Arts Institute was founded in 1871, making it one of the oldest art schools in America. It started out as the San Francisco Art Association but took its current name in 1961. The school offers BAs, MAs, BFAs, and MFAs, as well as post-baccalaureate certificates and honorary doctorates.

The institute was located in four different places on Nob Hill before moving to its current campus on Russian Hill in 1925. (There is a separate graduate campus elsewhere in the city.) Legend has it that the Arts Institute was built atop or adjacent to an abandoned cemetery. If the rumor is true, it might explain why the campus **tower** is overrun with spirits. Disembodied footsteps echo as they make their way up the staircase. Lights go on and off without human assistance; doors open and close. At least one group of workers has felt a malevolent presence there. Other people have seen an unidentifiable apparition climbing the stairs.

SAN JOSE STATE UNIVERSITY

1 Washington Square, San Jose, CA 95192; (408) 924-1000
www.sjsu.edu

San Jose State University is the oldest institution of higher learning on the West Coast. It is also the founding member of the California State University system. It was established as Minn's Engineering Normal School in 1857 and was originally located in San Francisco. After a century of changes, the school became San Jose State University in 1974.

In a shameful blot on American history, from 1942 to 1945 some 110,000 US citizens and residents of Japanese descent were rounded up and forced into internment camps. Government officials claimed that the men, women, and children might somehow be a threat to national security while the country was fighting World War II in the Pacific theater. Detainees from the San Jose area were processed and temporarily held in buildings at San Jose State College, including the old gymnasium. The sounds of disembodied cries, Japanese-speaking voices, slamming doors, and disembodied footsteps continue to echo through the former gym when it's vacant. In 1997 the building was renamed **Yoshihiro Uchida Hall** in honor of San Jose State's long-time head judo coach.

University of California, Berkeley

2200 University Drive, Berkeley, CA 94720; (510) 642-6000
www.berkeley.edu

The University of California, Berkeley was formed in 1868 when the College of California merged with the Agricultural, Mining, and Mechanical Arts College. Often referred to as UC Berkeley, it's the oldest and also the flagship campus of the University of California system.

The **Campanile,** located in the center of campus, is the school's most notable landmark. The first report of its having a ghost took place in 1964 when a female student noticed a male spectre following her as she walked past the tower. In the latter part of the 1960s, a photographer took a photo of the Campanile, only to discover a ghostly hand in the image when the film was developed. Some say the phantom is a graduate student named Pedro who had been studying Sanskrit at the university. When his thesis proposal was rejected, he jumped from the observation deck at the top of the tower and died. Besides the hauntings attributed to him, students sometimes look to him for help during final exams. They superstitiously believe he'll find a way to jinx their professors.

The Faculty Club, tucked away in a wooded glen next to Strawberry Creek, is a haven for alumni, staff, administration, VIP members of the UC community, and the faculty. Opened in 1902, the building is a perfect example of Craftsman architecture. Books and other objects fall off shelves all the time, but paranormal nonbelievers point out that the phenomenon could be caused by frequent minute, indiscernible tremors that occur in the Berkeley area. Earthquakes can't explain away the ghost in Room 219, however. People walking past the empty room have heard someone on the other side of the door reciting poetry, and when Japanese academic Noriyuki Tokuda stayed there during a March 1974 visit to campus, he saw an apparition sitting in a chair by the bed. (He was quietly moved to a different chamber after mentioning the ghost at dinner.) Many people think the phantom is Professor Henry Morse Stephens, a history professor who resided in Room 219 for many years. Others claim he's an unknown Native American, one of several Ohlone tribe members whose buried remains were accidentally disturbed during the building's construction.

As an example of how hard it is to nail down facts—or even a consensus of opinion—in ghost lore, at least one source says Stephens lived in Room 219 for twenty years; another says thirty-six. But Stephens died in 1919. The Faculty Club was built in 1902. The longest he could have stayed there was seventeen years. Even Tokuda's part of the tale varies. In an alternate version of the story, he wasn't relocated until the next day, after he had seen a second ghost in the room, a two-headed spectre floating high over his head.

UNIVERSITY OF CALIFORNIA, LOS ANGELES

405 Hilgard Avenue, Los Angeles, CA 90095; (310) 825-4321
www.ucla.edu

Known by everyone as UCLA, the University of California, Los Angeles was founded in 1919 as the second campus in the statewide University of California system. It's considered to be a co-flagship campus with UC Berkeley. With about 41,000 students, UCLA is the largest university in the Golden State.

Residents in **Dykstra Hall,** which opened in 1959, complain of spooky noises coming from one of the third-floor restrooms at night. Legend has it that the sounds are caused by the unhappy spirit of a student who lived right across the hall and hanged himself in his dorm room closet. One of the tenth-floor bathrooms is haunted as well. For some unknown reason, the showers repeatedly turn themselves on when no one's around.

From around 1967 through 1978, UCLA was home to a parapsychology lab that conducted research into extrasensory perception (ESP), alternative medicine, hypnosis, and psi phenomena. Out in the field, it investigated claims of hauntings by ghosts, poltergeists, and other spirits. The facility was not a department of the university, but it was housed on the fifth floor of the Semel Institute (then, the Neuropsychological Institute, or NPI) at UCLA's Center for the Health Sciences. The lab's director was Dr. Thelma Moss, an assistant professor (then later associate professor) of clinical psychology at the NPI. In Moss's last years at UCLA, her personal focus turned to Kirlian photography, a process that many believed showed proof of a human aura. Among the lab's main researchers was Dr. Barry Taff, a noted paranormal investigator, parapsychology consultant, and author. The laboratory's two most famous cases were probably its 1974 examination of a Culver City home belonging to Doris Bither—which became the basis for the novel and film *The Entity*—and the 1976 study of a private residence on Hollymont Drive in the Hollywood Hills.

University of California, Santa Cruz

1156 High Street, Santa Cruz, CA 95064; (831) 459-0111
www.ucsc.edu

Founded in 1965, the University of California, Santa Cruz sits on 2,001 redwood-forested acres on the Monterey Peninsula. Much of the land is the former Cowell family ranch, which the University of California bought in 1961.

After being accepted into UC Santa Cruz, students become affiliated with one of ten colleges based on their academic preferences. Each college has its own residential housing. **Porter College** in particular has a reputation for being haunted. The spirit visitor at A Building is a student who allegedly killed himself by jumping off the fifth story (even though the building doesn't actually have a fifth floor). His ghost walks through the building, dressed in the same clothes as the night he died. Meanwhile, over in B Building, it's said the basement, nicknamed "the batcave," is haunted by the phantom of a student who committed suicide in the downstairs bathroom. The first floor supposedly contains three adjacent rooms that are collectively referred to as the Bermuda Triangle because of all the paranormal activity that occurs in them. Objects sail through the air poltergeist-style, and people hear strange voices and feel an unseen evil presence. (Rumors persist that the rooms have been taken out of service and remain empty.) In the north wing on the third floor of the dorm, students wake up to find themselves being strangled or pressed down against the bedding.

A female apparition frequently has been seen wandering across the **Great Meadow** on the southern half of campus, most often in the sections directly below Porter, Cowell, and Stevenson Colleges. Some people have nicknamed the spectre Lily, but most folks believe she's Sarah Agnes Cowell, the youngest daughter of Henry Cowell, the land and cattle tycoon who once owned the property. On May 14, 1903, the defiant forty-year-old woman, accompanied by a servant, took out a buggy against her father's wishes and headed down a path across the grassy expanse. When the buggy hit a rock, either the carriage overturned or the horse bolted. Sarah was thrown from the cart and fatally injured. Henry Cowell died from grief before the year was out, and Sarah's sisters, Isabella and Helen, considered the ranch cursed and never set foot on it again.

University of La Verne

1950 Third Street, La Verne, CA 91750; (909) 593-3511 www.laverne.edu

The University of La Verne, located about thirty-five miles east of Los Angeles, was founded as Lordsburg College in 1891 by the Church of the Brethren. The school is still associated with that denomination. When the local town took the name La Verne in 1917, the college followed suit. Eventually it became the University of La Verne in 1977.

The school is not shy about its ghosts, and there are several links concerning their haunted facilities on the university website.

Founders Hall holds administrative offices, the computer science center, and Morgan Auditorium. When people are alone in the building, they occasionally hear the sound of doors being slammed and disembodied footsteps running through the halls. Lights in the auditorium flick off and on—even when power to them is cut. It's thought that the spirit causing the paranormal activity may be Gladdys Muir, a part-time professor of Latin and Spanish who died after falling down an exterior flight of stairs on the east side of the building in 1967. Others say the hauntings come from David Glasa, a former AV director who killed himself in his basement office in August 1978 after his girlfriend called things off. Glasa's presence is still felt in his old office. Also, odd sounds emanate from the room, and equipment stored there is tampered with when the place is empty.

Studebacker-Hanawalt Hall, or Stu-Han, as everyone calls the residence building, is a two-story structure divided into five separate wings. Residents who are assigned to one particular room in Wing Two sometimes have to endure unmistakable yet inexplicable thumps coming from the walls and ceiling. They also hear what sounds like someone snoring, breathing hard, or gasping for breath. According to rumors, at some vague time in the past a female student committed suicide in the haunted room, and the noise people hear is the dearly departed as she chokes to death.

Hanawalt House, another building on campus, was constructed in 1905 by W. C. Hanawalt, who was then president of Lordsburg College. The historic Victorian home was almost destroyed by fire in December 2004 but has been meticulously restored. Guests have encountered an apparition they believe to be "Grandma Hanawalt," a family member who lived there.

Staff members at the **International and Study Abroad Center** often felt an unseen pair of eyes watching them when they first moved into the building, which had previously been a private home. They never knew why until 1993, when a little girl wandered in and started moseying around. Asked if she could be helped, the youngster revealed that her grandmother had once lived there. The unfortunate woman had burned to death in a fire in the kitchen—the same room the director was using as an office. The child soon left and never returned. Before long, small objects in the director's office began to move on their own or would disappear from one area and turn up in another. At one point, reproductions of paintings by Frida Kahlo removed themselves from the walls overnight.

In 1979 a ULV theater student named Jim Henderson went to the desert with a friend to shoot footage for a film. Two men approached them for a ride, but when they refused, the strangers shot them. In around 1983, Henderson's ghost began to appear in the two dressing rooms of the Daily Theatre, a small auditorium on campus.

COLORADO

Johnson & Wales University

7150 Montview Boulevard, Denver, CO 80220; (303) 256-9311 or (877) 598-3368; www.jwu.edu

Johnson & Wales University was founded as a business school in 1941. Today it is a full university, best known for its culinary arts program, with four campuses scattered across the country. The Denver campus—the one with the ghosts—opened in 2000.

A bit of background is necessary. Many sources have confused or misidentified the places where the school's hauntings have occurred because of various changes in buildings' names and ownership of the property. Johnson & Wales's campus sits on the former site of Colorado Women's College. That school was established in 1888, but in 1982 it was absorbed into the University of Denver, whose main campus was across town. Subsequently, the University of Denver moved its law school and music conservatory to the former CWC grounds, calling it their Montview campus. In 1999 Johnson & Wales University purchased the Montview space and renamed most of the structures located there.

Johnson Hall used to be called Dunklee Hall. The building was constructed by CWC in 1965 as a residence hall. Supposedly a female music student committed suicide in a practice room on the second floor, the last room on the right after exiting the elevator. An odd phenomenon takes place there: Its door closes itself behind people as they leave the room.

Many ghost sources say Dunklee Hall was the name of a dormitory owned by the Lamont School of Music. Perhaps the confusion exists because Lamont, once a separate institution, merged with the University of Denver in 1941. One way or another, the story about the Dunklee ghost was firmly established by the time JWU acquired the building.

Aspen Hall, formerly Laura W. Porter Hall, was CWC's library. (It's now JWU's admissions building.) Several security guards and members of Johnson & Wales's cleaning staff have reported paranormal activity inside, including the door to the foyer creaking open by itself and the elevator doors opening even though no one else was in the building. One female custodian saw the apparition of a woman dressed in mid-twentieth-century clothing sitting in a chair on the second floor. The janitor quit soon thereafter, but before leaving she claimed that she had recognized the spectre from a photo as being Gertrude Johnson. The founding mother of JWU died in 1961, however, long before the Denver campus opened. Gertrude might have chosen to come to the Mile High City from the Other Side, but she obviously had never visited the campus—at least not while she was alive.

Treat Hall retained its name after JWU bought the campus. At one time in the early 1900s, it was the only building on the CWC grounds, and it acted as a multipurpose building for classrooms, housing, and dining. A maintenance man and his family lived in the basement, and his seven- or eight-year-old daughter purportedly fell down the elevator shaft and died. The building wasn't used by the University of Denver after it took over Colorado Women's College, but during its ownership the fire alarm was known to go off for no discernible reason, and campus security and firefighters heard the disembodied laughter of a young girl in the then-empty structure. JWU has since restored the edifice, listed as a National Historic Landmark, so perhaps students will see more of the little lady.

University of Colorado Boulder

Boulder, CO 80309; (303) 494-4144; www.colorado.edu

The University of Colorado system has three campuses, and the one located in Boulder was its first. The territorial legislature established the university in March 1876, five months before Colorado became a state. The school opened its doors in September of the following year. Two buildings on campus have resident ghosts, but the spooks' identities are unknown.

Macky Auditorium hosts two or more of the spirits. Construction on the arts building began in 1910, but it didn't open for another thirteen years. One of Macky's ghosts is said to be a young female opera student. She was alone, practicing in the hall, when she was attacked and killed by a custodian in the 1960s. Her unsettled phantom now roams the building. A man, thought to be connected to another murder in the building, appears in one of the towers, always clad in brown clothing. Late at night the sound of organ music fills the auditorium, although no one is seen playing the instrument.

Cockerell Hall is centrally located on the Quadrangle. Most of its residents are first-year students majoring in engineering and applied sciences. A spectral woman with long brown hair wearing a flowing white nightgown appears by a door to the attic, but her home is thought to be a third-floor bathroom.

UNIVERSITY OF COLORADO DENVER

1250 Fourteenth Street, Denver, CO 80217; (303) 556-2400
www.ucdenver.edu

The University of Colorado Denver is a member of the University of Colorado system. The university's 127-acre downtown location is known as the Auraria campus. It was developed between 1973 and 1976 and is split among three institutes of higher learning: UC Denver, the Metropolitan State College of Denver, and the Community College of Denver.

All three schools share **Tivoli Student Union,** which means they also share its ghosts. The building was once a brewery that operated on the site from around 1870 to 1969. After passing through several owners, the structure was transformed into the Tivoli Union, opening in 1994. No one is sure what era the spectres come from because most of them remain invisible. Instead, people hear their disembodied voices (from whispers to normal speaking volume) throughout the building. Sometimes the sound of a large group of ghosts, obviously enjoying a convivial party, comes through air vents on the third floor. One apparition that *can* be seen is that of a sad young girl who shows up in the Multicultural Lounge. She keeps to herself and disappears on the spot if anyone tries to approach her. She's also heard on every floor.

Sigi's Cabaret inside the Tivoli Union is named for German-born Moritz Sigi, who built the brewery. Sigi himself used the room as a rathskeller. Again, its phantoms don't usually show themselves, but the staff knows they're there. The room mostly sits empty, but it's occasionally used as a conference space. Employees will set up before leaving for the night only to come in the next day to see everything rearranged, even though the doors had been locked. The room's ghosts are thought to be a Native American, a nineteenth-century immigrant, and possibly an early twentieth-century arrival to Denver.

UCD's **Mary Reed Hall** opened in January 1933 as the university library. Today it houses office space for the administration, including the chancellor and provost. Several rooms are haunted. The entire place is filled with unexplainable cold spots. Doors will momentarily stick as if someone is holding them shut, and lights will go out on their own. The seat of one particular chair is always warm as if someone had been sitting there. Books are scattered about in locked rooms, and alarms go off by themselves. Occasionally visitors see a vaporous, glowing female apparition in the DuPont and the Renaissance Rooms, quietly sitting and reading in the semidarkness. Many think the revenant is the building's namesake, Mary Reed, widow of mining, ranching, and banking tycoon Verner Reed. Her $350,000 donation to the university allowed the school to build the hall as a replacement for the aging Andrew S. Carnegie library. Some say the ghost is the Reeds' daughter Margery, an alumna of the school who died from an unknown disease in 1925 after visiting South America. Still others suggest that the spectre is Mrs. Marcella Miller DuPont, whose largesse helped build the study named for her. The apparition seldom interacts with the living, but one female custodian claimed she was shoved from behind by an unseen spirit on several occasions. When the woman turned, no one was there.

University of Northern Colorado

1700 Ninth Avenue, Greeley, CO 80631; (970) 351-1890
www.unco.edu

Founded in 1889, the University of Northern Colorado opened a year later as the State Normal School of Colorado. The insitution took its current name in 1970 to reflect the expansion of its offerings.

The university's most popular ghost story involves Edith, purportedly a resident assistant in **Wiebking Hall,** which was built in 1957 and renovated in 1999. Perhaps because Edith was so introverted, her fellow students liked to play tricks on her. She often would go to the attic to play marbles by herself. One spring break when no one was around, Edith hanged herself in that very garret. Her spirit now haunts the third floor.

The disturbances are minor, such as turning lights on and off and changing channels on TVs. Students also hear the sound of furniture being moved in other rooms, even though nothing ever seems to have been rearranged when they go to check. A few residents have reported seeing Edith's shadowy apparition in their rooms.

Some believe the phantom also haunts the third floor of **Wilson Hall,** another dormitory built in 1957.

HAWAII

UNIVERSITY OF HAWAII AT MÀNOA

2500 Campus Road, Honolulu, HI 96822; (808) 956-8111
www.manoa.hawaii.edu

The University of Hawaii at Mànoa was founded in 1907 and is the flagship of the state's university system. At least three spectres haunt its campus. The first is Mary Dillingham Frear, a longtime university regent who occupies **Frear Hall**—along with the dorm's living residents, of course. Frear's easily recognizable ghost, an aged woman dressed all in white and carrying a ring of keys, is seen throughout the building. Even when she doesn't materialize, people have smelled her distinctive perfume and heard her footsteps.

Two phantoms, both male, haunt **Hale Kahawi,** a four-story dormitory. "George," who sticks to the fourth floor, repositions personal items and plays with the lights. The other, "Herman," spends most of his time on the second floor. He'll grab accessories from students' hair or move around objects in their rooms. Supposedly Herman was from the mainland and lived on the second floor while taking classes during the summer. He fell in love with a local girl, but when classes ended, he had to return home. Before he left, he swore he would come back, but he died in a car accident before he could fulfill his promise. Perhaps Herman actually made it back after all.

WINDWARD COMMUNITY COLLEGE

45-720 Keaahala Road, Kāneohe, HI 96744; (808) 235-7400
www.windward.hawaii.edu

The University of Hawaii system consists of ten campuses—three of them universities and the rest community colleges. One of the latter, Windward Community College, was founded in 1972 and has several main buildings. A friendly but mischievous spirit nicknamed Bob makes his presence known in **Hale Iolani,** or Hall of the Royal Hawk. The building contains art and photography studios as well as other classroom space, but it served as a hospital before it was repurposed for the college. It's thought that Bob was a patient there at one time. He's certainly a "neat freak." He likes to straighten up and put things away.

IDAHO

BOISE STATE UNIVERSITY

1910 University Drive, Boise, ID 83725; (208) 426-1156
www.boisestate.edu

The Episcopal Church founded Boise Junior College in 1932. The school began offering baccalaureate and master's degrees in 1965. Nine years later it became a full university.

A student union building that opened in 1942 was one of the three original structures on the Boise Junior College campus. When a new SUB opened in 1967, the music and theater departments moved into the old building. Soon after, a ballroom on the second floor was turned into a theater, the Subal (an acronym for Student Union Ballroom). In 1984 music and theater students got a new playhouse, the Morrison Center, and the original student union became the **Communications Building.** According to legend, back when the theater was still a ballroom an unidentified young man stood up his date to a dance. She was so upset that she went into the women's powder room by the entrance and killed herself. (In one version of the tale, it was a Sadie Hawkins dance. Either way, the boy didn't show.)

The fact that no such suicide in the hall has ever been recorded hasn't stopped the ghost stories. Although no apparition has been seen, rumors that the girl's ghost haunts the theater started circulating soon after the playhouse was opened. Students called the spectre Dina because the name appeared on a chalkboard in one of the classrooms and also showed up written in lipstick on dressing-room mirrors.

One of the more popular tales about Dina involves Frank Heise, a professor in the Theatre Arts department. As a technical director for a production of *Stop the World, I Want to Get Off* during the 1971–1972 academic year, he assisted in painting the flats (large canvas-covered frames that are raised to form the set's walls) and then sat down in the auditorium while they dried. When he and a student went back onstage, they found one of them covered in footprints from the small heels and pointed toes of a woman's shoes—Dina's!

Other phenomena included stage lights and houselights operating themselves. Students working in the space heard various odd noises, including a piano playing "London Bridge Is Falling Down." The song could have been drifting up from practice rooms on the lower level, but not the other sounds. One night some students followed disembodied footsteps up a staircase heading to the wardrobe room. When they opened the door, the footsteps abruptly stopped. Even the theater department chairman, whose office was in the building, would sometimes hear taps at his door but found no one there when he opened it.

Lights also shone out from under the doors to unoccupied rooms that, when checked, were totally dark. Office file drawers opened themselves. A secretary inside one of the rooms saw a human shadow pass by the door, even though the hall was empty. On at least one occasion after an actor onstage had trouble striking a match it suddenly lit without being struck. It then supposedly shot out of his hand and flew across the room.

Spirit activity has slowed down since the theater department moved out of the building, but it hasn't ended. People still hear footsteps and see lights flicker. Meanwhile, over at the **Morrison Center for the Performing Arts,** students still blame Dina's ghost when anything out of the ordinary takes place.

Idaho State University

921 South Eighth Avenue, Pocatello, ID 83209; (208) 282-0211 www.isu.edu

Idaho State University was founded in 1901 as the Academy of Idaho. Today the university has six colleges that offer almost three hundred graduate and undergraduate degree programs.

The university has a theater ghost who lives in Frazier Auditorium, now called the **Diane and Chick Bilyeu Theatre,** located inside Frazier Hall. The building and its playhouse were constructed in 1924. If he materializes at all, the Frazier phantom appears as an elderly man, though sometimes he's seen only as a bluish-gray aura. His face and clothing give no clues about his identity. The spectre acquired the name Alex during an incident in the 1980s. A female theater student was backstage waiting for her cue to go on when a window high on the wall opened. Despite the girl's repeated attempts to shut it, the window kept reopening itself. Finally in frustration the girl called out to "Alex" to stop playing around—even though she had no idea why that particular name popped into her head. She was cold, she told the invisible spirit, and she wanted him to close the window. And the ghost did! The name Alex stuck.

The spectre has been blamed for opening and shutting doors, lighting candles, and moving objects. People have also heard items being dragged across the stage when it was empty and the sound of a piano being played, even when no instrument was nearby. Alex has popped up throughout the building, but he mostly keeps to the stage and the hallways.

NORTH IDAHO COLLEGE

1000 West Garden Avenue, Coeur d'Alene, ID 83814; (208) 769-3300
www.nic.edu

Founded in 1933 as Coeur d'Alene Junior College, the community college moved to its present forty-five-acre campus in 1939. At that time the name was changed to North Idaho Junior College. The school, which offers associate degrees, took its present name in 1971.

Seiter Hall was constructed around 1964. For most of its existence, the multistory brick building has held offices and classrooms for the math and science departments. Its ghost haunts the halls dressed in a dark blue peacoat like the ones soldiers wore at the turn of the twentieth century. (The campus stands on what was once part of an army outpost.) The apparition is an old man with a beard, but he doesn't materialize often. When he does, he's blurry or is caught out of the corner of one's eye. Most folks only hear him. He opens doors, moves furniture, and walks the halls. And he may not be alone: Some people have reported hearing disembodied voices in conversation. Almost all the spooky activity takes place between 11:00 p.m. and 1:00 a.m.

MONTANA

CARROLL COLLEGE

1601 North Benton Avenue, Helena, MT 59625; (406) 447-4300
www.carroll.edu

Carroll College was established in 1909 by Bishop John Patrick Carroll as Mount St. Charles College. It was renamed to honor its founder in 1932. Originally admitting only men, the private, Catholic liberal arts institution is now coeducational.

The first and still-largest building on campus is **St. Charles Hall.** Two spirits, both unidentified males, haunt its corridors. One of them supposedly killed himself by jumping from a window at the top of the north stairwell. His spectre seems doomed to repeat the tragic leap throughout eternity. The second phantom is said to have been a student who fell and struck his head on the sink in a fourth-floor bathroom.

He died of a cerebral hemorrhage. Soon after the student's death, residents began to claim the restroom was haunted and that it was impossible to remove the boy's bloodstains from the sink. The college closed off the room until it was determined that the "blood" was actually red paint. The door to the bathroom now locks itself, however, and the young man's ghost wanders the halls and disturbs folks by knocking on doors.

Montana State University

Bozeman, MT 59717; (406) 994-0211; www.montana.edu

Montana State University was established in 1893 as the Agricultural College of the State of Montana, but it had adopted its current name by the 1920s.

The **Student Union Building** was constructed in 1940. It was later renamed the Strand Union Building in honor of A. L. Strand, who was president of the college from 1937 to 1942. In 1955, part of the SUB was converted into a playhouse. The theater closed in 2007, but after a major renovation it was turned into the Procrastinator Theatre, a second-run, two-hundred-seat cinema operated by the students.

Although they've been pretty quiet recently, two ghosts have haunted the union building. One is the spectre of a woman dressed in 1930s apparel. Legend has it that she hanged herself in the SUB ballroom. She's appeared throughout the building, including near the sound and light booth of the old theater. The other apparition is of more recent vintage. In the early 1970s one of the theater professors fell down a metal staircase behind the stage and suffered a major head injury. He soon began to have wild mood swings.

Then one night he removed a gun from the prop room, took it to his office, put in real bullets, and shot himself. Before long, students and staff started sensing an otherworldly presence whenever they were in the former office, and his darkened shadow started appearing there in the mid-1980s.

Hamilton Hall was built in 1910 as a women's dormitory. It was later converted into offices and is now home to Gallatin College and the Army and Air Force ROTC programs. An unidentified phantom haunts the fourth floor at night, but usually only the cleaning staff encounters it.

University of Montana

32 Campus Drive, Missoula, MT 59812; (406) 243-0211
www.umt.edu

Founded in 1893 and opening its doors two years later, the University of Montana is the flagship and largest campus of the state's university system. Although all of the original buildings were set around a centrally located green known as the Oval, sixty-four major buildings now dot its 220-acre location.

At least four buildings on campus are haunted. The oldest, **Main Hall** (also called **University Hall**), was constructed in 1898, and most of the administration offices are located there. At night after everyone but the cleaning staff is gone, an unidentified, invisible spirit stomps around, makes heavy breathing noises, and slams doors to the restroom stalls.

Rankin Hall was built in 1908. The structure, the university's only example of Neoclassical architecture, is on the National Register of Historic Places. Jeannette Rankin was a 1902 UM graduate and the first female member of Congress. She supposedly haunts her namesake building by closing doors. Her footsteps also echo in the halls. Supposedly if you say hello to her invisible spirit and touch her oil portrait as you enter the building, you'll find a little gift from her in a nearby trash can. The building has another haunting: An entire group of phantom students can sometimes be heard in a vacant classroom on the second floor.

Brantly Hall, formerly known as North Hall, dates from 1923. The Alumni Association, UM Foundation, and University Relations offices are there today, but it was a three-story women's dorm until 1986. Its ghost is a female student who committed suicide when her father lost his fortune in the stock market crash.

Constructed in 1956, the four-story **Fine Arts Building** can be found just east of Brantly Hall. It's the home of the George and Jane Dennison University Theatre, so it's suspected that the unpleasant ghost causing poltergeist-like activity inside the building was once a drama student or theater professor.

NEVADA

University of Nevada, Reno

1664 North Virginia Street, Reno, NV 89557; (775) 784-1110
www.unr.edu

The University of Nevada, Reno was founded in Elko in 1874 as the State University of Nevada. Seven years later it became Nevada State University, and it moved to Reno in 1885. Its current name dates from 1906. Also called the University of Nevada or simply Nevada, it was the only institution of higher learning in the state until 1965.

Morrill Hall, built between 1885 and 1886, is the oldest building on campus and was listed on the National Register of Historic Places in 1974. The building's architectural style is Second Empire, with its first floors in redbrick and its third story designed as a mansard roof with dormer windows. Not much is known about its ghost, a woman who appears throughout the building dressed in 1920s wardrobe. Minor paranormal activity has also been reported on occasion.

NEW MEXICO

NEW MEXICO STATE UNIVERSITY

1600 Stewart Street, Las Cruces, NM 88003; (575) 646-2222 www.nmsu.edu

New Mexico State University grew out of Las Cruces College, which was established to teach agriculture in 1888. The following year the school changed its named to New Mexico College of Agriculture and Mechanical Arts. It became New Mexico State University in 1960.

The **Rhodes-Garrett-Hamiel Residence Center** was built between 1941 and 1955. A ghost occupies the laundry room and makes itself useful. Students return to find their clothes folded for them. The spirit is thought to be a young woman who committed suicide in the building or another who died from a fall while going down the stairs to the laundry room. As is often the case in ghost legends, there's no record of either death.

Another phantom freaks out folks in **Goddard Hall,** the engineering building. Constructed in 1913 with an annex added in 1936, the building was named for a former engineering dean, Ralph Willis Goddard. He was accidentally electrocuted in the KOPB radio station's FM transmitter room while preparing for a New Year's Eve broadcast in 1929. Many think his ghost is responsible for the building's disembodied foot-steps, doors that open and shut themselves, and unexplained odd noises. The old bell tower on Goddard Hall is closed to students, and some say it's haunted, too, even though there are no specific reports of activity. According to one rumor, a student hanged himself there several years back.

Lastly, the **Hershel Zohn Theatre** is haunted by an apparition nicknamed George. Some say he was an actor who fell from the catwalk above the stage. The ghost often appears on the overhead walkway, sometimes tinged in a green, glowing light and usually wearing a nineteenth-century top hat and cape. The phantom creates the sound of loud crashes around the playhouse, but nothing is ever discovered out of place.

OREGON

Pacific University

2043 College Way, Forest Grove, OR 97116; (503) 352-6151
www.pacificu.edu

Pacific University is a private institution of higher learning affiliated with the United Church of Christ. It's an outgrowth of Tualatin Academy, which was founded in 1849. The school took its current name in 1854.

Knight Hall was constructed around 1879 as a private residence. For a little more than a decade, it was a women's dorm. At various points it served as a fraternity house, a coed residence hall, and headquarters for the music depart-ment. Since 2004 it's been the admissions office.

It's also been home to a ghost. Folks have named her Vera, and reports of her existence date from around 1949.

According to the most popular legend about her, Vera was a music student who lived on the top floor of Knight Hall. One night she looked down from her window and saw her boyfriend outside the dorm. Rushing down the back staircase to meet him, she tripped, fell, and broke her neck. (Another version of the tale says her fall occurred during the time the music department was located in the building, and she had been upstairs practicing piano. Still other variations claim Vera died a suicide, was shot by a gun, or was killed during an Indian uprising.)

Her ghost has been credited with opening and closing doors, locking doors, shutting windows, moving furniture, playing with lights, turning on fans, moving objects, creating odd odors, writing on chalkboards, turning off radios if she didn't like the music, and touching people (including a young man in the shower). People have heard her walking the halls, using the stairs, whispering, singing, and playing the piano, and her apparition is seen in upper-story windows at night.

Back when the building contained music practice rooms, her apparition once walked in on a female student, asked her to stop playing the piano, and strolled back out. (Vera apparently didn't approve of the piece or the player's technique.) The student ran into the hall to confront the rude stranger, but by then the phantom had disappeared.

Vera has even wandered next door to another residence building, **Walter Hall.** On at least one occasion, a student there has woken up in the middle of the night to find the spectre sitting at her desk, watching her sleep.

Two séances held in Knight Hall around 1969 suggested clues to Vera's past, but they led to dead ends. To this day her true identity remains unknown.

University of Portland

5000 North Williamette Boulevard, Portland, OR 97203
(503) 943-8000; www.up.edu

The University of Portland, a private Roman Catholic institution affiliated with the Congregation of the Holy Cross, opened in 1901. Portland University, founded by the Methodist Episcopal Church in 1891, had previously stood on the site overlooking the Williamette River, but financial troubles forced them to abandon the campus five years later.

West Hall was the only building standing there when the Portland diocese acquired the property. In 1992 the building's name was changed to **Waldschmidt Hall** to honor Paul Waldschmidt, a former university president. Today the building houses the administrative offices and a few classrooms.

According to school tradition, one of the University of Portland students drowned in the Williamette in 1911 and has haunted the former West Hall ever since. Most often students only hear the spectral boy's footfalls following them in the hallways, but now and then the apparition materializes. The shadowlike form quickly disappears as soon as it's spotted.

Western Oregon University

345 North Monmouth Avenue, Monmouth, OR 97361
(503) 838-8000; www.wou.edu

Pioneers founded Western Oregon University as Monmouth University in 1856, three years before Oregon became a state. The school has gone through seven name changes throughout the years, taking its present appellation only in 1997.

Rice Auditorium, built in 1976, is the home of the school's Department of Theatre and Dance. The building is haunted by George J. Harding, who was a popular theater professor. During his time at the university, Harding also taught classes in English, speech, dramatics, and humanities, and he directed many student productions, particularly in the 1950s. His ghost didn't arrive at WOU until Rice Auditorium opened. No one has ever seen him, but it's believed he's the one who messes with the theater lights and whose disembodied footsteps pace the stage. He's also a bit of a practical joker, so guess who gets blamed if something goes wrong during a production. Perhaps it's the spirit's way of telling the actors, director, and production staff to step up their game.

UTAH

Brigham Young University

Provo, UT 84602; (801) 422-4636; www.byu.edu

Brigham Young University, founded in 1875, is a private institution of higher learning owned and administered by the Church of Jesus Christ of Latter-day Saints. It's the largest religious university in the United States, and its main campus in Provo offers undergraduate, graduate, and doctoral degrees in eleven colleges.

The **Harold B. Lee Library** on the Provo campus is the second-largest private university library in the United States. The five-level facility—with collections housed both above and below ground—is said to contain almost ten miles (that's right, *miles*) of shelving. Apparently the building also contains several ghosts. Not much, if anything, is known about the spirits other than the fact that their voices are heard moaning in the Music Library on the fourth floor.

UNIVERSITY OF UTAH

201 Presidents Circle, Salt Lake City, UT 84112; (801) 581-7200
www.utah.edu

The University of Utah was founded in 1850 as the University of Deseret. The school lasted just three years, but then it was re-established in 1867. It became the University of Utah in 1892.

The school has had a library since 1850. Its current facility, the **J. Willard Marriott Library,** opened in 1968. Its Special Collections department, located mostly on the fifth floor, preserves essential documents related to the university, the founding of the state, the Church of Jesus Christ of Latter-day Saints, the West, and the Middle East.

For some unknown reason, the Special Collections area also seems to preserve the ghost of a Civil War soldier. Students, faculty, and staff have all seen the spectre—or at least half of him. The unidentified man appears only from the waist up, and if anyone meets his eye, he instantly vanishes. Normally he doesn't interfere with work or study at the library, but some people have reported coming back to their materials after a few minutes away to find that things have been disturbed in their absence.

UTAH STATE UNIVERSITY

1400 Old Main Hill, Logan, UT 84322; (435) 797-1000; www.usu.edu

Caine Lyric Theatre, 28 West Center Street, Logan, UT 84321
(435) 752-1500

Utah State University was founded in 1888 to concentrate on agricultural studies, but throughout the years its mission has expanded exponentially to encompass eight colleges, offering more than 175 undergraduate degree programs as well as master's and doctoral degree programs.

The haunted **Caine Lyric Theatre** is owned by the university. It was opened by a notable local family, the Thatchers, in 1913, but heirs donated it to the school in 1959. After a complete restoration, the theater was reopened in 1961, and it was placed on the Utah State Register of Historic Sites ten years later.

The theater's ghost is a former actor named Everett. He was playing the second gravedigger in the production of *Hamlet* that opened the playhouse in 1913. He was getting more laughs than the first gravedigger, who became insanely jealous even though both are minor roles. One day Everett disappeared, and somehow the production had a new prop skull. Everett has yet to take his final bow. He's been spotted on the catwalks and in a loge seat in house right. Sometimes his disembodied voice calls out to actors or to the tech crew during rehearsals. He also makes the rear house-right chandelier sway to let people know he's there.

WASHINGTON

SEATTLE CENTRAL COMMUNITY COLLEGE

1701 Broadway, Seattle, WA 98122; (206) 934-3800 www.seattlecentral.edu

Although it can trace its roots to earlier vocational schools, Seattle Central Community College began teaching college-level classes in 1966. Its **South Annex** was originally the Booth Building, constructed sometime around 1907. From 1914 to 1921, it was the Cornish School of Music. The Burnley

School of Professional Art, headed by Edwin and Elise Burnley, moved into the building in 1946. Jess Cauthorn bought the Burnley School (and the building) in 1960. In time the academy became part of the Art Institute of Seattle, after which the college was able to acquire the property.

Now, for the hauntings. Back when the building belonged to the Burnleys, their daughter Marilyn worked as the receptionist. She often would arrive in the morning to find that the door had unlocked and opened itself overnight.

The building's spectre was most active during Cauthorn's tenure in the 1960s. People came in to discover that the furniture had rearranged itself overnight, desk drawers and doors had opened, and trash cans were toppled. The phantom set off security alarms after hours. During the day there were strange noises, including footsteps, rotary phones being dialed, papers being shuffled about, and coffee being poured. Students would see items shift on the tables, feel themselves being pushed from behind, and walk into sudden cold spots. Random objects would appear out of thin air—a phenomenon known in Spiritualist circles as an apport—and students occasionally saw the blurred phantom of a young man. Also, during this period the phantom would occasionally leave the school and go down to the ground floor, where there was a bank. It would flick the lights, clatter dishes in the break room, and brew coffee. At some point the ghost was nicknamed Burnley.

Mediums and psychics investigated. They claimed the spectre was an eighteen-year-old student at Broadway High School, which had also once occupied the building. In 1913 the boy got into a fight after a game of basketball in the gym on the third floor and fell (or was shoved) down the stairs to his death. Some recent ghost hunters, however, believe that the ghost was a young man who committed suicide in the building. There's no evidence to support either scenario.

Seattle Community College purchased the former Booth Building in 1986. The following year a staff member said she ran into the apparition. The ghost has been quiet in recent years, but his antics continue. Objects continue to move on their own, papers crumple, and there are still those darned footsteps. One female student in the second-floor microcomputer lab even had a stack of discs rain down on her, which is not surprising: According to several accounts, these days the spirit seems to prefer taunting ladies.

UNIVERSITY OF WASHINGTON

1410 Northeast Campus Parkway, Seattle, WA 98195 (206) 543-2100; www.washington.edu

The University of Washington was founded in 1861. The school has three campuses, the first and largest of which is in the University District in Seattle.

Nestled in a wooded area on the north side of campus and dating from the 1930s, **Hansee Hall** was the first residential building on campus. One entire floor is said to be haunted by a male student who committed suicide in the dormitory in 1958.

The school's most famous, or rather infamous, phantom is Theodore Robert "Ted" Bundy, the serial killer who terrorized the nation in the 1970s. A full profile of this evildoer and his gruesome murders of young women is best left for elsewhere, but he had a very strong association with the Pacific Northwest and the University of Washington in particular. His known killing spree began in January 1974, although it's now assumed there were several earlier murders as well. There have been claims of Bundy's ghost appearing in several states since his death in the Florida State Prison electric chair on January 24, 1989. It's impossible to find specific paranormal activities credited to Bundy at the University of Washington, but many people feel his unsettling spirit pervades **McMahon Hall,** the dorm where he lived while at UW.

Washington State University

1630 NE Valley Road, Pullman, WA 99163; (509) 335-3564 www.wsu.edu

Washington State University was founded in 1890 as Washington Agricultural College and School of Science. It became a university in 1959 and now offers bachelor's, master's, and doctoral degrees in approximately two hundred programs.

Built in 1895, **Stevens Hall** is the oldest women's residence hall on campus, and it's been listed on the National Register of Historic Places. In the early 1900s there was a tradition that every Halloween students would gather in Stevens Hall for a reading of Edgar Allan Poe's "The Black Cat." Before long a legend emerged that a real black cat stalked the building on the night of October 31, and chaos followed in its wake. One All Hallows' Eve the girls thought someone was joking around when they saw a black cat sitting outside the housemother's door. When they went back later that evening to remind her about the annual reading, they found the woman dead. Supposedly she died of natural causes, but had the black cat been a death omen—a ghost—and not a real feline at all?

During the summer of 1971, custodians cleaning Stevens Hall during summer break discovered blood on the wall in one of the rooms. Police feared it belonged to Joyce LePage, a student who sometimes snuck into the empty building for solitude but had been missing since July. Nine months later her remains were found in a ravine ten miles away, wrapped in a piece of carpet remnant that had been cut from the front hallway of the building. There was speculation at one point that she may have been a victim of serial-killer Ted Bundy, who spent a great deal of time in Washington (and whose ghost is said to haunt the University of Washington), but her murder didn't match his normal modus operandi. Her killer has never been found. There are rumors that LePage's ghost now haunts Stevens Hall, especially the basement. Doors open themselves, the piano sometimes plays itself, and people hear muffled screams and other odd noises.

Twelve-story **Orton Hall** on the south side of campus was completed in 1964. Its ghost, Railroad Sam, restricts himself to the top floor. The apparition shows up only when a train is passing through town. Sam will stand in one of the windows watching the railroad cars go by. No one knows who he is or how he was connected to the university, if at all.

Regents Hall is an all-women's dorm housing mostly first-year students. The female spectre that roams the building at night was a resident in the 1970s. Supposedly her parents came to meet her on graduation day, but when she didn't come down to the lobby, the RA let them into the girl's room. She had hanged herself in the closet but left no suicide note. Sightings of the apparition are rare. More often, she opens doors to the rooms and opens and shuts closets.

Streit and Perham Halls opened in fall 1962. They share a connecting building that contains a dining hall, lounge, and other facilities. On December 18, 1979, a student named John Stickney set off explosives on the fifth floor of Perham after his ex-girlfriend refused to get back together with him. Damage to the building was extensive, but he was the only one killed. According to legend, his spectre has returned to **Streit Hall,** not Perham. It's also claimed that many of the doors in Streit no longer close properly. They do, of course, and there's no reason the unhappy spirit would show up in the wrong place. But that's the nature of ghost stories.

WYOMING

NORTHWEST COLLEGE

231 West Sixth Street, Powell, WY 82435; (307) 754-6000 or (800) 560-4692; www.northwestcollege.edu

Northwest College opened in 1946 as the University of Wyoming Northwest Center. By 1953 the school was known as Northwest Community College. It took its current name in 1989. Today, Northwest College offers more than eighty-five associate degree and skill certificate programs.

All of the school's otherworldly guests show up in the **Nelson Performing Arts Center.** The building, one of the oldest on campus, holds the student-run radio and television facilities, recording studios, music instruction and practice rooms, and the five-hundred-seat Nelson Auditorium, home of the Northwest Civic Orchestra.

Hauntings have been reported as far back as the 1970s. There are unexplainable cold spots, including one that often appears in the middle of the stage. Phantom actors have been seen as well as their shadows. A menacing black haze once appeared in the left rear section of the auditorium during a rehearsal, and a dark spectral figure has material-ized during performances in the front row.

Throughout the building there's the standard paranor-mal activity often associated with visits from the Beyond, such as lights that go on and off, objects that shift around on their own, unrecognizable noises, and chairs that move or rock by themselves. There's also at least one apparition backstage: a smiling female phantom who shows up in the green room. Nobody knows who she is. In fact, none of the spectres in the building has ever been identified.

Appendix: School Library

Although there have been hundreds, if not thousands, of books written about ghosts and paranormal activity, there have been remarkably few that specifically examine the apparitions haunting colleges and university campuses. This is particularly surprising because there are perhaps as many as five hundred post-secondary schools in the United States that have resident spirits.

The scarcity of material is remedied somewhat by the number of works focused on a particular region of the country or an individual institution of higher leaning. There are also many tales shared online and in other media. Here is a representative sampling of the resources used to research *Haunted Colleges and Universities*.

Books

Baltrusis, Sam. *Ghosts of Boston: Haunts of the Hub*. Charleston, SC: History Press, 2012. Part of the Haunted America series.

Barefoot, Daniel W. *Haunted Halls of Ivy: Ghosts of Southern Colleges and Universities*. Winston-Salem, NC: John F. Blair, 2004.

Brennan, Genevieve. *College Prowler: Wellesley College Off the Record*. Pittsburgh, PA: College Prowler, 2005.

Bronner, Simon J. *Piled Higher and Deeper: The Folklore of Campus Life*. Little Rock, AR: August House Publishing, 1990.

Campbell, Allen. *Ghosts at Carlisle Barracks Army War College*. Columbus, GA: Brentwood Christian Press, 2002.

Ciochetty, John. *The Ghosts of Stuyvesant Hall and Beyond: Volume 1*. Bloomington, IN: AuthorHouse, 2007.

Glass, Debra Johnson. *Skeletons on Campus—True Ghost Stories of Alabama Colleges and Universities*. Amazon Digital Services, 2007.

Hulan, Richard H., project historian, and Robert C. Giebner, project supervisor. *Historical American Buildings Survey. Brinkley Female College. (Ghost House)*. Washington, DC: Department of the Interior, 1972.

Kleen, Michael. *Legends and Lore of Illinois, 17: University of Illinois*. Amazon Digital Services, 2012.

———. *Legends and Lore of Illinois, 39: Illinois State University*. Amazon Digital Services, 2012.

———. *Legends and Lore of Illinois, 45: Western Illinois University*. Amazon Digital Services, 2012.

Lunis, Natalie. *Spooky Schools*. New York: Bearport Publishing, 2013. Part of the Scary Places series.

MacDonald, Margaret Read. *Ghost Stories from the Pacific Northwest*. Atlanta: August House, 1995.

Mallett, Renee. *Haunted Colleges and Universities of Massachusetts*. Charleston, SC: History Press, 2013. Part of the Haunted America series.

McCarthy, Stephanie E. *Peoria's Haunted Memories*. Charleston, SC: Arcadia Publishing, 2009.

Norman, Michael. *Haunted Homeland: A Definitive Collection of North American Ghost Stories*. New York: Tor Books, 2008. Part of the Haunted America series.

Powell, Jack. *Haunting Sunshine: Ghostly Tales from Florida's Shadows*. Sarasota, FL: Pineapple Press, 2001.

Provine, Jeff. *Campus Ghosts of Norman, Oklahoma*. Charleston, SC: History Press, 2013. Part of the Haunted America series.

Robertson, James R. *The Brinkley Female College Ghost Story*. Memphis, TN: Floyd & Co., 1871.

Swayne, Matthew L. *America's Haunted Universities: Ghosts That Roam Hallowed Halls*. Woodbury, MN: Llewellyn Publications, 2012.

———. *Paranormal Pitt: Ghost Stories and Legends of the University of Pittsburgh*. Amazon's CreateSpace Independent Publishing Platform, 2010.

Thuma, Cynthia, and Catherine Lower. *Creepy Colleges and Haunted Universities*. *True Ghost Stories*. Atglen, PA: Schiffer Publishing, 2003.

Tucker, Elizabeth. *Campus Legends*: *A Handbook*. Westport, CT: Greenwood Press, 2005.

———. *Haunted Halls*: *Ghostlore of American College Campuses*. Jackson: University Press of Mississippi, 2007.

White, Thomas. *Ghosts of Southwestern Pennsylvania*. Charleston, SC: History Press, 2010. Part of the Haunted America series.

Windham, Kathryn Tucker. *Jeffrey's Latest 13: More Alabama Ghosts*. Tuscaloosa: University of Alabama Press, 1987.

Articles

In addition to the articles found in independent newspapers and magazines, student periodicals at many colleges and universities publish stories about their campus ghosts. (Links can often be found on the schools' websites.) Here is a sampling.

Tom Anderson, "Tales of Supernatural Haunt ULV," *Campus Times*, October 29, 2004.

Annette Barnette, "Glenville State College: A Picturesque Campus with a Haunting Past," college press release, October 21, 2013.

Chay Dallas Baxley, "Beaty Beauty—Fact, Fright, or Just for Fun," *Summer Times 2007*, July 2, 2007.

Renee Dillard, "Rumors of Wendy Williamson Auditorium's Haunting Draws Spirits, Skeptics, Speculation," *The Northern Light*, October 30, 2007.

Marilyn Fernandez, "Hauntings Are Plentiful, but They're Not Always Scary," *Cambridge Day*, October 31, 2005.

Cara Hillstock, "Legendary Ghost Haunts Purple Masque Theatre," *The Collegian*, October 17, 2012.

Karl Joas, "Campus History Haunted with Ghost Stories, Unexplained Events," *Ripon College Days*, October 13, 2004.

Marilyn Lim, "Local Haunts Well-Known for Supernatural Suspicions," *Baylor Lariat*, October 28, 2005.

Melanie Pawlyszyn, "Haunted at Marquette: An Investigation into the Paranormal," *The Warrior*, October 31, 2010.

Jessica Rubio, "Haunted by a Tragic Past," *Orange County Register*, Cal State Fullerton section, October 30, 2013.

Scott Swindells, "The Ghosts That Haunt Us," *The Daily Collegian*, October 30, 1998.

Peggy Townsend, "43 Things You Might Not Know about UC Santa Cruz," *UC Santa Cruz Review*, October 6, 2008.

Television

www.syfy.com/schoolspirits

In summer 2012, television's Syfy channel ran a six-episode series entitled *School Spirits* featuring tales of ghost encounters and paranormal activity that occurred at various colleges and universities. The stories were told by interviews with students, alumni, and staff as well as through reenactments—although almost none of the footage was shot at the actual haunted locations. The six colleges profiled on the series were the University of Michigan, SUNY Geneseo, Lebanon Valley College, Sweet Briar College, Eastern Kentucky University, and Slippery Rock University. All but the first episode (about a haunted sorority house at U of M) can be watched online.

Websites

There is no end to the number of websites about ghost phenomena. Some of them have directories of haunted places, but so far there doesn't seem to be a site that allows users to search its pages according to the type of venue (e.g., university, library, etc.). Instead, the sites that deal with American hauntings are broken down by city and state. These sites can be problematic because the capsule descriptions are often repeated verbatim from one site to the next, including any mistakes or misleading information.

Here are two of the better paranormal websites out there:

www.theshadowlands.net

This is the granddaddy of them all. Dave Juliano has maintained this excellent site and directory since 1994. Follow the link to "Ghosts and Hauntings" to be taken to the section on paranormal experiences. Shadowland probably has the most popular and most copied online ghost directory.

www.prairieghosts.com
Rather than a directory, you'll find a blog, a bookstore, and links to ghost tours and ghost-hunting expeditions. The site concentrates on hauntings in the Midwest, hence the phrase "prairieghosts" in the site's address.

Many colleges and universities provide links on their official websites to online articles about the ghosts found on their campuses. Go the school's main site, find the window that provides a "Campus Search" (as opposed to a search of the whole Internet), and enter the word "ghost" or "haunting." Also try the plural forms "ghosts" and "hauntings." You'll sometimes get different results.

Be creative. Try an Internet search for hauntings in a particular region (such as "college ghosts in New England"), a specific kind of building (maybe "university theater hauntings" or "dormitory ghosts"), or using some other qualification (say, "Big Ten ghost stories" or "13 Most Haunted Schools"). You'll be pleasantly surprised by what you find.

About the Author

Tom Ogden is one of America's most celebrated magicians. His television work has included appearances on NBC's *The World's Greatest Magic II* and Fox's *The Great Magic of Las Vegas*. He's twice been voted "Parlour Magician of the Year" at the world-famous Magic Castle in Los Angeles and has received a dozen more nominations in other categories.

Ogden's background in magic and "the unexplained" led to an interest in the supernatural, apparitions, and hauntings. Now, as a recognized author on the subject of ghosts, he is a popular speaker on spirit phenomena and paranormal activity.

His books include *200 Years of the American Circus* (which was named a Best Reference Work by both the American Library Association and the New York Public Library); *Wizards and Sorcerers; The Complete Idiot's Guide to Magic Tricks; The Complete Idiot's Guide to Ghosts and Hauntings; The Complete Idiot's Guide to Street Magic;* and seven other works in the Globe Pequot Press *Haunted* series. He also has been profiled in *Writer's Market*.

Ogden resides in haunted Hollywood.